THE Horticulture GARDENER'S GUIDES
PERENNIALS

Andrew McIndoe and Kevin Hobbs

HORTICULTURE
BOOKS
www.hortmag.com

A HORTICULTURE BOOK

Horticulture Publications, Boston, Massachusetts

First published in the US in 2005 ISBN 1-55870-764-6

Text Copyright © Andrew McIndoe and Kevin Hobbs 2005
Copyright © David & Charles 2005

Horticulture is a subsidiary of F+W Publications Inc. Company
Distributed by F+W Publications Inc.
4700 East Galbraith Road, Cincinnati, OH 45236
1-800-289-0963

Andrew McIndoe and Kevin Hobbs have asserted their right to be
identified as authors of this work in accordance with the Copyright,
Designs and Patents Act, 1988.

Printed in Singapore by KHL
for Horticulture Publications, Boston, Massachusetts

Visit our website at www.hortmag.com

Commissioning Editor Mic Cady
Art Editor Sue Cleave
Production Beverley Richardson

Series Editor Sue Gordon, OutHouse Publishing
  Winchester, Hampshire SO22 5DS
Designer Robin Whitecross
Editors Lesley Riley, Jo Weeks
Proofreader Audrey Horne
Indexer June Wilkins

American edition by
Creative Plus Publishing Ltd.
53 Crown Street
Brentwood, Essex CM14 4BD

ORNAMENTAL PLANT OR PERNICIOUS WEED?

In certain circumstances ornamental garden plants can be
undesirable when introduced into natural habitats, either
because they compete with native flora, or because they act
as hosts to fungal and bacterial disease pathogens and insect
pests. Plants that are popular in one part of the world may be
considered undesirable in another. Horticulturists have learned
to be wary of the effect that cultivated plants may have on
native habitats and, as a rule, any plant likely to be a problem
in a particular area if it escapes from cultivation is restricted
and therefore is not offered for sale.

Contents

Introduction

Both of us are passionate about herbaceous perennials: Kevin about growing, introducing, and discovering new varieties for our gardens; I about selling them, planting them, and using them in my own garden and in gardens I have designed or have visited to give advice. With such a large and diverse group of plants to deal with, our problem has been selecting those to feature in this book.

We could not include everything. The number of varieties of our favorite perennials increases every year as breeders, hybridists, nursery managers, and gardeners work their magic. In keeping with the current interest in English-style planting schemes, this book describes plants that suit a traditional herbaceous border (or perennial border) and the illustrations are of old European gardens. The gardener looking for a specific plant should always be open-minded and prepared to accept a substitute. Perhaps the cultivar available is a more recent one, and an improvement on our recommendation. The selections Kevin and I have made for this book will undoubtedly change and be added to as time moves on.

We aim to whet the reader's appetite, to inspire the use of perennials in as many ways as possible. Perennials should be considered not only essential elements in the border but also serious contenders for use in any other situation in the garden. For example, they can bring color to a woodland, add texture and interest in a low-maintenance gravel planting, and provide a luxurious display at the waterside. They are about flowers, certainly, but they are also about foliage, structure, and texture. Most are easy to grow and maintain; some require special conditions and attention—qualities that appeal to the experienced gardener who likes a challenge.

Although the typical English-style perennial border is at its peak at the height of summer, you can have interest from herbaceous perennials for a much longer period, and this book will help you to achieve it. Because most perennials are available as container-grown plants, we are able to select varieties when we see them at their best.

Because of the variety offered by herbaceous perennials, there will always be one that can be fitted into even the most crowded garden. That quality is irresistible to any gardener. All of us who care deeply about plants want more of them; and when we find what we want, we can always make room for it. We hope you find something new in this book, along with many old favorites that have proved their worth.

Andrew McIndoe

SELECTING HERBACEOUS PERENNIALS

The breeding of new cultivars has increased in recent years due to the ease with which herbaceous perennials can be accommodated in smaller gardens, and their ability to give almost instant results.

Availability

Some of the species mentioned are new cultivars and others are traditional British varieties, which, if you can find them, will give authenticity to your design. The following sources should help you on your way to your traditional, English-style perennial border:

Plant Delights Nursery, Inc., 9241 Sauls Road, Raleigh, NC 27603, tel (919) 772-4794

Select Seeds – Antique Flowers, 180 Stickney Hill Road Union, CT 06076-4617, tel 1-800-684-0395

USDA HARDINESS ZONES

Most species described in this book will thrive in temperate areas (around zone 7) and the seasonal changes described apply to these areas. With the exception of annuals, zones are indicated next to each species name, and cultivars are suitable for the same zones unless otherwise stated. Remember that a plant's site can also affect its hardiness.

Zone	Avg. annual min. recorded temp.	Zone	Avg. annual min. recorded temp.
1	Below -50°F	7	0°F to 10°F
2	-50°F to -40°F	8	10°F to 20°F
3	-40°F to -30°F	9	20°F to 30°F
4	-30°F to -20°F	10	30°F to 40°F
5	-20°F to -10°F	11	Above 40°F
6	-10°F to 0°F		

To find your zone, see the USDA zone map on the back flap of this book.

LEFT: *Delphinium* 'Magic Fountains Lilac Rose' and *Centranthus ruber*

INTRODUCING HERBACEOUS PERENNIALS

Sometimes unfairly considered hard work, herbaceous perennials prove their worth with their reliable performance and, in most cases, ease of cultivation. Unlike woody plants, they do not need pruning, just a little tidying up. Many perennials fill their space in the border in a season or two; some need dividing only rarely. Taller varieties must have support to give their best display. If you follow just a few rules of cultivation, perennials will reward you with a variety of form, leaf shape, and flower color unsurpassed by other plant groups.

RIGHT: *Iris sibirica* 'Flight of Butterflies'

What are herbaceous plants?

Understanding a little of the nature of herbaceous plants—what they are, why they grow the way they do, and where they come from originally—will help you to give them the care and conditions they need in your garden. In return, they will give you their very best performance.

The term "herbaceous" is applied to those plants that do not produce wood. Trees and shrubs, or "woody plants," undergo a process called secondary thickening, whereby their stems are strengthened with woody tissue. This enables them to gain height year on year and to support leaves and flowers. Because secondary thickening does not happen in herbaceous plants, their size may be more limited, although this is not always the case: the banana, for example, is an herbaceous plant. The "trunk" of the banana "tree" consists of layers of leaf bases, reinforced by fibers. Once the banana has fruited, the trunk dies and is replaced by offsets that grow from the root.

Some annuals and biennials such as the common foxglove, *Digitalis purpurea*, are grown as perennials because they survive in the garden from year to year by seeding themselves freely.

DECIDUOUS OR EVERGREEN?

Most herbaceous plants from temperate regions are deciduous; that is, they lose their leaves and die down to ground level in winter. However, some are evergreen, their leaves having developed protective layers that prevent water loss and help them withstand extremes of temperature. Most herbaceous plants from tropical zones are evergreen: Conditions in their native habitat allow the plants to continue to grow all year round, so they have no reason to die down and go dormant.

PERENNIAL?

The term "herbaceous" can be applied to annuals and biennials, but it is usually used with reference to perennials. Deciduous herbaceous perennials survive from year to year by shedding their leaves and stems at the end of the growing season and overwintering by means of adapted stems or roots that store food and water in readiness for growth to start the following spring. This life cycle may be an adaptation to climates where there is insufficient light, water, or warmth for part of the year to allow growth to be continuous; or it may be a result of habitat.

In gardening, the term "herbaceous plants" often includes annuals and biennials that seed themselves freely so are perennial in the garden, even if not perennial as individual plants. *Digitalis* (foxglove) and *Lunaria* (silver dollar) are two examples, and these may be found in garden centers alongside true herbaceous perennials.

HABITATS

The herbaceous perennials that we grow in our gardens have originated in a variety of habitats throughout the world: woodland, prairie, mountain, riverside, and bog. Their members include water plants such as *Nymphaea* (water lily), which grow virtually submerged with only their flowers and leaf surfaces in contact with the air. At the other end of the spectrum are tropical plants that live entirely in trees; all parts of these plants are in contact with the air, and they absorb atmospheric moisture by means of aerial roots.

As with all plants, knowledge of the natural habitat provides clues about the conditions a plant will enjoy in the garden and the contribution it will make to a planting scheme. For example, many herbaceous perennials, particularly those from woodlands, are adapted to grow, bloom, set seed, and die down before competition from other plants robs them of water and light. *Corydalis flexuosa* is one such. Its light fernlike foliage appears from fleshy underground tubers early in the growing season. The foliage will work to replenish the food supply in the tubers, and as soon as it is in place, flowers are produced. In summer the flowers fade and set seed, and the foliage dies down; the plant then becomes dormant below ground until the following spring. This is perfect timing, as the foliage of the trees has by now stolen the light, and tree roots have drained the ground of moisture.

In some cases, the opposite conditions have led to similar growth habits. *Papaver orientale* (oriental poppy) is from Turkey and the Caucasus. It has long tuberous roots that enable it to grow, bloom, set seed, and die back quickly in the early part of the year, before the fierce summer sun parches and bakes the earth in its native environment. The gardener needs to know this when positioning the plant in the garden, not only from the point of view of the poppy's preferred growing conditions but also because of the gap it will leave in the border from early summer onward.

(For more information about siting herbaceous perennials see pages 36–83.)

The water lily *Nymphaea* 'Marliacea Chromatella' grows almost submerged, using the water as support for the stems and floating leaves and flowers.

HARDINESS

Because in winter most garden herbaceous perennials have no leaves to be desiccated by freezing winds or stems to be ruptured by frost, their roots and underground stems are generally able to survive the coldest days of the year. Exotic appearance is not necessarily an indication of a tender constitution. Herbaceous peonies, for example, are extremely tough; despite luxuriant flowers and lush foliage, they can survive temperatures of −4°F (−20°C) or lower. Some evergreen herbaceous perennials, such as agapanthus, are also fairly hardy, simply becoming deciduous when grown in cold areas.

The USDA hardiness zone information is normally a safe indicator of whether a plant is a good choice for your garden. With the exception of plants normally grown as annuals, zone information for the plants in this book is provided next to each species name. Cultivars are suitable for the same zones unless otherwise stated. To find your zone, see the map on the back flap of this book. Plants that are half-hardy and tender in your zone will usually thrive outside through the warmer months but either die when the weather gets cooler or survive the cold only if they are given protection, such as heavy mulching, or are dug up and stored under cover. If you really like a plant, try giving it the best protection you can and seeing what happens.

Perennials in the garden: a history

People have been gardening in Europe since Roman times, but it is only in the last century and a half that herbaceous perennials have become a major feature of our gardens. Inspired by the work of key Victorian gardeners, modern horticulturalists have taken up these versatile plants and shared their passion for them, so that today herbaceous perennials are more popular than ever.

Topiary punctuates the parterre at Cliveden, Buckinghamshire, England. Trees and shrubs featured strongly in early gardens. Neat clipped hedges contained areas near the house and joined the garden to the landscape.

The first plants cultivated in gardens were mostly those with a culinary or medicinal use. Even when gardens became more ornamental, gardening and collecting plants remained a pastime for the prosperous. And because of the sheer size of the gardens of their wealthy clients, early designers often favored trees and shrubs above herbaceous perennials, displaying them in open parkland settings; even smaller gardens or areas closer to the house consisted largely of shrubs, including neat clipped hedges in the knot-garden style. Nowadays, however, many of us have the opportunity to cultivate plants purely for their ornamental qualities, and here, to a great extent, lies the appeal of herbaceous perennials.

HOW PLANTS CAME TO GARDENS

Our passion for gardening has its roots in the early days of worldwide trading and the prosperity it generated. By the 16th century, the European seafaring nations were beginning to expand their empires, funded by wealth earned from trading foodstuffs, spices, and materials from exotic crops. The 17th century saw many nations continue to flourish, and industrialization led to further trading. Many traders would have brought home plants found during their travels, perhaps via Cape Horn or South Africa; wealthy merchants traveling the world established gardens wherever they settled and brought specimens with them on their return.

In addition, there were those people who traveled specifically to study the flora of other lands and who brought back some of what they found. These "plant hunters" were often the first Europeans to visit remote regions, and they faced hardship and danger there. To add to their trials, much of the seed and plant material they collected perished on the journey home. Despite this, they made many successful introductions that have added to the glorious wealth of plants we now enjoy.

John Tradescant Senior and his son John are recognized as the most important of the 17th-century plant hunters. *Tradescantia virginiana* is a reminder of Tradescant Senior's successful introductions to Europe of North American species while associated with the Virginia Company. In 1768, the *Endeavour* set sail from Plymouth, England, on its famous voyage of discovery of

The Royal Botanic Gardens at Kew, England (left) were founded by Sir Joseph Banks. David Douglas collected in America and introduced the California poppy, *Eschscholzia californica* (right) to Britain.

The lovely *Primula bulleyana* (left) was collected by George Forrest. William Robinson devised a new style of planting, using bold perennials and wildflowers in naturalistic settings (right).

"Terra Australis" under the command of Captain Cook. On board was Joseph Banks, a brilliant young scientist with a passion for botany. On his return to Britain, Banks founded the Royal Botanic Gardens at Kew with the help of King George III and so began the golden age of plant hunting, which lasted two centuries. The Royal Horticultural Society was founded in 1804. Along with Kew, it helped to fund a number of plant-hunting expeditions. Commercial nurseries, such as the famous Veitch Nursery of Chelsea, were hungry for new plants to enrich their catalogues and sponsored expeditions.

The plant hunters brought back both woody and herbaceous plants. David Douglas is best known for woody plants and conifers collected in America, but he also brought species of lupine, penstemon, mimulus, and the California poppy (*Eschscholzia californica*). Robert Fortune traveled in the Far East and collected such treasures as *Dicentra spectabilis* and *Primula japonica*. Ernest "Chinese" Wilson introduced the beautiful *Lilium regale*; George Forrest found *Primula bulleyana*, and Frank Kingdon Ward *Meconopsis betonicifolia*: the catalogue of introductions is seemingly endless.

ESTABLISHING THE ROLE OF HERBACEOUS PERENNIALS

It was not until the 1870s that herbaceous perennials evolved into their present role as a major ornamental part of our gardens. Using both wildflowers and bold and beautiful herbaceous plants in a naturalistic setting, William Robinson (1838–1935) started a new era in planting, superseding the typical Victorian combination of dark evergreen shrubberies alongside formal colorful bedding schemes. Gertrude Jekyll (1843–1932) built on Robinson's ideas. Although known for color-themed plantings, her borders also had structure, instilled partly through the repetition of bold plants such as acanthus, bergenias, and stachys. She used subtle shades to enhance an effect—introducing yellow or white to blue plantings, for example—and often also introduced an element of surprise, such as orange lilies alongside blue delphiniums, to accent the planting. Plants that were more difficult to combine with others, such as ferns and hostas, were grown in pots, an idea that gardeners are just adopting today.

In her planting schemes for gardens such as those at Hestercombe, Somerset, in England, Gertrude Jekyll used subtle color progressions, adding bold surprises—perhaps orange lilies with blue delphiniums.

11

SPREADING THE WORD

Many herbaceous perennials and bulbs were introduced and promoted by E.A. Bowles (1865–1954). Known more as a plantsman than as a gardener, he loved the rare and the unusual. He was also perhaps the most important garden writer of the early 20th century, and his thoughts and ideas are quoted by all influential plantsmen who have followed him.

The writings of Vita Sackville-West (1892–1962) about the garden at Sissinghurst, Kent, in England, also aroused interest in herbaceous perennials. Sissinghurst, now in the care of the British National Trust, is still one of the best gardens in the world for herbaceous perennials: gardeners everywhere have imitated the plantings found there, particularly the associations created with fine old roses. Sissinghurst combines the formal design and structure devised by Harold Nicolson, Sackville-West's husband, with her informal and luxuriant style of planting. Their unusual lifestyle (both had homosexual affairs although they remained friends) undoubtedly added an element of intrigue: successful gardens often reflect the personality of the gardener, and perhaps the passion of an artist comes through not only in the wealth of plant material at Sissinghurst but also in how it is put together.

Hidcote Manor, in Gloucestershire, England, now also owned by the British National Trust, was the work of an American, Major Lawrence Johnston. Developed from 1903 onward, the garden is renowned for its structure—a series of garden "rooms" divided by immaculate hedges—and for the plants that have been named after it. Johnston exchanged ideas with Sackville-West and other influential gardeners. Within the strong structure of Hidcote, herbaceous perennials are used in sumptuous mixed plantings in both formal and informal settings. The red borders—a cocktail of red foliage and flowers—are perhaps the best known of the color-themed plantings: a rich mix against dark yew hedges, the traditional backdrop of a perennial border. The woodland garden provides informal contrast with its hydrangeas and shade- and moisture-loving perennials.

CARRYING ON THE TRADITION

Gardens adviser to the National Trust for many years, the late Graham Stuart Thomas (1909–2003) carried on the herbaceous perennial tradition begun by these early pioneers. His books, published from 1940 onward, have become the definitive works on old roses and herbaceous perennials. He established the National Collection of old roses at Mottisfont Abbey, Hampshire, England. Here visitors can meet not only his much-loved classic roses but also his herbaceous perennial "old friends," as he knew them.

East Lambrook Manor, in Somerset, England is another place that has been immortalized in the names of several herbaceous perennials that originated there: *Euphorbia characias* ssp. *wulfenii* 'Lambrook Gold', for example. The garden was the inspiration of journalist-turned-gardener Margery Fish (1889–1969), who had an enthusiastic interest in plant combining.

At Bressingham, in Norfolk, England, Alan Bloom pioneered the idea of island beds containing perennials surrounded by lawn, a more informal and less labor-intensive approach. By selecting sturdy varieties and

Carol Klein's subtle and exuberant plantings have taught gardeners to look differently at perennials: the way they move in the breeze, the effect of light on both color and outline, and how they work together.

using them carefully, he ensured that plantings were largely self-supporting, with a long season of interest. As befits a nurseryman and plant breeder, he introduced many new varieties—work that is continued by his son Adrian and grandson Jason.

Two other important names in modern herbaceous perennial gardening are Beth Chatto and Carol Klein. Beth Chatto is well known for her writings on the selection and cultivation of herbaceous perennials for specific growing conditions and for her clever use of foliage and plant forms. She has introduced us to many unusual plants. Carol Klein, through her enthusiasm and sincere interest in her subject, has taught gardeners to look more closely at the detail of plants: how they move in the breeze, the effect of light, and the sheer wonder of their luxuriance.

As creative use of plants in gardens has developed, gardeners have gained the confidence to develop their own styles. Through his experiences in the garden at Great Dixter, in Sussex, England, Christopher Lloyd has become an advocate of bold experimentation with color and form, asserting that subtle (or "dull," as he describes it) is not the only option. Robinson would have approved of Lloyd's use of exotic plants such as cannas to enrich more traditional plant combinations.

NEW STYLES AND NEW VARIETIES

Meadow gardens and prairies are relatively new styles of planting that combine herbaceous perennials and bulbs with grasses. Emulating natural habitats, they bring a different kind of informality to the garden setting. In Europe, their early use in public parks and other open spaces was in stark contrast to the stiff, ordered coniferous plantings that preceded them. Through use of native species, these schemes also fulfill a conservation function, and with current levels of environmental awareness, the prairie and the wildflower meadow have become highly popular in the last few years.

Although herbaceous perennials are such a feature in English gardens, interest in them is by no means confined to Britain. From the 20th century onward,

Perennials fit into any garden, even those with modern, minimalistic planting. This has led to increased interest in bold foliage subjects such as hostas (left) and rodgersias (right).

American nurserymen have been active particularly in the breeding of new hostas, daylilies, and irises. Many parts of North America and continental Europe have very cold winters and warm summers; since deciduous herbaceous perennials die down in winter, they are often highly suitable for gardens in these areas, whereas woodier plants tend to find the contrasting temperatures and icy winds more of a challenge.

Even gardens with a minimalist, low-maintenance approach have space for herbaceous perennials. The foliage of architectural subjects such as angelicas, rheums, and rodgersias is ideally suited to such a setting, the big leaves perfectly balancing strong architectural lines and bold masonry. In addition, these plants require no complicated pruning and training: just let them grow and give an impressive display, then clear up when they get knocked back in the winter.

THE FUTURE

In recent years herbaceous and evergreen perennials have gained ever-increasing popularity. These affordable plants offer good value, reliably performing year to year. Many of them are extremely easy to grow and maintain, and they are available in such variety that there is more than enough choice for every size and type of garden. As gardens get smaller and fuller, perennials will become even more popular with enthusiastic gardeners. There may not be space for another shrub or tree, but there is always room for just one more herbaceous perennial.

Speaking botanically

Latin names are essential for accurate communication. A plant's common name may vary from one area to another; and when it comes to using common names in a different country, the confusion can be greater still. The origins of botanical Latin date back to the 1700s, to the work of the Swedish botanist Carl Linnaeus. The dual name system he devised is still in use today.

PLANT CLASSIFICATION

FAMILY In plant classification flowering plants are divided into families. Each of these contains a number of genera that have similar characteristics. Members of the family Leguminosae, for example, all have pealike flowers and carry seed in a pod (the Latin word *legumen* means pulse). Genera within this family include *Baptisia*, *Lathyrus*, and *Lupinus*. A plant's botanical name consists of the genus and the species.

GENUS The generic name is something like our surname. The generic name always starts with a capital letter and is always a noun. It is often derived from names found in an ancient language such as Latin, Greek, or Arabic. *Artemisia*, for example, is named after Artemis, one of the goddesses of ancient Greece. Other generic names commemorate people—in some cases the person that discovered the plant. For example, *Lobelia* is named after Mathias de l'Obel, a botanical author, plant collector, and physician to James I of England; *Dahlia*, after Anders Dahl, a Swedish botanist.

SPECIES A plant's specific name, or epithet, is more like our first name, although it is written after the genus and always starts with a lower case letter. It cannot stand alone as a name. As a Latin adjective, it takes the gender of the generic name, so its ending agrees with the noun (although there are exceptions to this, as there are in any language). The specific name is descriptive, telling us something about the plant.

SUBSPECIES, VARIETAS, AND FORMA These are the botanically recognized subdivisions of a species

where distinct forms occur in the wild. These are variously known as subspecies (ssp.), varietas or variety (var.), and forma or form (f.). A popular example is *Euphorbia characias* ssp. *wulfenii*.

Subspecies and forms are less common as cultivated forms of herbaceous perennials than they are in the world of trees and shrubs.

CULTIVAR A cultivar is a distinct form of a species that has been selected from wild or cultivated stock and has then been maintained in cultivation by vegetative propagation. In other words, all offspring come from one original plant. The cultivar name is written with an initial capital letter within single quotation marks and follows the specific name. For example, *Campanula lactiflora* 'Loddon Anna'. Sometimes the cultivar name immediately follows the generic name. This often occurs with genera that have many garden hybrids, sometimes of uncertain parentage. For example, *Iris* 'Langport Wren' and *Hemerocallis* 'Gentle Shepherd'.

In gardening nomenclature, the terms 'cultivar' and 'variety' are used interchangeably. Often, too, the term 'form' is used in a general way to refer to a variety, subspecies, or cultivar.

GROUP A cultivar shows little or no variation, because it has originated from a single individual. Members of a group can show considerable variation, but not enough to separate them botanically. For example, *Aquilegia* McKana Group includes a range of hybrids of variable flower color but with similar flower form.

HYBRID Species are collected from the wild; hybrids are usually born in gardens. Over the years, gardeners have interfered with nature by hybridizing species and, in some case, genera. Where a hybrid has originated from a cross made between two species, the new "hybrid epithet" is always preceded by a multiplication sign. For example, *Nepeta* × *faassenii* is a hybrid between *Nepeta racemosa* from the Caucasus and *Nepeta nepetella* from Europe and North Africa.

In some cases, where two genera are closely related, it is possible to create a hybrid between them. In this case, the multiplication sign always appears before the generic name. For example, × *Heucherella alba* 'Bridget Bloom' is a hybrid between *Heuchera* × *brizoides* and *Tiarella cordifolia*.

NAME CHANGES

The naming of plants using botanical nomenclature is an ongoing process. As botanists' knowledge increases, it sometimes becomes apparent that plants that appeared

---

---

similar at the outset are in fact sufficiently different to require separate classification, so it becomes necessary to make changes to nomenclature. Old names, when they are particularly well known, are often shown in parentheses after the new name. For example, *Leucanthemum* × *superbum* (*Chrysanthemum maximum*).

Plant nomenclature is controlled by two international codes. The botanical names (in other words, the generic and specific names) are covered by the International Code of Botanical Nomenclature. This is applied to wild and cultivated plants. The cultivar names, which are used in addition to the botanical name, are covered by the International Code of Nomenclature for Cultivated Plants. This relates only to garden plants.

PLANT NAMES ARE FUN!

Whether the gardener is a natural linguist or not, botanical Latin is a satisfying language. Just as a feel for plants grows the more you work with them, so a feel for plant names develops over time. Not only are the names in a language that can be used anywhere in the world, they also provide immediately accessible information about the plant to which they refer. A few examples:

Specific epithet	Meaning	Example
argenteus, -a, -um	silvery	*Salvia argentea*
bonariensis, -e	of Bonaria (Buenos Aires)	*Verbena bonariensis*
grandiflorus, -a, -um	large flowered	*Epimedium grandiflorum*
latifolius, -a, -um	broad leaved	*Campanula latifolia*
mollis, -e	soft	*Alchemilla mollis*
perennis, -e	perennial	*Linum perenne*
spinosus, -a, -um	spiny	*Acanthus spinosus*
spectabilis, -e	showy	*Dicentra spectabilis*
vulgaris, -e	common, familiar	*Pulsatilla vulgaris*

For a fuller exploration see Horticulture's *Plant Names Explained*.

Buying perennials

Herbaceous perennials are available in a number of different forms, including seed, bare-root plants, young pot-grown plants, and larger, more mature specimens. All these have their advantages and disadvantages. Which form you choose depends to a large extent on how much money you want to spend—and how impatient you are to see results.

Many herbaceous perennials, such as delphiniums, are easily raised from seed.

SEED

For the admirably patient gardener who is prepared to start from scratch, seed is the ideal way of acquiring a number of plants at relatively little cost. Growing from seed is most attractive where a large area needs to be filled, or drifts of plants are required. Lupines, delphiniums, and *Digitalis* (foxgloves) are all easily raised from seed, as is *Verbena bonariensis*; all these flower relatively quickly from seed. However, not all herbaceous perennials can be grown successfully in this way; named varieties, for example, do not come true from seed, while the seed of some others may be sparse or difficult to germinate.

Perennials with fleshy roots or rhizomes can be bought bare root in the dormant season.

BARE ROOTS

In the days before nurseries used pots for raising plants, perennials were grown in fields and then lifted, divided, and sold as bare-root plants during the dormant season. Some are still sold in this way. While those with delicate roots must be protected in soil mix or moss in order to survive such treatment, there are many with tough swollen roots or underground stems that can live in a semidry state for several weeks out of the ground.

Buying bare-root plants can be an inexpensive way of acquiring perennials such as *Gypsophila* (baby's breath), *Incarvillea,* or *Papaver orientale* (oriental poppy). They are often sold alongside summer-flowering bulbs in colored packets. However, do not expect to acquire the choicest varieties in this way; plants are often sold by flower color rather than by cultivar name. The divisions of more select plants, such as peonies, may be small and will take several years to flower and make a sizable plant in the border.

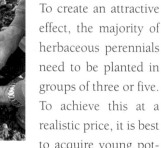
Young pot-grown perennials planted in groups early in the season will make substantial clumps by midsummer.

SMALL POTS

To create an attractive effect, the majority of herbaceous perennials need to be planted in groups of three or five. To achieve this at a realistic price, it is best to acquire young pot-grown plants in early spring. Because most perennials grow and establish quickly, these will soon catch up with larger, more mature specimens planted later in their life. It is important to buy and plant such

16

Buying choice perennials such as hellebores when they are in flower means you can see what you are getting, rather than relying on the label.

specimens early in the season: the amount of soil mix in the pots is small, and the plants soon become starved. If they are not planted out, they may be stimulated to flower instead of producing good root systems and healthy foliage first.

LARGE POTS

Because of the growing modern trend toward "instant" gardening, specimen-sized container-grown plants have become very popular. This is one of the most expensive ways of buying plants, but may be worth it if the gardener wants a quick result.

Some plants are worth the extra cost, because of the role they play in the garden. Architectural and statuesque perennials that will be used as features in planting schemes are examples: one good plant of *Cynara* (cardoon) or *Actaea* (*Cimicifuga*) will make an instant impact. In the case of *Actaea*, growth can be slow, so a large plant is a good investment. Large plants of easy-to-grow perennials such as *Alchemilla mollis* (lady's mantle) and most hardy geraniums really are an

extravagance; the money would be better spent else-where in the garden. The same is true of biennial plants and short-lived perennials such as foxglove; if you buy a mature foxglove it is often near the end of its lifespan.

Soil preparation and planting

Although some plants are very particular about the conditions in which they grow, most do best on neutral, fertile, well-drained soil that does not dry out. As perhaps only one in a hundred gardeners has these ideal conditions, the rest of us have to help our plants thrive through good cultivation techniques and adding nutrients to the soil.

Prepare the site well, mixing in compost and fertilizer. Dig a hole larger than the rootball.

Water the plant thoroughly, then carefully turn it out of its pot, without disturbing the roots.

Situate the rootball surface just below ground level. Replace soil, firm gently, then water well.

CULTIVATION

Thorough cultivation of flower beds is essential for good soil structure and healthy plant growth. Breaking up the soil with a fork will facilitate air and water penetration, which will help perennials develop a good root system. Prior to planting, digging should be deeper, since this will encourage newly planted specimens to establish deep roots. Even apparently shallow-rooted perennials have fine roots that grow down into the soil in search of water. These roots are especially important for plants growing on soil that dries out in summer; they will be better able to withstand these conditions if their root systems are well developed.

Dig new beds in the fall, leaving the ground rough to allow the penetration of frost, which will continue the cultivation process through a freeze-thaw action. Using a fork or border spade rather than a traditional digging spade will make the task less arduous and will break up the soil more thoroughly. Where plants are being added to existing beds, cultivate the area deeply, adding compost or manure to the hole, along with a slow-release fertilizer; this will help to give the newcomers a head start over competing neighbors.

ORGANIC MATTER

Organic matter is good for just about all types of soil. Well-rotted manure or compost increases the soil's water-holding capacity and its potential to retain nutrients. By increasing the humus content it also improves the overall structure of the soil. For example, humus separates the fine particles of a clay soil, helping it toward a more open, crumbly texture, while in sandy soil it forms a gel-like layer around the large particles, helping in the retention of moisture and nutrients.

DRAINAGE

Some plants like wet conditions, but most appreciate good drainage, even if they do not like to dry out. Along with organic matter, sharp grit or gravel is useful to improve the drainage of heavy clay soils. Roughly dig a layer of sharp grit into the soil in the fall; this will work in during winter as the ground freezes and thaws.

FEEDING

Most soils, especially clay, are adequately fertile for the majority of plants. Bulky organic manures add readily available nitrogen (for growth), but little else in the way of nutrition. Use a general slow-release fertilizer to ensure that plants receive all the main plant nutrients, and trace elements, if required.

PERENNIAL WEEDS

Perhaps the most important task when planting is to eradicate perennial weeds beforehand. Digging out is rarely entirely successful on the first attempt; fragments of root of weeds such as goutweed and bindweed quickly regrow. It is better to treat growing weeds with

Perennial weeds must be eradicated before any planting is undertaken.

a systemic herbicide, such as glyphosate, wait for any regrowth, and re-treat before carrying out permanent planting. Bear in mind that perennial weeds themselves are herbaceous perennials, and herbicides are unable to distinguish between those that the gardener strives to cultivate and those that he or she wishes to eradicate. Remember, too, that systemic herbicides work only on actively growing weeds with plenty of top growth; they are inactivated by contact with bare soil.

Impatience to plant will not save time and effort in the long run. If perennial weeds persist in the flower beds, they will become a real problem to eradicate as the planting becomes established.

INVASIVE SPECIES

Many useful plants may become invasive pests in favorable conditions. Examples in this book include *Aegopodium podagraria*, *Anthriscus sylvestris*, *Centaura* species, *Lamium maculatum*, *Ranunculus acris* and *R. ficaria*, *Trifolium pratense*, *Verbascum thapsus*, *Verbena bonariensis* and *Vinca minor*. Be aware of the invasive plants in your state (see www.nps.gov/plants/alien), and consider growing an alternative.

PLANTING

Most herbaceous perennials establish quickly and easily. The ideal planting time is early spring, just as the plants start growing. Bare root specimens will quickly start to produce leaf and stem growth and develop root systems. Container-grown stock planted at this time behaves in the same way. Whenever you plant, water well immediately afterward and until the plant is established.

When planting pot-grown specimens, aim to get the potting mix surface just below the soil surface. It is easy to plant too deeply and this can affect performance. For example, plants with rhizomes that need ripening by the sun, such as *Iris germanica*, will not thrive if the rhizomes are covered by soil. Similarly, peonies fail to flower if their crowns are covered by more than about 1 in. (2 cm) of soil.

Maintenance

Herbaceous perennials are generally easy to cultivate and maintain, with one of the most important jobs being to ensure that those that need support are well staked before flowering time. Most perennials grow quickly and fill space effectively, so may need control in future years, but there is less mystique attached to their pruning than with woody plants, and most can be increased through simple propagation methods.

DIVIDING AND REPLANTING

Most herbaceous perennials eventually become over-crowded, and the clumps they form grow too large for their position in the flower bed. When this happens, it is necessary to lift the clumps, divide them, and replant some of the divisions, allowing space for them to develop. The frequency of this operation depends on the growth habit, rate, and vigor of the individual plant. Some, including *Hemerocallis* (daylily) and *Helenium*, may benefit from this treatment every three to five years, while others, such as peonies, will live for many years without attention. There is no hard and fast rule; it is up to the discretion of the gardener.

Where winters are mild and wet, as in the Pacific northwest, divide plants in early spring. Because of the lack of growth over the winter, autumn transplanting brings the risk of any damaged roots' rotting in wet soil. In drier zones, transplanting in the fall is preferable, as the plant then has the maximum time to re-establish before it is faced with summer drought.

Lift clump-forming perennials using a fork: work around the plant, carefully prising it from the soil and

A large clump of hemerocallis is split into smaller pieces.

Three of the divisions are replanted, leaving 12 in.(30 cm) between them.

DIVIDING BEARDED IRISES

Some perennials are best divided and replanted after flowering. The most important example is the bearded iris: Its clumps gradually become overcrowded, which reduces vigor and flowering. Take young pieces of rhizome from the outside of the clump, shorten the leaves to one-third of their height to avoid wind disturbance, and replant the divisions, anchoring them onto the soil using wire pegs or hoops if the plants seem to need securing.

TAKING ROOT CUTTINGS

Root cuttings can be used to renew and propagate perennials with thick, fleshy roots: *Pulmonaria* (lungwort), *Papaver* (poppy), *Anemone × hybrida* (Japanese anemone), and *Acanthus* (bear's breeches), for example. Use pots of general-purpose potting mix with added sand and insert pieces of root 1 in. (2–3 cm) long so that the top cut end is just below the surface. Stand the pots in a frame or a sheltered, shaded corner and keep the soil moist.

Perennials such as hemerocallis need dividing every three to five years.

keeping the clump intact, if possible. Then simply pull the clump apart by hand. With a stubborn clump, plunge two forks back to back into the clump and work them outward to pry it apart. If all else fails, chop the clump into divisions using a spade. For replanting, choose divisions from around the edge of the original clump, as these will be the youngest and most vigorous, and they will not have suffered from overcrowding. Pot up some spare divisions to fill gaps or in case any of the planted ones fail.

Herbaceous perennials with deep, fleshy roots, such as poppies and peonies, are more difficult to divide, as it is virtually impossible to keep the root balls intact (see Moving peonies, below). In the case of oriental poppies, any pieces of root that break off may be used as root cuttings. This type of perennial is the sort that grows like a weed in one garden and fails in another.

Some herbaceous perennials are woody at the base and more shrublike in habit. These usually deteriorate with age, so propagation is necessary for replacement of the plant as well as increasing your stock. Woody-based perennials are not usually suitable for division and are best propagated by stem cuttings. *Dianthus* (pinks) and *Penstemon* are good examples of plants that are easy to propagate from cuttings but never seem to recover after division. Take cuttings in summer from nonflowering shoots, and overwinter them in pots, under protection, before planting out the following spring.

COPING WITH RAMPANT VARIETIES

Some plants, such as those that spread by underground stems or long, thin rhizomes, may need containing to prevent them from taking over the border. *Macleaya* (plume poppy), for example, has long rhizomes that quickly find any available space and then send towering stems of jigsaw-puzzle leaves rocketing skyward. This can be overpowering for less robust shrubs and perennials growing in the area. Mint is often grown in a bottomless bucket plunged into the herb bed, and other plants of a similar habit can be grown in the same way. Inexpensive plastic pots are readily available from garden centers; choose ones at least 18 in. (45 cm) across and of similar depth, in black or brown, in case the rim becomes visible in the border. Either remove the bottom or drill plenty of large holes in it to prevent the container from becoming waterlogged.

Less invasive perennials with rhizomes near the soil surface, such as hardy geraniums, can be contained by inserting terracotta roofing tiles vertically into the ground to form a box around the plant. *Aegopodium podagraria* 'Variegatum' (variegated bishop's weed) makes a very attractive edging plant when grown in this way, sandwiched between two rows of tiles.

Some vigorous perennials can be contained using a physical barrier in the soil. Here, *Aegopodium podagraria* 'Variegatum' is held back by roof tiles.

MOVING PEONIES

The peony has a reputation for being the most difficult herbaceous perennial to move successfully. Peonies have a tuberous root and little in the way of fibrous roots. Lift them in fall, after you have cut off the foliage but before the onset of the first frosts. Replant immediately to the same depth as before. No more than about 1in. (2.5 cm) of soil should cover the crown of the plant: deep planting will result in lack of flowers.

If lupines are cut back to ground level immediately after flowering, they will produce a second crop of flowers later in the season.

TIDYING AND CUTTING BACK

Since most gardeners were born to prune, herbaceous perennials will be their targets at some point in the year. Tidying up and cutting back at the right time can enhance the performance and appearance of most perennials. For inexperienced gardeners, there is little risk of inflicting a permanently damaging cut because the underground part of the plant will generate new stems next season.

Although tidying has its place in late summer, take care not to remove stems that still have decorative potential. While hardy geraniums and *Alchemilla mollis* (lady's mantle) will produce a new low mat of foliage if cut back after the main summer flowering, similar treatment of plants that color well in the fall will rob you of a season of glory. Autumn color is mainly a feature of

After flowering, cut back *Alchemilla mollis* (left), but leave *Euphorbia griffithii* 'Fireglow' (right) so as to enjoy the fall color of its foliage.

deciduous shrubs and trees, but some herbaceous perennials also play their part. *Euphorbia griffithii* 'Fireglow' is a good example. After its spectacular spring display of glowing bracts on upright shoots, 'Fireglow' grows branches and can become a rather untidy mass of stems and narrow green leaves. The temptation to cut it back at this point is strong, but to do this would be to sacrifice a superb show of orange and red shades that lasts for several weeks in fall.

In addition, some herbaceous perennials have stems and seed heads that remain decorative late into the year. Although dead, and usually devoid of leaves, these stems and seed heads stand proud in the winter garden, making an eye-catching feature, especially when etched with frost; many are also appreciated by birds, which search out their ripe seeds. *Rudbeckia* and *Echinacea* are two that retain straight stems with cone-shaped seed heads, particularly attractive against the fine waving leaves of parchment-yellow winter grasses. The dark purple-pink flowers of *Sedum spectabile* (ice plant) become more sophisticated as they fade to chestnut on their fleshy stems.

Those perennials with soft, nonpersistent stems and leaves, such as hostas, are the easiest to deal with. They quickly collapse and decay with the first frosts and the onset of winter. Tidy gardeners remove the leaf waste and commit it to the compost heap at any time between late fall and early spring. In cold areas there may be an advantage in delaying this because the leaf waste provides an extra layer of protection on the soil surface. Take into account early-flowering bulbs planted among the perennials—late clearing may be made difficult by their emerging shoots.

DEADHEADING AND REMOVING FLOWERS

Some early-flowering perennials will produce a second crop of blooms if cut back immediately after flowering. Delphiniums and lupines are notable examples. When the first main spike fades, it is tempting to trim this back and preserve the weedy lateral flowers until the very last

Penstemons will bloom throughout the season if regularly deadheaded. This keeps the plants in trim without the need for hard pruning.

Verbena bonariensis self-seeds prolifically. To prevent unwanted spread, cut back the flower stems as soon as the blooms have faded.

bloom has faded. A positive approach is needed: once the main blooms have faded, cut the stems right back to ground level. Water plants well and apply a general-purpose fertilizer, in liquid form if conditions are dry. New foliage will quickly appear, followed by a new crop of flowers in early fall. These colorful summer beauties are particularly welcome alongside autumn favorites such as *Crocosmia* and *Rudbeckia*.

Some herbaceous perennials can become pests if allowed to set seed, especially in light, sandy soil where seed germination is particularly good. If lady's mantle is not prevented from getting a hold, it will produce seedlings in profusion and can become too successful as a ground-cover plant. To prevent such spread, cut off the flowers as soon as the lime color of the blooms starts to yellow. Alternatively, stems can be pulled off established plants by tugging firmly. Where the foliage has flopped and become untidy, the whole plant can be sheared off to ground level and allowed to regrow: a fresh crop of leaves and a few late flowers will result. Also consider removing the faded flowers of *Knautia macedonica*, *Verbena bonariensis*, and *Verbascum* before seed is sprinkled liberally all over the border.

Some plants are grown mainly for foliage effect, and these also benefit from the removal of the flower stems before seed is set. Flowering and seed production are part of a plant's life cycle; when seed is produced, the plant knows that its job is done for the season. If the cycle is not completed, because seed is not allowed to set, there is more chance of the foliage staying in good condition. In other cases, the faded flower stems simply detract from the beauty of the leaves, and for that reason should be removed.

Stachys byzantina is wonderfully silver as the new "lamb's ear" leaves appear in spring. The plant becomes more noticeable as the flowering stems rise from the silver felted mat beneath. Once the lilac flowers open, however, these stems become untidy and the foliage starts to deteriorate. Cutting it back at this point will encourage the plant to produce new silver foliage, which will look good throughout the fall. Statuesque *Cynara cardunculus* (cardoon) is a magnificent plant, but it

Stachys byzantina (left) looks better if flower stems are removed. Cut back *Cynara cardunculus* (right) after flowering, and new leaves will appear.

declines after the flowers have produced their thistlelike mauve stamens in late summer. Cut the plant to ground level now, and new silver leaves will emerge; these remain on the plant throughout winter, surviving all but the most severe weather.

Several hostas retain their leaf variegation better if the flower stems are removed as they appear. Hosta flowers are not unattractive, so it is up to the gardener to decide whether the flowers or the variegated leaves are preferable. The foliage of rheums also remains more attractive if the flower stems are removed at an early stage: allow them to develop but not to set seed. Keep pulmonarias looking better and encourage them to produce their new foliage more quickly by removing flower stems as the blooms fade in late spring. Do this to brunneras, too, especially the lovely silver-variegated *Brunnera macrophylla* 'Jack Frost'.

The foliage of variegated hostas (left) is preserved by removing flowers as they appear. The lovely *Brunnera macrophylla* 'Jack Frost' (right) remains in good condition if the flowers are removed as they begin to fade.

PROVIDING SUPPORT

Support in some form or other can make or break perennial planting, whether the subjects form part of a classic perennial border or are contributing to a mixed scheme. In mixed borders, shrubs lend some support and shelter to their herbaceous companions. In prairie-style planting, grasses may perform a similar function, filtering the wind and so reducing its impact. In traditional-style perennial borders, however, artificial support will always be necessary for the taller-growing perennials, whatever the situation.

Birch twigs put in position during early spring are natural supports for herbaceous perennials; they are hidden as the plants grow.

Traditional birch and hazel twigs are ideal for use as grow-through supports for individual plants in the perennial border. If you have a good local supply, they are generally inexpensive and easy to tailor to the height of the plants. Put them in position in early spring, well ahead of the perennials' main growing season. They look

REDUCING STAKING PROBLEMS

Grow strong, wind-resistant varieties. Choose plants that require little or no support, rather than those that need every shoot staked. For example, *Aconitum* (monkshood) varieties are more upright and reliable than delphiniums. You may like the delphiniums' color and habit, but are you prepared for the amount of maintenance they need?

Herbaceous perennials whose stems have collapsed under the weight of flowers, foliage, and summer rain—like the peonies shown here—are never a pretty sight. Stay ahead of the game. Remember that perennials grow quickly, and introduce support when they are still in good condition—not when the stems are starting to fall into one another.

Linked green metal plant supports, through which the developing stems grow, are strong and unobtrusive.

natural and in any case quickly disappear from view as the border billows in midsummer.

A similar effect is achieved with grow-through metal supports, which are basically metal hoops supporting a wire grid. These are held above individual plants on three or four legs, and their height can be adjusted. Put them in position when the plants are just showing above ground. The stems grow up through the grid, gradually concealing it. In some cases, grids can be left in position through the winter. Metal supports are comparatively expensive, but good-quality galvanized ones last for many years. As they give support only to the lower part of the stem, they are most suitable for stouter subjects.

In perennial borders that do not contain any woody plants, large-gauge netting can be used over the whole planting area. Put this in position at the beginning of the season; as the plants grow through it they will be held upright by the mesh. Netting is extremely effective where all the border plants peak at the same time. If any cutting back is required, however, it can be done only down to the level of the netting, which would otherwise be exposed. Gaps in the border are difficult to fill during the growing season if netting is used in this way.

Bamboo canes are popular for supporting plants with tall spikes, such as delphiniums. Put them in place when the plants are knee high, and tie the stems in with twine or raffia as they grow. Thin, strong canes are the most discreet. Various metal and wire stakes that can be put in place during the growing season are also available.

Semicircular metal hoops on legs can be put into position later in the season to support tall perennials such as heleniums.

These are designed to support individual stems or whole clumps. The best ones are fairly inconspicuous and are useful to have on hand to solve unexpected problems due to abnormally lush growth or wind and rain damage.

WATERING AND MULCHING

When herbaceous perennials are planted during the fall or early spring, a thorough watering helps to settle the soil particles around the roots and ensure easy establishment as new roots develop. Additional watering is rarely required during the early stages of growth, as perennial roots grow vigorously to balance the developing stems and leaves.

When growth above ground is at its maximum, some perennials are particularly sensitive to drought, responding by wilting of foliage and of developing flowers. If dry conditions persist, their performance can be severely impaired. If they are watered liberally at the first signs of stress they quickly recover.

Generous mulching around the plants with compost, composted bark, or well-rotted farmyard manure at the start of the season helps to conserve moisture and prevent water loss from the soil surface; it also helps to suppress weeds and will benefit the plants throughout the growing season.

Where do herbaceous perennials fit in?

Herbaceous perennials are extremely versatile and are as useful in new gardens as they are in established ones. They grow quickly, and most show results in their first season (perfect for the impatient gardener). Many are inexpensive and offer exceptional value. In addition, they can be moved around within the garden and respond well to being divided and replanted.

LAYERING, STRUCTURING, AND DECORATING

Trees, tall shrubs, and climbers provide height in our gardens—they make them three-dimensional. The plants at eye level are the first that grab our attention, so are perhaps the most important. Woody shrubs play a leading role, as do taller perennials, particularly many favorites such as delphiniums, foxgloves, heleniums, lupines, phlox, and asters. The lowest layer—below eye level—is the detail. It is often the closest to us and has become even more important in small modern gardens. Dwarf shrubs and annuals, bulbs and container plants

are found here, but herbaceous perennials predominate because of the variety they offer. They include corydalis, hellebores, geraniums, hostas, and pulmonarias.

Trees and shrubs form the basic structure of a garden. However, the average plot has space only for a certain number of these, so there are few opportunities for planting more once the selection has been made. Dwarf shrubs and container plants can be added, as can climbers, which occupy little space horizontally but fill the vertical space above them. But the biggest scope for adding plants comes in the form of bulbs, annuals, and herbaceous perennials. All these may be seen as short-term propositions. Just like the accessories in a room, they are easily changed to alter the look, color scheme, and mood of a garden, as the gardener chooses.

COVERING GROUND

Besides being useful in their own right, herbaceous perennials are excellent for planting between newly planted shrubs and trees, to fill space and provide color until the woody plants become established. Many are well adapted to poor soil or otherwise difficult sites, so can be left in such positions as ground cover or used in other unpromising areas of the garden.

The choice of suitable herbaceous perennials is vast, and with a little thought, areas of ground cover can be made interesting and varied. The pretty *Erodium pelargoniiflorum* (zone 6–8) is a spreading perennial that will colonize poor soil in sun or shade, seeding freely on sandy soil. It resembles a hardy geranium, but with

Herbaceous perennials predominate in the lower layer of planting, below eye level. Here they are used both in the open ground and in pots.

stiffer foliage, rather like that of a zonal pelargonium, in grayish green. The rosettes of leaves give rise to soft pink flowers in early summer. *Geranium* 'Ann Folkard' (zone 5–7) is often described as compact, but in semishade it will spread vigorously, its creeping stems carrying lime yellow leaves and vivid magenta flowers, like those of its parent *Geranium psilostemon*. Spreading and twining, it makes very effective ground cover, particularly under shrubs with gold foliage such as *Philadelphus coronarius* 'Aureus' (zone 4–8). On really challenging sites, such as beneath the canopy of mature rhododendrons, the tough and vigorous *Symphytum ibericum* (zone 4–8) will quickly create a bold, leafy layer, with the benefit of pretty, creamy yellow flowers in spring.

EXTENDING THE SEASON

Our gardens contain many shrubs that flower through spring into early summer. Fewer woody plants flower in summer, and herbaceous perennials are ideal for filling the color gap. Where roses predominate in a garden, cottage-garden favorites such as *Phlox paniculata* (zone 4–8), *Leucanthemum* × *superbum* (shasta daisy) (zone 4–7), and *Campanula persicifolia* (zone 4–8) perform as the first flush of rose blooms fade. Not only do they provide color in the garden, but they are also valuable for cut flowers. Before the roses bloom, some perennials start the period of interest: early peonies, oriental poppies, lupines, and aquilegias bloom in late spring as color from spring-flowering bulbs and shrubs fades.

PROVIDING VARIETY IN FORM AND TEXTURE

Many herbaceous perennials are soft in form, and this softness brings movement into the garden. Perennials also come in a variety of shapes, from rounded to spiky, vertical to spreading—all forms that bring borders to life. There is such contrast between, for example, the upright spires of flowers produced by delphiniums and lupines and the mounded domes of hardy geraniums and some asters, that gardeners have a hard time choosing among them. (See also pages 28–33.)

BROADENING THE COLOR PALETTE

Herbaceous perennials are unrivaled in both the range and the intensity of color they provide in our gardens. Bright gems are fitted into a planting scheme with partners that either soften or accentuate their display. For example, the solid blaze of flowers produced by star performers such as heleniums, rudbeckias, gaillardias, phlox, and crocosmias is most effective diluted by foliage plants and other gentle companions. Adventurous gardeners have experimented with such neutral partners as grasses; in such associations the grass provides a foil for the strong color of the flowers.

Plant shapes

Borders consist of plants of different shapes and colors that work together to create a picture. Each plant shape contributes to the character and texture of the border as a whole. Changing the relative proportion of each shape in the composition has as much of an effect on the border's appearance as changing the proportions of the constituent colors.

The look of a planting scheme alters all the time, not only according to what is in flower, but also depending on the stage of growth of the plants. A successful scheme is a continuously changing picture, with enough variety to maintain interest throughout the seasons. Although herbaceous perennials are considered here, the majority of successful plantings use a mixture of perennials, trees, shrubs, annuals, and bulbs, each making a contribution in shape, color, and texture.

SPREADING MATS

Often associated with hostile conditions, such as exposed situations and dry soils, mat-forming perennials lie low to avoid desiccation. Examples include *Acaena microphylla* (zone 6–7), *Sedum aizoon* (zone 4–9), and *Euphorbia myrsinites* (zone 5–9). These plants hug the ground, spreading out on it so their leaves can soak up the maximum amount of sunlight. Some develop long

These herbaceous borders at Ilnacullin, Ireland, are a symphony of different plant shapes, colors, and textures.

stems that grow out on the surface of the soil; some have underground stems or rhizomes that throw up short vertical shoots. However they grow, the overall plant shape is similar. Use these plants at the front of the border, where they will provide a gentle foreground for the plants behind. They associate well with paving and with gravel and are ideal for softening the edges of hard landscaping. Alongside a lawn, however, they make mowing difficult, unless contained.

Euphorbia myrsinites (left) and *Acaena microphylla* (right) are both herbaceous perennials that form low, spreading mats.

SPACE AND SHAPE

The space around a plant affects its overall shape and appearance. For example, to produce the impression of one large soft mound of herbaceous geraniums, plant several close together, but for several individual mounds, increase the planting distance to allow each plant enough space to develop fully.

Many perennial geraniums (left) and *Alchemilla mollis* (right) are perennials that form soft mounds near the front of the border.

Penstemon heterophyllus 'Catherine de la Mare' (left) and *Paeonia lactiflora* 'Bowl of Beauty' (right) both form mounds of solid structure.

SOFT MOUNDS

Soft mounds of foliage and flowers that melt into one another and billow across the border epitomize English-style gardens. Geraniums, *Anthemis tinctoria,* fine-leaved artemisias, and *Alchemilla mollis* belong in this category. These plants are good at filling space either under or beside other plants. They are excellent companions for taller perennials and shrubs in a mixed border, and perfect under hybrid tea roses. Plant them at the front of a border or farther back, or alternate them with lower spreading plants. The latter scheme accentuates the forms of the individual plants and makes the planting more interesting. Soft mounds can be monotonous *en masse*—relieve them with spiky and architectural forms.

Plants with narrow strap-shaped leaves, such as *Hemerocallis* and *Agapanthus,* create a different type of

soft mound. Out of flower, these two plants are fairly discreet, but when they are in bloom, their shape and presence change dramatically; their exotic flowers are produced on relatively tall spikes in midsummer.

SOLID DOMES

Some plants are generally mound shaped, but have a more solid form. Most penstemons and *Euphorbia characias* varieties are good examples, forming shrublike plants with persistent stems. Penstemon flowers rise on spikes above the mounded plants, which provide structure even when out of flower. The foliage of herbaceous peonies is also in this category; their blooms are short-lived, though spectacular, so the plant shape plays an important part. The foliage is attractive and provides long-lasting, bold, rounded structure.

BROAD COLUMNS

Common among herbaceous perennials is the short, stout column. Plants of this form have many stems growing close together, all to the same height. The effect is of a green cylinder rising as the season progresses, and usually culminating in a sheet of flowers at the top of the column. Heleniums bear masses of daisylike flowers, which open from dark buds, creating a rich velvet tapestry in late summer. Other examples include *Monarda, Aster, Heliopsis,* and *Leucanthemum.*

Often these plants originate from grassland habitats, where they need to grow tall to survive among the

REPEATING SHAPES

In larger borders repeat plant shapes at intervals. This simple technique holds the scheme together, regardless of what is planted in between. It was often used by Gertrude Jekyll to give her planting structure. She used blocks of the same plant, but a similar effect can be achieved with different plants of the same shape: a more practical solution in smaller areas.

Clumps of *Helenium* 'The Bishop' (left) and *Helianthus* 'Lemon Queen' (right) both make broad columns consisting of many upright stems.

Digitalis lutea (zone 5–8), and *Linaria purpurea* (zone 4–7) create gentle vertical brushstrokes in the border. They seed freely on most soils, increasing the sense of informality. *Sisyrinchium striatum* (zone 7–9) is a more definite spike and a good cream color. It has few flowers, but these, together with the gray-green sharp foliage, make it a good foil for frothy *Alchemilla mollis* (zone 4–7) or flowing *Nepeta* × *faassenii* (zone 3–9). On poor soils sisyrinchium seeds freely; thin as necessary.

The white form of fireweed, *Epilobium angustifolium* 'Album' (zone 6–8), produces soft spikes atop graceful grasses. In borders, the size of their clumps may need reducing regularly to prevent them from predominating and being too large and solid in effect. The interesting part of this shape of plant is at the top of the stems; they need lower, softer forms in front of them.

LIGHT SPIKES

Light spikes are among the most valuable plant forms because they provide vertical interest that lifts any planting scheme. Plants such as *Veronica spicata* (zone 5–8),

Sisyrinchium striatum (left) and *Epilobium angustifolium* 'Album' (right) have slender, upright flower stems that provide light spikes in the border.

MAKING THE MOST OF BULBS

Bulbs are useful plants for prolonging the season of herbaceous perennials.

Alliums Ornamental onions naturally have poor foliage, so plant them where companions will hide this, such as beneath soft silver herbaceous plants. *Artemisia schmidtiana* (z. 3–7), with its finely cut foliage, is the perfect setting for *Allium cristophii* (z. 4–10), with its silvery lilac firework flowers.

Camassias For color before many herbaceous perennials have gotten going, choose *Camassia leichtlinii* (z. 3–8). Its spikes appear with the bluebells, and the flowers are a similar color. Plant it to grow through the emerging plumes of bronze fennel, *Foeniculum vulgare* 'Purpureum' (z. 5–8).

Triteleias The long-lasting sapphire flowers of *Triteleia laxa* 'Queen Fabiola' (Koningin Fabiola) (z. 6–10) are similar to agapanthus and add vibrant color to mounds of lime green *Alchemilla mollis* (z. 4–7). Both plants enjoy well-drained soil.

Tulips Create the effect of exotic poppies in the border by including well-spaced tulips among herbaceous perennials. The glorious simple dark flowers of *Tulipa* 'Queen of Night' (z. 4–8) are stunning above a lime green carpet of *Euphorbia cyparissias* 'Fens Ruby' (z. 5–9).

stems clad with willowlike gray-green leaves. On a larger scale *Veronicastrum virginicum* (zone 4–8) is a taller, slimmer spike, reaching 6 ft. (2 m) high. Where less height is needed, herbaceous salvias, such as *Salvia × superba* (zone 5–8), contribute a glowing mass of low spikes from midsummer onward.

STATELY SPIRES

For a strong vertical statement, choose the stately spires of delphiniums, *Aconitum* (monkshood), lupines, *Alcea,* (hollyhock), and *Digitalis purpurea* (foxglove). These plants look spectacular, but no less impressive is their ability to achieve this height without producing permanent stems. The vegetative parts of the plant are not tall, only the flower stems, which thrust the flowers skyward to render them unavoidable to pollinators. Grandiose though these plants are in flower, their impact is lost at other times, so bear this in mind when planning their position. Also important are support, which needs to be in place before the flower stems arise, and access, which is necessary to allow them to be cut back after flowering to encourage a repeat performance.

In traditional English herbaceous borders, spire-forming plants are placed at the back, where their transient nature is disguised by more solid structures, such as a high wall or a yew hedge, perhaps with clipped hedges dividing the scheme into sections and providing height when the plants are not in full growth. This is rarely the way these plants are used in modern gardens. They need space but with their foundations screened behind more permanent subjects such as taller penstemons, whose main flowering season follows the peak of the lupines and delphiniums. Light foliage shrubs such as *Cornus alba* 'Sibirica Variegata' (zone 2–8) are another solution: they will grow on to fill the gaps created as the spires are removed. Alternatively, tall annuals such as the tobacco plant *Nicotiana sylvestris* may be planted to take over the role of height provider, and make an equally arresting display later in the year.

Of all the plants in this group, *Acanthus spinosus* (spiny bear's-breech) (zone 5–8) is in a league of its

The stately spires of *Acanthus spinosus* (left) and *Digitalis purpurea* (right) create points of strong vertical interest in a planting scheme.

own. It contributes stately, self-supporting spires above a mound of bold architectural foliage. A favorite of Gertrude Jekyll, this plant can be used nearer the front of a border to provide structure throughout the season.

BOLD BLOOMS

Some plants contribute little in terms of form, but their flowers can be used to make bold statements. Although the plants of *Papaver orientale* (oriental poppy) (zone 3–8) are of little substance in themselves and die down

Achillea filipendulina 'Gold Plate' (left) and *Paeonia lactiflora* 'Lord Kitchener' (right) both provide bold flower forms of strong color.

early in the season, the blooms are flamboyant. Plant them beside more solid subjects that will hold the scheme together when the poppies have flowered and their foliage has faded. The larger achilleas, such as *Achillea filipendulina* 'Gold Plate' (see page 31), have an indistinct form with light fernlike foliage at the base of stiff stems. However, this is an advantage when they flower, as the bright blooms seem to fly above the border. The eye-catching flowers of tulips and alliums have a similar effect (see Making the most of bulbs, page 30).

Peonies, like acanthus, double up on effect. Their luxuriant floating blooms draw attention as they open (see page 31), and for the rest of the season the solid domes of strong green foliage contribute structure.

RISING CLOUDS AND DRIFTING MISTS

With their masses of tiny flowers or finely cut foliage, cloudlike plants add a magical lightness to planting schemes, softening the shapes and colors of their neighbors. Some grasses are particularly effective—the lovely *Stipa gigantea* (giant oat grass) (zone 8–10) for example. Its fine golden flowers reflect the light, especially in the low sun of evening. A smaller relative, *Stipa tenuissima* (zone 7–9) produces a soft mist toward

The smoky foliage of purple fennel, *Foeniculum vulgare* 'Purpureum' (left), and the white cloudlike flower heads of *Crambe cordifolia* (right) rise and drift above the border.

HEIGHT IN THE FOREGROUND

It is tempting to position tall plants at the back of a border and work forward in order of decreasing height. Including some taller, lighter plants in the foreground makes the scheme more three-dimensional; this changes the perspective and the picture appears deeper and so more interesting.

the front of a border and looks wonderful with short, smoldering *Crocosmia* (montbretia). The feathery foliage of bronze fennel, *Foeniculum vulgare* 'Purpureum' (zone 5–8), provides a drifting vapor throughout the season. Its soft color is an excellent partner to most other perennials, and it is especially useful to fill positions where seasonal interest is to follow: Try it with *Dahlia* 'Bishop of Llandaff'. However, *Crambe cordifolia* (zone 6–8) is the definitive cloud plant. Growing up to 6 ft. (2 m) tall, it forms a white cumulus above the border in summer, the perfect setting for sapphire delphiniums or steel blue monkshood. On chalk soils *Gypsophila paniculata* (zone 4–8) gives a similar, but lighter effect. It is beautiful with scabious and other cottage-garden flowers.

SEE-THROUGH PLANTS

Plants that you can see through have two purposes in the border. In the foreground, they bring delicate height to the planting, something to look through, thereby increasing the perspective and depth of the scene.

SUPPORT—THE SECRET OF SUCCESS

Remember to provide support for plants before they need it. The beauty of a plant's shape is lost if it collapses just before it reaches its prime. Support is particularly important for plants with tall, upright stems. Grow-through supports, put in place at an early stage of growth, are more satisfactory than trying to prop up fully grown stems. They also help to define the shape of a plant and the space it occupies.

Plants with tall, fine stems and small flowers, such as *Verbena bonariensis* (left) and *Knautia macedonica* Melton Pastels (right), can be used near the front of the border to add depth to the planting.

ACCENT ARCHITECTURALS

The shape of some perennials is unimportant compared to their bold distinctive stems and/or foliage. Use these plants as exclamation marks in mixed planting, giving them plenty of space to develop; if you do not, most will take it anyway, overwhelming weaker neighbors. With its huge steely leaves and statuesque stems, the cardoon *Cynara cardunculus* (zone 6–9) will need more than a square yard (square meter) by midsummer. It is a good plant to take over where oriental poppies leave off, as an accent point in the border. Its strong leaf form may fight with other bold subjects, so soften it with rounded mounds and light foliage. Another strong candidate is *Macleaya microcarpa* 'Kelway's Coral Plume' (zone 3–9). Its jigsaw-puzzle blue-gray leaves on tall stems are more of a feature than the plumes of pinkish flowers. It is also an excellent choice for the back of a border against dark evergreens or growing through the soft fronds of bronze fennel. For an exotic touch, use cannas, with their fabulous foliage and brilliant flowers. Since they are tender, add them seasonally in temperate zones.

Accent plants increase the sense of the exotic in a border, and their effect can be stunning, so long as they are appropriate to the style of the garden.

Farther back, they can be drifted through the other plants: a thread holding these lightly together. *Verbena bonariensis* (zone 8–9) is the ultimate see-through, drifting plant. It has height without weight, and its rich purple color and deep green stems are good mixers. Its other good qualities are a long flowering season and resistance to weather. *Valeriana phu* 'Aurea' (zone 4–8) has similar qualities, with tall, branched stems, small white flowers, and golden yellow young foliage. *Knautia macedonica* Melton Pastels (zone 5–8) has scabiouslike blooms that come in crimson, pink, and mauve and float above the border on wiry stems.

For temporary drifts through mixed planting, use hardy annuals. *Nigella* (love-in-a-mist), *Cosmos*, *Salvia viridis* var. *comata*, and the annual grass *Briza maxima* are all easy and associate well in informal schemes.

ADDING TO EXISTING PLANTING

Most herbaceous perennials arrive in the garden as additions to existing planting, rather than as part of a new scheme. When choosing a plant for a particular position, think about the shapes the scheme might lack, and at what time of the year. When positioning a new plant, think about the shape and texture of its potential neighbors, as much as their color. A good combination of plant forms is just as important as a clever color combination.

The bold foliage and flowers of *Cynara cardunculus* (left) and the tall stems and jigsawlike leaves of *Macleaya microcarpa* 'Kelway's Coral Plume' (right) add dramatic effect to any planting scheme.

Color: themes and continuity

In the planning stages, careful thought is often given to the color scheme of a bed or border. Later, we tend to choose what appeals, often with little regard for perfect coordination. This is entirely acceptable. The most important rule of color is to remember that it is a matter of personal taste. If you like a plant, and it looks good in your garden, it is the right choice.

A yellow border at Hadspen Garden, Somerset, in England, with a wonderful selection of soft yellow flowers set against an exuberant variety of foliage.

THEMING

Color-themed planting is dependent upon what is in flower or otherwise performing at any one time. There are two ways to approach the planning: either go for a scheme that will look absolutely stunning over a few weeks at a certain time of the year by choosing plants that grow together and bloom together, or try to achieve continuity by choosing plants that reach their peak at different times so that the effect will last more than one season. The results will be quite different. The first will have a lively short-lived crescendo, and the second will be quieter, gentler, and longer lasting.

Foliage is the key to success in holding a color scheme together, and can be provided by deciduous or

ADDING COLOR WITH ANNUALS

Make full use of seasonal color to ensure a continuity of interest in perennial borders. Annuals are excellent for providing high summer color, often lacking in our gardens. Choose those with a tall, loose habit, rather than compact bedding types, as these will sit more happily with the perennials. If annuals are to be a regular feature, keep spaces clear for them. The following annuals are all easy to grow and combine well with perennials. Some, such as the antirrhinum, are available in a variety of heights and colors.

Antirrhinum majus

Cleome hassleriana

Cosmos bipinnatus

Nicotiana alata

Nigella damascena 'Miss Jekyll' (left)

Salvia viridis var. *comata*

evergreen shrubs and trees or herbaceous perennials. Get the foliage plants right, and the flowers will act as seasonal highlights. For example, a yellow border might be based around shrubs such as the gold-variegated *Elaeagnus pungens* 'Dicksonii' (zone 6–9) and the yellow-leaved *Philadelphus coronarius* 'Aureus' (zone 4–8), with additional foliage interest being introduced by perennials such as *Hosta* 'Gold Standard' (zone 4–8) and the light, airy *Valeriana phu* 'Aurea' (zone 4–8). To this add a long succession of perennials to continue the theme from early spring to late fall: *Euphorbia polychroma* (zone 5–8) for early spring, *Ranunculus acris* 'Flore Pleno' (zone 4–7) for late spring, *Achillea filipendulina* 'Gold Plate' (zone 2–9) in early summer, followed later by *Helenium* 'The Bishop' (zone 3–8) and, finally, *Rudbeckia fulgida* var. *sullivantii* 'Goldsturm' (zone 4–8) in the fall.

FILLING GAPS

As borders grow and establish, they often need fine tuning. Gardeners usually choose plants that look good together, but this often means that they all flower together, too, leaving the garden dull at other times. In a large garden, this is not such a problem, as the action can be concentrated in different areas, the various corners of the garden performing in rotation. It is less desirable in a small garden, where the interest is best distributed through as much of the year as possible. To ensure continuity of flower, go out when you spot a gap and deliberately obtain plants that are currently in bloom.

Whatever the scale of the planting, there will always be peaks and troughs in performance; you may wish to plan for these. For example, there is little point having everything flowering in midsummer, if that is when you are normally away on vacation.

INTRODUCING NEW PLANTS

One of the great advantages of container-grown plants is being able to buy them in flower. Not only can you see what you are getting; you can also experiment with the plant's position in the garden. Try the pot in different

sites, and see for yourself where the plant will fit best into a color scheme. If you find that the ideal site is already taken, leave the new plant in its pot until the fall and then just relocate the existing occupant. Herbaceous perennials are generally easy to transplant, so try moving things around if you can see a combination that can be improved by a little rearrangement.

LINK PLANTS

Color-themed borders are most successful when some linking plants are incorporated. Select plants that do not need much space and that can be planted in subtle drifts among the other occupants. *Digitalis lutea* (zone 5–8) is useful to trail through yellow color schemes. Its delicate spikes of creamy yellow flowers are noncompetitive but gently conspicuous. *Verbena bonariensis* (zone 8–9) is useful in pink, lilac, and burgundy themes. The flowers are blue enough to be a good linking color, and the small blooms on tall stems create a great see-through effect.

BLUE: THE PERFECT MIXER

Blue combines well with just about any other color, so perennials such as nepetas and blue-flowered salvias and herbaceous geraniums are invaluable in any planting scheme where something is needed to unite two or more contrasting colors. Even clashing pinks and oranges will live together when blue is used to dilute and complement them.

SITUATIONS

All gardens have their different growing conditions. Most have places that get little or no direct sunlight; many have hot, dry areas with little moisture in the soil. Some have water or wet soil, a few trees or woodland, a little pasture or meadow. All these can support fascinating and desirable plants, and by choosing the right herbaceous perennials, you can give them color and interest throughout the year. When it comes to perennials, no situation is a problem; any is an asset if the right selection of plants is made.

RIGHT: Royal Horticulture Society Garden, Rosemoor, Devon, England

The perennial border

A formal perennial border at its peak is one of the most spectacular sights in the English garden. An essential feature of English Edwardian and Victorian gardens, it is rarely seen today, having largely been replaced by the mixed border and other, less formal styles of planting. Yet fresh ways of looking at the traditional perennial border can make it fitting for modern times while retaining the spirit of the original.

True herbaceous perennial borders are long, formal beds, often backed by yew hedges, which provide shelter as well as serving as a backdrop to the display. Some borders are arranged as mirror images of one another; occasionally they are double sided.

The perennial border can have up to eight months of interest in a year, but most have their moment of glory at one point during mid- to late summer; it is virtually impossible to achieve the same level of interest the whole year through. Even with careful planning, gaps will be left by early flowering plants (although these can be filled by annuals or tender perennials), and the ground is always left empty in the dormant season.

Traditional perennial borders are often said to be labor intensive. Undoubtedly plants require support, cutting back, weed control, and periodic lifting and division. Whether this is more demanding than other styles of planting is debatable; perhaps it is the focus of these activities on one area of the garden, and on one group of plants, that has fostered the belief that the perennial border is hard work.

SELECTION AND PLANNING

The secret of success in any perennial border is the selection and placing of plants. Shape, height, flower color, and timing all have a contribution to make.

Mirrored herbaceous perennial borders at Bramdean House, Hampshire, in England.

Plants tend to be arranged with the tallest at the back and the shortest at the front, but the most successful schemes use variations on this pattern. Exclamation marks of tall, spiky plants and light, airy, see-through subjects increase depth and perspective as well as creating focal points in the long expanse of planting. Repetition of key plants is important to hold the scheme together, especially in double-sided or mirrored perennial borders.

EXOTICS IN THE BORDER

Tender, exotic perennials are often used in herbaceous borders to provide focal points and to fill the gaps left by early perennials, such as oriental poppies (*Papaver orientale*). Cannas, with splendid foliage and brilliant flowers, are a natural choice, as are dahlias, particularly those with dark chocolate leaves. In warm, sheltered situations, dark-leaved aeoniums are stunning additions to hot color schemes.

THE MAINTENANCE SCHEDULE

Work in the perennial border takes place mainly in the dormant season and includes soil cultivation, manuring, division and preparing supports. Once the border is in full growth, there is no stopping its progress, nor any room to maneuver between the plants. Selective cutting back and some watering in dry periods is all that is needed.

Asters growing through twiggy supports.

Support is a vital element of any perennial border. The perennials grow in close proximity, particularly as clumps increase in size from year to year. There is a certain amount of competition between them, and they are drawn upward towards the light, increasing the need for support. This has to be in position before the plants require it; staking and tying once they have grown is difficult and results in an awkward, unnatural appearance.

Perennial weeds are perhaps the biggest problem in planting of this kind. They retreat below ground with the ornamentals, reemerging as the young perennial shoots push through the soil in spring. Bindweed is a particular pest, using both perennials and their supports as a means to climb and smother the display. Using an herbicide is impossible without damaging the plants. The only solution is to save plants that are free of infestation by moving them to a nursery bed, then sacrificing the rest while dealing with the problem (see page 19).

HERBACEOUS PLANTING IN ISLAND BEDS

As gardens became smaller over the years, it became more difficult to find room for the traditional rectangular perennial border, and gardeners began to experiment with other styles of herbaceous planting. Alan Bloom, at Bressingham Gardens, in Norfolk, England, pioneered the planting of perennials in informal island beds. Here the environment is less enclosed, promoting better air circulation and allowing more light to reach the plants from all sides; as a result, plants are sturdier, with a stockier habit, and the need to provide supports is often reduced. Because island beds are visible from all angles, they also allow more opportunity for variety and interest in the planting: as one aspect is entering its quiet phase, another can be reaching its peak. In the average garden this style of bed is far easier to accommodate than the grand formal border.

PERENNIAL BORDERS BASED ON FOLIAGE

Herbaceous perennials requiring no support or cutting back during the season are a much less demanding option. Beds of hostas, ferns, astilbes, aruncus, rodgersias, and other lovers of semi-shade can be used to create a different type of perennial border that suits an informal garden with light tree cover. Using the effect of foliage more than the seasonal impact of flowers maintains interest over a long period. This can be further extended by planting bulbs that flower in early spring, such as narcissi, camassias, and leucojums, which perform before the perennial leaf cover is established. As the perennial growth develops, it hides the fading foliage of the bulbs.

Perennial borders based on foliage have a long season of interest.

CLASSIC HERBACEOUS BORDER PERENNIALS

Here is a selection of the key plants traditionally used in the perennial border. They have a variety of shapes, sizes, and forms, and between them provide a wealth of color from early summer to autumn.

The **asters** were adopted from the cottage garden because of their tall stems of colorful daisylike flower heads that are produced so reliably throughout late summer and fall. Rich blue and purple asters contrast beautifully with the deep orange, yellow, and flame shades of autumn, while pink and lilac varieties enliven the deepening burgundy heads of sedums and blend with the soft pink of anemones.

Aster novae-angliae 'Pink Victor'

Most cultivars of **Aster novi-belgii**, or the Michaelmas daisy (zone 2–8), mostly grow to about 4 ft. (1.2 m). Strong stems and an upright habit suit them to a midway position in the border. Sadly, their handsome, dark green foliage is often plagued with mildew, so they tend to be shunned by gardeners. Given good air circulation and regularly sprayed with a fungicide, they can be enjoyed in the border and make lovely cut flowers. **'Eventide'** is a good semi-double violet-blue, **'Marie Ballard'** a double light blue, and **'Patricia Ballard'** a semidouble, vibrant pink.

Campanula glomerata 'Superba'

Aster novae-angliae (zone 2–8), the New England aster, is woody stemmed with coarser, slightly hairy foliage, which seems immune to mildew attack. It lacks the excellent blue shades of some *Aster novi-belgii* hybrids but has some good pink and red varieties. All grow to 40 in. (1 m) or more. (See also page 174.) **Aster novae-angliae** 'Pink Victor' has semidouble medium pink flowers with golden yellow centers. Ruby red **'September Ruby'** ('Septemberrubin') looks lovely behind the late flowers of wine red penstemons and with the indigo blooms of *Aconitum* 'Spark's Variety' (see page 46).

Campanulas come in many shapes and sizes, and both tall and shorter forms find their place in the herbaceous border. (See also pages 83 and 155–56.) **Campanula glomerata** (zone 3–8), the clustered bellflower, produces rounded heads of upturned bell-shaped flowers on stout stems, 12 in. (30 cm) high, and is useful to provide early color at the front of the planting. The deep violet-blue blooms of *Campanula glomerata* **'Superba'** are lovely with lime green *Alchemilla mollis* (see page 46) and add depth and contrasting flower form to an edging of *Nepeta* × *faassenii*.

Varieties of **Campanula persicifolia** (peach-leaved bellflower) (zone 4–8) mix easily with other plants. From rosettes of shiny, evergreen leaves arise slender

Campanula lactiflora 'Loddon Anna'

stems, 3 ft. (90 cm) tall, carrying the nodding, cup-shaped flowers in early and midsummer. The single white blooms of *Campanula persicifolia* var. *alba* or the double white *Campanula persicifolia* **'Fleur de Neige'** mix well with the bright indigo blue *Baptisia australis* (see page 132). **'Telham Beauty'** is an icy, light blue; **'Chettle Charm'** is white with a pale blue frosting.

Campanula lactiflora (zone 5–7), or milky bellflower, finds its place farther back in the border. Forming clumps of upright stems, 5 ft. (1.5 m) high, with large heads of bell-shaped flowers, it needs support in most sites. It blooms from early to midsummer, its pastel shades mingling happily with stronger pinks and blues (see Good Companions, right). Its shape contrasts well with the upright spikes of delphiniums. Soft pink **'Loddon Anna'** and deep lavender-blue **'Prichard's Variety'** are two of the best named varieties. **'Alba'** is pure white.

CUTTING BACK CAMPANULAS

When the flowers of campanulas have faded, there is a temptation to cut them back immediately.
This is the right course of action with most varieties except for *Campanula persicifolia*. When the first flush of flowers is over, leave the stems in place; new flower buds will quickly appear.

Perennial borders always conjure images of the magnificent spires of delphiniums soaring above mounds of flowers in the foreground. Undoubtedly delphiniums are essential border plants, not only for their imposing stature but also for their brilliance of color. No other plant delivers the intensity of blue in quite the same way, along with delightful pastel shades of pink, lilac, purple, and white.

Delphinium **Pacific hybrids, New Century hybrids,** and **Magic Fountains** series (zone 4–7, see Good Companions, below right) are easily raised from seed sown in summer or early fall, and young pot-grown stock grows quickly when planted in spring. All need deep, fertile soil with adequate moisture but resent being waterlogged, and are best in large, deep borders where they can be given space. The emerging shoots need early protection from slugs; and grow-through supports should be put into position before plants reach 12 in. (30 cm) tall. After the first flowering in early summer, the plants must be cut back hard to encourage new shoots that will produce more flowers in fall. Because of this they are best positioned behind later per-formers: phlox, asters, heleniums, and kniphofias are all good choices. (See also pages 134–35.)

Heleniums (zone 3–8) have the ideal habit for the perennial border, the clumps growing to broad, stout columns topped with a brilliant display of long-lasting blooms from midsummer right through to fall. Shades range from yellow to deepest red-brown, and they work well alongside subjects in the same part of the color spectrum, such as kniphofias (see page 42), crocosmias, dahlias, and achilleas, as well as with rich blue asters. The shorter varieties, such as *Helenium* **'Wyndley'**, with brown-eyed, yellow and copper flowers, can be planted in front of taller kniphofias to hide their untidy foliage.

Tall spires of delphiniums provide impressive eye-level interest in early summer and again in fall.

GOOD COMPANIONS

Campanula lactiflora (1) (z. 5–7) and *Phlox paniculata* (2) (z. 4–8) are similar in shape and flower form. The phlox blooms as the campanula flowers are fading.

The bold magenta-pink of *Geranium psilostemon* (3) (z. 5–7) gives strength of hue to the softer shades of *Delphinium* 'Magic Fountains Lilac Rose' (4) (z. 4–7) .

41

Kniphofia 'Atlanta' with heleniums

They are also an excellent choice behind the earlier-blooming hemerocallis, their color taking over as the daylilies fade. (See also pages 52 and 159–60.)

Kniphofias (red hot poker or torch lily) (zone 6–9) are a must in any border using hot colors. Their upright spikes offer a strong contrast to the softer, rounded flower heads of so many perennials. Enjoying an open, sunny position and adequate moisture, they do not like to be swamped by their neighbors; planted forward from the back of the border, their rising spikes provide relief from the contrived graded height from the back to the front of the planting. They are usually associated with late summer and fall, but there are varieties that bloom in early, mid-, and late summer. Careful selection will achieve continuity. Most early varieties are smaller than later ones. **'Atlanta'** is early, with 4 ft. (1.2 m) spikes of red and creamy yellow flowers above blue-green evergreen foliage. **'Toffee Nosed'** starts to bloom in midsummer; it has cream flowers ticked with brown in slightly shorter spikes, 40 in. (1 m) high.

'Bressingham Comet' is at its peak in the fall, with spikes, over 5 ft. (1.5 m) tall, of flame red and yellow flowers. (See also pages 68 and 175.)

Nepeta **'Six Hills Giant'** (zone 4–7) is one of the essential blues of the summer border. Reaching 40 in. (1 m) high, this is not an edging plant but a definitive mixer, ideally planted between other subjects that will help to hold it up. It benefits greatly from a grow-through plant support or twiggy props of hazel or birch. The soft gray-green, aromatic leaves, and lavender blue flowers are a delightful combination that works with hot colors as well as soft shades and pastels. Plants can be cut back halfway through the season if they get too untidy, but left untouched will continue to flower through late summer. (See Good Companions, right.)

Peonies may have a relatively short flowering season, but when in bloom they steal the show. Most come into flower early, making a spectacular start to summer. They are best near the front of the border, where their beauty and fragrance can be admired; they also have the advantage of foliage that stays looking good all season and provides

Nepeta 'Six Hills Giant'

some structure among less robust plants. Growing up to 40 in. (1 m) tall, most benefit from some support in case heavy rain strikes when the plants are in bloom. Their colors are both subtle and vibrant. The popular *Paeonia lactiflora* **'Bowl of Beauty'** (zone 4–8), with its soft pink and cream flowers, is essential in any border of warm summer colors.

Paeonia lactiflora 'Bowl of Beauty'

OTHER PERENNIALS FOR THE BORDER *Agastache • Astrantia • Centaurea • Clematis recta •*

Phlox paniculata

Salvia × sylvestris 'May Night' ('Mainacht')

Paeonia lactiflora 'Lord Kitchener' (zone 4–8) is upright in habit, with dark green leaves and gold-centered, bright scarlet flowers. (See Good Companions, right, and see pages 146–47.)

Peonies are especially useful planted in front of *Phlox paniculata* (zone 4–8); their early flowers will hold the spotlight until the phlox is ready to produce its pretty heads of fragrant blooms, from midsummer onward. The phlox's sweetly spicy scent is as much a feature of the border as the bonbon shades of the flowers. (See Good Companions, page 41.) Most varieties grow to about 40 in. (1 m) high, with light green foliage. *Phlox paniculata* 'Dodo Hanbury-Forbes' has large heads of pure pink flowers. 'Prospero' is lavender, with dark foliage. 'Starfire' is deep red, 'Prince of Orange' is salmon, and 'Border Gem' violet-blue. Phlox also offer some of the purest whites in the border: 'White Admiral' and 'Mount Fuji' are two of the best.

Phlox like a well-drained, fertile soil enriched with well-rotted manure. They need watering in dry spells, particularly

just before flowering. Where plants are not growing vigorously, the foliage is prone to leaf spot and mildew. It is worth thinning mature plants in spring, removing weaker shoots to allow strong ones to develop. Dry weather can cause yellowing and browning of the foliage. If plants suffer from eelworm, causing poor growth and distorting leaves and stems, they should be disposed of, and new plants should be sited elsewhere in the border rather than in the same spot.

Herbaceous **salvias** provide some wonderful long-lasting, deep blue spikes that need little or no support and contribute superb depth of color from midsummer to fall (see also pages 166–67). *Salvia × superba* (zone 5–8) is an easy, hardy plant with deep violet-blue flowers and red-purple bracts, which persist long after the flowers have fallen. It grows to 3 ft. (90 cm) high, so is perfect in the middle of the border with later perennials such as heleniums

and phlox. *Salvia × sylvestris* 'May Night' ('Mainacht') is shorter and earlier but with the same color intensity (see Good Companions, below). It makes a stunning combination with the pale yellow *Achillea* 'Moonshine' (zone 2–9), whose flat, platelike flower heads float above it on silver-green stems.

GOOD COMPANIONS

The frothy flower heads of *Centranthus ruber* 'Albus' (1) (z. 4–8) are the perfect background to the large, flamboyant blooms of *Paeonia lactiflora* 'Duchesse de Nemours' (2) (z. 4–8).

Salvia × sylvestris 'May Night' ('Mainacht') (3) (z. 4–8) strengthens the blue in the border and reaches the peak of condition when *Nepeta* 'Six Hills Giant' (4) (z. 4–7) may need a mid-season trim.

Helenium 'The Bishop' (5) (z. 3–8) and *Hemerocallis* 'Hyperion' (6) (z. 4–10): the sunny flowers of the helenium are at their best when those of the yellow daylily are fading.

The mixed border

The mixed border is the most common planting ground for herbaceous perennials today. Here, trees and shrubs give structure, contribute foliage effect, and in some cases offer seasonal flowers. Perennials provide color from the ground to eye level, mainly during the most important time of the year, from late spring to autumn. Spring- and summer-flowering bulbs, annuals, and climbers may also be used to add to the variety of color and form.

The mixed border combines herbaceous perennials with evergreen and deciduous shrubs and roses to provide interest all through the year.

A well planned mixed border can be attractive throughout the year; unlike perennial borders (see pages 38–43), mixed borders have no empty, dormant season. Even in winter deciduous shrubs have branch framework and form, and evergreens come into their own when herbaceous perennials die down and deciduous shrubs lose their leaves.

Mixed borders are regarded as being less labor intensive than traditional perennial ones. Although herbaceous plants require maintenance of one form or other every winter, the woody plants do not necessarily need annual attention; the decision as to when and how much to maintain is very much in the hands of the gardener.

THE IMPORTANCE OF FOLIAGE

The proportion and importance of foliage is greater in a mixed planting than it is in a truly herbaceous border, since foliage provides the setting for the blooms of both shrubs and perennial plants. Colored foliage perennials and variegated shrubs and trees can form the basis of a color scheme, with high-lights supplied by the perennial flowers.

Shrubs with purple or plum foliage work well with most flower shades and are especially useful to bring depth of color to planting schemes.

Silver foliage helps to lighten mixed plantings, particularly those in full sun.

Papaver orientale 'Patty's Plum' seen against the subtle foliage of *Elaeagnus* 'Quicksilver'.

Silver shrubs or small trees are invaluable to plant with sun-loving perennials: they combine very well with pink and blue shades and are sparkling with whites. The silver pear *Pyrus salicifolia* 'Pendula' (zone 4–7) is an excellent small tree for a border with roses, geraniums, nepetas, and lavender. The sizable shrub *Elaeagnus* 'Quicksilver' (zone 3–6) will create a silver-gray backdrop from late spring, just in time to show off the vibrant blooms of oriental poppies (*Papaver orientale*) (zone 3–8) planted in front; it makes a superb companion for *Papaver orientale* 'Patty's Plum'.

Shrubs with white-variegated foliage are good mixers in sun or shade. Those with yellow variegation need to be used more carefully, but can be stunning with yellow- and orange-flowered perennials.

SHRUBS WITH PURPLE FOLIAGE TO MIX WITH PERENNIALS

Acer palmatum 'Bloodgood' (z. 6–8)
Berberis thunbergii f. *atropurpurea* 'Rose Glow' (z. 4–8)
Cotinus coggygria 'Royal Purple' (z. 4–8)
Physocarpus opulifolius 'Diabolo' (z. 2–7)
Pittosporum tenuifolium 'Tom Thumb' (z. 9–10)
Salvia officinalis 'Purpurascens' (z. 5–10)
Weigela florida 'Wine and Roses' ('Alexandra') (z. 5–8)

The ever-popular *Helenium* 'The Bishop' (see page 43) and *Rudbeckia fulgida* var. *sullivantii* 'Goldsturm' (see page 53) intensify the golden yellow variegation of *Elaeagnus pungens* 'Maculata' (zone 6–9) and *Euonymus fortunei* 'Emerald 'n' Gold' (zone 5–8).

ROSES IN MIXED BORDERS

When the herbaceous perennial was confined to the perennial border, the rose was at home in the rose bed, surrounded by its own kind. The two are now combined in the mixed border, and it is a marriage made in heaven. The perennials extend the flowering season of the border and complement the roses at their peak. Shrub roses, English roses, and floribundas are the types most often grown here, since their relaxed habit and soft colors allow them to mix well with many perennials. Compact herbaceous geraniums, *Alchemilla mollis* (see page 46), and heucheras are good subjects for soft ground cover around shrub roses. *Viola cornuta* (see page 49) will grow tall and twine through open-branched rose bushes, producing delicate blue or white blooms from late spring to fall. The tall-growing *Geranium psilostemon*, with black-eyed magenta flowers (see page 48), mixes well with pink and dark wine red roses, especially with plum-colored foliage.

EASY-CARE ROSES TO PLANT WITH PERENNIALS

Rosa 'Amber Queen' (z. 4–9)
Rosa 'Blanc Double de Coubert' (z. 3–7)
Rosa 'Bonica' (z. 5–9)
Rosa 'Cornelia' (z. 4–10)
Rosa 'Crocus Rose' (z. 4–9)
Rosa 'Golden Celebration' (z. 5–10)
Rosa 'Queen of Denmark' ('Königin von Dänemark') (z. 4–9)
Rosa 'Rhapsody in Blue' (z. 6–9)
Rosa 'Roseraie de l'Haÿ' (z. 2–7)
Rosa 'Rosemoor' (z. 5–9)
Rosa 'Valentine Heart' (z. 6–10)

A mixed border with roses in the Jardin d'Angélique in Normandy, France.

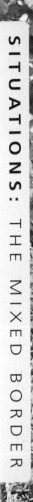

PERENNIALS FOR MIXED PLANTINGS

Most of the commonly available garden perennials can, of course, be used in mixed plantings, but there are some that are particularly suitable. This may be because they have a long season of interest or because they are a useful color to blend with most others. Some perennials are especially valuable for mixed borders because they add that certain something: an exclamation mark in the planting that is not contributed by other subjects.

Aconitum 'Spark's Variety'

Aconitum cultivars are a better choice than delphiniums in mixed borders. Also known as aconite, monkshood, or wolfsbane, aconitums have more attractive, finely cut foliage and do not require the same degree of support as delphiniums (see pages 41 and 134–35). Because the plants stay in good condition after flowering, there is no immediate need to cut them back, so there are no large holes left in the border. *Aconitum* 'Spark's Variety' (zone 3–7) has tall, branching stems, 5 ft. (1.5 m) high, of dark violet blue flowers in late summer, associating well with the rich reds and golds of the season. The equally tall *Aconitum* 'Stainless Steel' (zone 3–7) is an exceptionally good mixer; with its straight spikes of steely blue-gray foliage and gray-blue flowers, it has an eryngium-like quality. The variety *Aconitum*

Anemone × hybrida 'Honorine Jobert'

carmichaelii var. *truppelianum* 'Kelmscott' (zone 4–8) is a real delphinium alternative with spikes reaching nearly 6 ft. (2 m) and rich violet blue flowers borne in early fall.

Alchemilla mollis (lady's mantle) (zone 4–7) is invaluable in the garden. Useful at the front of the border, with paving, and as an edging plant, it is also excellent ground cover on any soil, in sun or shade. It has soft green foliage and, from early summer, clouds of lime green flowers on stems 12 in. (30 cm) high. The color mixes well with any other (see Good Companions, right) and is especially lovely with soft blue. Its one failing is that it scatters seeds freely and can become a pest. A few seedlings are useful to transplant; to prevent it spreading farther, cut off the flowers as they start to turn yellow.

On soils that are heavy and moist, the cultivars of *Anemone × hybrida* (Japanese anemone) (zone 5–7) will spread freely, throwing up their fine stems of perfect white or pink flowers, which enliven the border from late summer on (see pages 170–71). They mix well with strong-growing shrubs, which can cope with their interference. Japanese anemones are useful to plant among shrub roses to lengthen the season of color, very important with roses that flower only once in summer. The vigorous 'Honorine Jobert', with large, single white flowers, combines well with white-variegated shrubs such as *Cornus alba* 'Elegantissima' (zone 2–8). Pink cultivars such as 'Königin Charlotte' are lovely against the purple foliage of *Cotinus coggygria* 'Royal Purple' (zone 4–8).

Alchemilla mollis

Digitalis, the foxgloves, are mostly biennial plants (see pages 56–57). This does not make them any less effective in the mixed border; it just means they need to be managed to ensure that some are in flower each year. There are also perennial species, their light spikes and subtly colored flowers making them excellent mixers.

Digitalis grandiflora (which was formerly known as *Digitalis ambigua)* (zone 5–8) reaches only 18 in. (45 cm) high, with narrow, apple green leaves and delicate spikes of soft yellow flowers, daintily curved at the top. It is easy to grow on well-drained soil and is a useful plant to bring light spikes to the foreground of the border in a subtle but uplifting color. It looks pretty in early summer against the emerging foliage of bronze fennel, *Foeniculum vulgare* 'Purpureum' (see page 90).

Digitalis lutea (zone 5–8) has darker green, narrow leaves in starry rosettes. The fine spikes of tiny, tubular greenish yellow flowers are not spectacular, but have wonderful shape and presence. Reaching 20 in. (50 cm) in height, this is a superb plant to drift through the front of the border. After the flowers fade, the spikes remain attractive for several weeks. Leave a few in position for the seed to ripen; it sows itself freely and will provide ample young plants for use elsewhere in the garden.

Digitalis × mertonensis (zone 5–8) is reliably perennial, if often short-lived, especially on heavy, wet soils. It more closely resembles the European foxglove, *Digitalis purpurea*, which is one of its parents (the other is *Digitalis grandiflora*). Gray-green felty leaves in neat rosettes give rise to dumpy spikes of large strawberry pink flowers in early summer, making it a good partner for summer-flowering shrubs such as deutzia and weigela. It looks pretty with silver foliage, such as that of *Artemisia ludoviciana* 'Valerie Finnis' (see page

Eremurus stenophyllus

51), and with the deep wine red young foliage of *Lysimachia ciliata* 'Firecracker' (see Good Companions, below).

Eremurus (foxtail lily) have become increasingly popular in recent years, and few plants are as spectacular in bloom. Late spring sees the emergence of narrow gray-green leaves, which usually grow to a height of 12–16 in. (30–40 cm). The flowering stem arises from the center of the foliage rosette and grows quickly. In some species it can reach dramatic height, of up to 10 ft. (3 m); in others it remains at around

40 in. (1 m). In midsummer a sparkling bottlebrush, 2–3 ft. (60–90 cm) long, of starry flowers in pink, white, or yellow is produced at the top of the stem; it opens from the bottom upward, creating an attractive gradation of color.

Foxtail lilies are planted in fall as dry tubers; these are curious structures, like starfish, with one or two central "eyes." They should be given a sunny position, in a well-drained, fertile soil. Because of their height and stature, foxtail lilies suit planting with tall, upright perennials such as *Salvia × superba* (zone 5–8), a good solid companion, above which the foxtail lily spikes can rise majestically. *Eremurus himalaicus* (zone 5–8) is the hardiest and reaches 4 ft. (1.2 m). The flowers are pure white with orange stamens. The popular *Eremurus × isabellinus* Ruiter hybrids (zone 5–8) grow to 5 ft. (1.5 m), with spikes of yellow, apricot-, or peach-colored blooms. *Eremurus robustus* (zone 5–8) is the tallest and can reach 10 ft. (3 m). It has peach pink flowers marked with brown and green. The shorter *Eremurus stenophyllus* (zone 5–9) grows to 5 ft. (1.5 m), and has fine yellow flowers that look good with golden-variegated shrubs.

GOOD COMPANIONS

The reddish-pink flowers of *Digitalis × mertonensis* (1) (z. 5–8) and the deep coppery purple foliage of *Lysimachia ciliata* 'Firecracker' (2) (z. 5–8) make lovely partners.

The burgundy blooms of *Penstemon* 'Port Wine'(3) (z. 6–9) combine beautifully with the frothy lime flowers of *Alchemilla mollis* (4) (z. 4–7).

Herbaceous geraniums are a natural choice for mixed borders, especially the larger-growing blue cultivars that mix so easily with roses and deciduous shrubs, silver foliage, and lavenders. Geranium 'Johnson's Blue' (zone 4–8) is a border basic. It is planted so widely because it takes some beating when it comes to reliability. It forms a clump up to 12 in. (30 cm) high and 24 in. (60 cm) across, so requires no support. The dark-veined lavender blue flowers are produced over a long period in early to midsummer and it will usually perform again in fall.

The cultivars of *Geranium pratense*, (zone 4–7) the meadow cranesbill, are also good mixers. Taller growing, they reach 24 in. (60 cm), with long-stalked, deeply divided leaves. Their flowers are smaller but have prettily veined, tissue-like petals. **'Plenum Caeruleum'** is pale blue and double. **'Mrs. Kendall Clark'** is the loveliest of all, its pale blue-gray petals having a pink tint and delicate veining. (See also pages 91 and 164.)

Geranium 'Johnson's Blue'

Geranium psilostemon

Linaria purpurea

Geranium psilostemon (zone 5–7) grows up to 40 in. (1 m) high and can hold its own between medium-sized shrubs and taller perennials. The blooms are borne throughout summer; vivid magenta-pink with black centers, they are showy but mix surprisingly well with a wide range of colors. They look good against plum-colored foliage and with blue nepetas. Burgundy penstemons, such as Penstemon 'Raven' and 'Port Wine' (see Good Companions, page 47), are its natural companions. Brave gardeners could try it with lavender-blue Nepeta 'Six Hills Giant' (see page 42) and soft orange hemerocallis (daylilies).

Linaria (toadflax) is one of those cottage-garden perennials that seem so familiar that no one ever bothers to find out what they are. *Linaria purpurea* (zone 4–7) has tall clumps of slender stems clothed all the way up with narrow blue-green leaves. At the top of each stem is a spike of purple-blue flowers resembling those of a miniature antirrhinum. The spikes are often lightly branched, and the flowers fade to leave round seed capsules that distribute their contents liberally throughout the border. This is a plant to drift through the mixed border, its slender height working well to make the planting three-dimensional.

Persicaria amplexicaulis 'Atrosanguinea'

Penstemon hybrids (zone 7–9) are some of the most valuable plants in the garden. These are evergreen perennials with a woody base, and are more like shrubs than herbaceous plants. Flowers vary from narrow tubes to broader foxglove-like trumpets, but all bloom for a remarkably long period, starting in early summer and continuing until late fall. Those with purple and ruby flowers are superb in mixed planting, their rich coloring blending beautifully with the pinks and blues of summer, as well as with the orange-flame shades of autumn (see pages 162–63).

The robust *Persicaria amplexicaulis* 'Atrosanguinea' (zone 4–7) is much underrated. Perhaps because the foliage is rather coarse, some gardeners overlook its quality as a solid border plant that stays looking good from early summer until late fall. Healthy, dark green foliage and light spikes of red-brown flowers, 4 ft. (1.2 m) high, are a good foil for showier subjects. It grows on almost any soil in sun or partial shade and thrives in wet sites. There are other varieties, but this is the most versatile.

Thalictrums (meadow rue) (zone 5–8) are lovely foliage plants from the beginning of the season with their finely divided blue-green leaves that resemble

OTHER PLANTS FOR MIXED BORDERS *Chaenomeles* • *Foeniculum vulgare* 'Purpureum' • *Gaura lindheimeri* •

Thalictrum flavum subsp. glaucum

maidenhair fern (*Adiantum*). The foliage is a feature not only of the emerging plant but also of the rising flower stems later on. *Thalictrum aquilegiifolium* (zone 5–8) produces wide heads of fluffy mauve flowers during summer. There is also a white form, *Thalictrum aquilegiifolium* var. *album*. *Thalictrum delavayi* (zone 5–8) has daintier foliage and more airy heads of

The perennial sweet pea *Lathyrus latifolius* (z. 4–7) looks delightful with the delicate lilac-blue blooms of *Viola cornuta* (z. 5–7).

lilac flowers with white stamens. Ideal with companions that offer support, this is not a plant for an exposed position, as the stems are likely to be blown over. It is good for cutting as an alternative to gypsophila. The cultivar *Thalictrum delavayi* **'Hewitt's Double'** bears tiny, very double lilac flowers, which are pretty but without the appealing, soft fluffy stamens of the single form.

An excellent plant in any scheme, *Thalictrum flavum* ssp. *glaucum* (zone 5–8) has fine blue-green leaves and pale yellow flowers. The foliage stays in good condition throughout the season, after the blooms have faded.

PEAS AND VETCHES

Several members of the pea family are herbaceous climbers and scramblers that will use the branches of woody plants for support. They can add a new dimension to the border and extend the season of interest, often by performing later in the year than their hosts. Some, like the everlasting peas (*Lathyrus*), use tendrils to help them climb over and through nearby plants; others, like goat's rue (*Galega*), simply drape their lax stems over their nearest neighbor, or anything else that will give them the support they need.

Galega officinalis (goat's rue) (zone 4–8) is a native of Europe. A very lax plant, it depends on others to support its 5 ft. (1.5 m) stems and fernlike foliage. Spikes of small pea flowers in shades of purple, pink, and white appear in great profusion from early summer to early fall. It will grow happily in sun or partial shade.

Lathyrus latifolius (zone 4–7), the perennial sweet pea, is a vigorous herbaceous climber, growing happily to 12 ft. (4 m) in well-drained, fertile soil in full sun. It has flattened stems and fresh green foliage, and flowers over a long period from early summer to early fall.

Galega officinalis 'Alba'

The stout stems of silky, rounded blooms are weather resistant and are excellent for cutting. The species often has vivid rose-purple flowers, which look stunning against the purple elder *Sambucus nigra* f. *porphyrophylla* 'Gerda' (formerly called *Sambucus nigra* 'Black Beauty') (zone 5–7). *Lathyrus latifolius* **'Rosa Perle'** has pale pink flowers while **'White Pearl'** gives a profusion of pure white blooms. *Lathyrus latifolius* can be easily raised from seed or bought as container-grown stock and planted in spring. Named cultivars are propagated with difficulty from cuttings.

Lathyrus grandiflorus (everlasting pea) (zone 6–8) scrambles to 6 ft. (2 m) or more. It has sparse, fine blue-green stems and leaves and large flowers produced in twos and threes throughout summer. Deep purple-pink with varying shades of maroon, the blooms have an old-fashioned character. This is a lovely plant that sits lightly on its host.

Lathyrus vernus (zone 5–9) blooms in spring, forming clumps of 12 in. (30 cm) stems with pretty fernlike foliage and heads of tiny pea flowers. There are several varieties, in purple, pink, and white. All of them mix well with spring-flowering bulbs.

Hemerocallis • Paeonia • Polemonium • Sedum 'Autumn Joy' ('Herbstfreude') • Verbascum • Verbena bonariensis •

Prairie and meadow

Prairie planting and wildflower meadows both use plants hailing from grassland habitats to create a soothing, softly moving gardenscape that evolves and changes as the year progresses. Whether on a large scale or in a smaller bed, both planting styles can help to bring a real feeling of the countryside into the garden.

The Piet Oudolf prairie-style planting at RHS Garden Wisley, Surrey, in England.

PRAIRIE PLANTING

In a natural prairie habitat, herbaceous perennials and grasses exist in harmony, the mix of species varying according to the conditions: wet or dry. In all cases a succession of flowers and seed heads punctuates a changing background of grasses from spring to late fall. In most gardens the association of prairie plants and grasses can be used on a small scale to create a naturalistic effect that is at home in a rural environment or an urban setting. Some of the most innovative gardeners on both sides of the Atlantic have used prairie-style planting for a number of years.

In cultivation prairie plants require the minimum of maintenance and will tolerate quite hostile conditions. In their natural habitat, they will cope with drought, extreme heat and cold, and heavy grazing by elk and buffalo. Unlike the flowers typically found in a meadow, many are robust plants, able to compete with vigorous grasses growing in fertile soil. Bold and colorful, many are members of the daisy family, their individual flowers consisting of many small florets usually with a number of raylike petals around a central disk. Rich in nectar and prolific in seed production, they attract both insects and birds and are perfect for wildlife gardens.

Agastache foeniculum 'Alabaster'

Agastache foeniculum (giant hyssop) (zone 8–10) is a deadnettle-like plant with square stems, reaching over 40 in. (1 m) tall, and narrow, aromatic leaves.

The spikes of bluish purple flowers appear at the top of the stems from early summer to early fall. The whole plant smells of aniseed when touched. It suits a dry soil in full sun and is useful for its upright, spiky form and its blue color, mixing well with prairie daisies. Several cultivars exist, among them *Agastache foeniculum* 'Alabaster' (zone 8–10), with white flowers. (See also page 153.)

Artemisia ludoviciana 'Valerie Finnis'

Artemisia ludoviciana (zone 4–8) will introduce softer foliage and subtle color into prairie planting. The plant spreads to make loose patches of upright stems bearing willowlike silver leaves. The cultivars **'Silver Queen'** and **'Valerie Finnis'** are particularly fine and reach 30 in. (75 cm). Greenish yellow flowers appear in late summer, but the foliage is the feature of these plants.

The perennial **asters** (Michaelmas daisy) are a diverse group, invaluable for their autumn pinks and purples. Sadly, the susceptibility to mildew of some forms has put many gardeners off

---

---

these cottage-garden classics. The one aster that no garden should be without is *Aster × frikartii* 'Mönch' (zone 5–7). Raised in Switzerland in 1920, it is still considered the finest perennial aster, producing lavender-blue flower heads 24–36 in. (60–90 cm) high in late summer and fall. It is not a true prairie plant, but can be used in this style of planting. (See also pages 40 and 171.)

The small-flowered asters are most effective mixed with bolder perennials. *Aster ericoides* 'Pink Cloud' (zone 3–7) has a light, airy habit and fine, starry, pale pink flower heads over a long period in late summer and autumn. The stems are graceful and wiry and will reach 40 in. (1 m) high. It combines well with the purple coneflower, *Echinacea purpurea* (see below).

Aster ericoides is a true prairie native, as is *Aster lateriflorus* (zone 5–7). *Aster lateriflorus* 'Horizontalis' has fine, spreading, stiffly branched stems, 32 in. (80 cm) high, and clouds of tiny, starry, mauve-pink flowers with darker centers in late summer or autumn. This plant is quite different in habit from the other asters, and it contrasts well with light grasses such as *Stipa tenuissima* (see page 73) and *Panicum virgatum* 'Heavy Metal' (zone 6–8).

The purple coneflower, *Echinacea purpurea* (zone 4–8), is another prairie native, perfect with spike-flowered plants, such as verbascums, or with grasses. Borne on stout, upright stems up to 40 in. (1 m) high, the flower heads are a wonderful combination of rich red-purple petals and chestnut brown cones, laden with orange pollen when at their prime, in late summer. *Echinacea purpurea* 'Rubinstern' is especially pleasing, with glowing wine-red flowers on 24 in. (60 cm) stems. *Echinacea purpurea* 'White Swan', also 24 in. (60 cm) high, is elegantly beautiful, with its greenish cream blooms of reflexed petals. Plant it amid

Echinacea purpurea 'Kim's Knee High'

a cloud of smoky bronze fennel, *Foeniculum vulgare* 'Purpureum' (see Good Companions, page 52), or with the dancing butterfly-like blooms of gauras (see page 52). For exposed sites or the front of a planting scheme, look for *Echinacea purpurea* 'Kim's Knee High'. (See also page 175.)

Filipendula rubra 'Venusta' (zone 2–8) is a magnificent and stately prairie perennial reaching over 6 ft. (2 m) tall. Both leaves and flowers resemble those of astilbe. The large, fluffy, bright pink flower heads are produced over a long period from early summer into early fall. (See Good Companions, page 52.) Just

---

MAINTAINING PRAIRIE PLANTING

Do not cut back prairie grasses and perennials after flowering. Leave the dry grasses and seed heads over winter and cut them back in early spring. With their dry parchment leaves and dark silhouettes, prairie plants look wonderful etched with frost and lit by the low winter sun.

Gaura lindheimeri

like the native British meadowsweet, *Filipendula ulmaria*, it likes a fair amount of moisture in the soil.

Gaura lindheimeri (zone 6–9) forms a low clump of narrow, dark green leaves, usually with chocolate spots. Upright, wiry stems, 40 in. (1 m) tall, bear pointed pink buds that open into white butterflylike blooms from midsummer to late fall. It is easy to grow in full sun and tolerates hot, dry sites.

The rich bronzes, oranges, and reds of the **heleniums** (zone 3–8) have a wonderful period character. Their silky petals and velvet button centers are like shreds of rich upholstery. Old cottage-garden plants, they are popular for their reliable late display, their disease resistance, and their tolerance of almost any soil conditions other than very wet or very dry. Heleniums are commonly known as sneezeweed, a name that comes from the plants' use by the early settlers to make snuff.

Most garden heleniums are hybrids of *Helenium autumnale,* native to North America, *Helenium flexuosum,* from the Midwest, and *Helenium bigelovii,* from California. They flower profusely from midsummer through fall. *Helenium* **'Moerheim Beauty'** bears bronze-crimson flowers and grows to 32 in. (80 cm) tall. *Helenium* **'Wyndley'**, 24 in. (60 cm) high, has yellow and flowers marked with copper. *Helenium* **'Waldtraut'**, one of the loveliest, grows strong stems to 4 ft. (1.2 m), carrying brown-flecked, rich orange blooms over a long period. *Helenium* **'The Bishop'** is a robust plant, to 3 ft. (90 cm) high, and produces deep golden yellow flowers. (See also pages 159–60.)

Helenium 'Waldtraut'

Helianthus 'Lemon Queen'

Helianthus decapetalus (zone 5–8), the wild sunflower, is a very hardy plant, forming clumps of stems up to 5 ft. (1.5 m) tall and blooming in late summer and fall. The flower heads are yellow and dainty, only 2½ in. (6 cm) across. There are several garden varieties with larger, showier flowers. With finer foliage and prettier flowers, *Helianthus salicifolius* (zone 4–8) is a true prairie native with stems up to 6 ft. (2 m) in height. The cultivar *Helianthus* **'Lemon Queen'** is a softer yellow and is a better mixer. (See also page 160.)

The varieties of **heliopsis** are the more popular sunflowers for garden cultivation. *Heliopsis helianthoides* (zone 4–8) blooms through mid- and late summer and forms clumps of upright stems 5 ft. (1.5 m) tall. *Heliopsis helianthoides* var. *scabra*

GOOD COMPANIONS

The greenish cream blooms of *Echinacea purpurea* 'White Swan' (1) (z. 4–8) are displayed against a cloud of bronze fennel, *Foeniculum vulgare* 'Purpureum' (2) (z. 5–8), with its smoky foliage and ocher lace flowers.

The plumelike flower heads of *Filipendula rubra* 'Venusta' (3) (z. 2–8) provide light contrast to the larger daisy blooms of *Echinacea purpurea* (purple coneflower) (4) (z. 4–8).

MORE PERENNIALS FOR PRAIRIES *Asclepias tuberosa* • *Camassia leichtlinii* • *Cirsium rivulare* 'Atropurpureum' •

Rudbeckia fulgida var. sullivantii 'Goldsturm'

resulting in their transfer from one garden to another. As with other prairie plants, they are tough and tolerant. The originally cultivated species and hybrids tend to be rampant and invasive, but there are more compact, better-behaved alternatives. *Solidago canadensis* (zone 3–7), with broad yellow plumes on stems up to 40 in. (1 m) high, is well suited to a wild garden. *Solidago* **'Cloth of Gold'** (zone 3–9) and **'Crown of Rays'** (zone 5–9) are dwarf but lack the grace of the tall varieties. *Solidago* **'Goldenmosa'** (zone 3–9) grows up to 40 in. (1 m) high, with fluffy yellow flower heads, and is one of the best. *Solidago* **'Golden Wings'** (zone 5–9) is a tall hybrid reaching 6 ft. (2 m). *Solidago* × *hybrida*, now known as × *Solidaster luteus* (zone 5–9), is a group of generally less invasive garden hybrids.

Solidago 'Goldenmosa'

'Light of Loddon' has yellow single flowers, while *Heliopsis helianthoides* var. *scabra* 'Spitzentänzerin' has strong yellow and semidouble blooms. There are double-flowered forms but these lack the charm of the single forms and, like all double flowers, are useless at attracting pollinating insects.

The perennial **rudbeckias** start to come into their own in late summer, with a blaze of rich yellow that brightens the dullest of days. *Rudbeckia fulgida* var. *sullivantii* 'Goldsturm' (zone 4–8) is a true black-eyed beauty, up to 3 ft. (90 cm) tall, that will thrive in poor soil and the toughest situations, as long as it is not too dry. Leave the flower stems after the blooms have faded; the black, cone-shaped centers make a stunning contrast to frost-traced grasses on a winter's morning. (See also page 177.)

Solidagos, or goldenrod, are ancient garden plants mostly native to North America. They throw up fine stems that carry a shower of greenish gold flowers in late summer and fall. They seed freely and grow readily from root divisions,

GRASSES TO GROW WITH PRAIRIE PLANTS

Many true prairie grasses are large and vigorous and too big for smaller spaces. Several smaller grasses will give a prairie effect in mixed planting while allowing the flowering perennials to predominate.

Some of the best are:

Calamagrostis × *acutiflora* 'Karl Foerster' (z. 5–9)
Calamagrostis brachytricha (left) (z. 4–9)
Miscanthus sinensis 'Kleine Silberspinne' (z. 5–9)
Panicum virgatum 'Heavy Metal' (z. 6–8)
Panicum virgatum 'Warrior' (z. 6–8)
Stipa calamagrostis (z. 4–8)
Stipa tenuissima (see page 73) (z. 7–9)

Eupatorium purpureum ssp. *maculatum* 'Atropurpureum' • *Oenothera speciosa* • *Veronicastrum virginicum* •

For a mass of flowers in early summer, a wildflower meadow needs careful management.

FLOWERING MEADOWS

Just like the prairie, the wildflower meadow is a mixture of herbaceous perennials, annuals, and grasses that grow in harmony, adapted to the conditions of their natural environment.

The wildflower meadow suits gardens of all sizes, but so often the results are disappointing after the first season: annuals die out, many perennials fail to establish, and grasses and coarse weeds take over. The secret of success is to emulate the natural environment as closely as possible. Soil type and fertility are primary considerations. Flowering meadows tend to do best on thinner, less fertile soils; grasses are not so dominant here, giving the flowers the chance to shine.

Wildflowers that succeed in meadow plantings are those that can coexist happily with grasses. Clovers, vetches, and buttercups, for example, reappear year after year with little problem. Plants such as annual poppies, on the other hand, quickly die out in grassland because their seed germinates best in broken soil, hence their prevalence in grain fields and on disturbed wasteland.

Centaurea scabiosa, commonly known as greater knapweed (zone 4–8), thrives on poor, dry soils, especially those over chalk. With flowers like large purple cornflowers, borne on stems 24 in. (60 cm) tall, it is attractive to butterflies and bees, and the ripe seeds are a good food for wild birds.

Hardy orchids are an exciting addition to any wildflower meadow and plants are increasingly available through micro-propagation. Thriving in damp as well as dry sites, *Dactylorhiza fuchsii* (common spotted orchid) (zone 5–8) has

Dactylorhiza fuchsii

MAINTENANCE OF A FLOWERING MEADOW

Cutting is the key to a wildflower meadow. It needs to be treated like a field cut for hay, the environment where meadow flowers naturally thrive. Grass and flowers are allowed to grow through the spring and bloom through early summer. By midsummer their seed is set and ripe, at which point the meadow is cut and left to dry, and seed from flowers falls to the ground; all cuttings are then collected (as if hay is being made). The meadow is then cut again through fall and early spring, as if grazed by animals; all clippings are removed each time. It is then left from early spring onward to grow and to bloom.

Removing the plant cuttings is vital. Left on the meadow, they feed the grass with nitrogen, making it lush and thick and more competitive with emerging wildflower seedlings.

Clearly, a wildflower meadow is not a low-maintenance option. You will also need to remove undesirables: docks, thistles, willow seedlings, and so on. You may need to thin areas to open up space for seedlings to develop; strew plant cuttings over the ground to help disperse seed; and reseed patches by hand, if you wish to introduce other varieties.

green lance-shaped leaves, spotted with purple and bears its numerous lilac spotted flowers on 12 in. (30 cm) stems in early summer. Some sources list this plant as *D. maculata* ssp. *fuchsii*.

Chalky soils with thin grass are ideal for *Geranium pratense* (zone 4–7), the meadow cranesbill. This plant has earned its place as a cottage-garden favorite for many years on account of its large, bowl-shaped violet-blue flowers, carried on 12 in. (30 cm) stems above aromatic, finely cut leaves. It is the parent of many garden cultivars (see pages 48 and 91).

MORE PLANTS FOR FLOWERING MEADOWS *Briza maxima* • *Centaurea montana* • *Fritillaria meleagris* •

Knautia arvensis (field scabious) (zone 4–9) is a beautiful perennial for late summer so does not fit into the same regime as most other meadow flowers (see left). Up to 16 in. (40 cm) high, this plant can be grown in rough grass that is not mown; it, too, does well in poor, alkaline soil. The pale mauve flowers look lovely with the pink musk mallow, *Malva moschata* (see below).

Leucanthemum vulgare (zone 3–8), the white moon or oxeye daisy, is a short-lived perennial that requires thin grass and space for the clumps of deep green, spoon-shaped leaves to become established. Where it is happy it seeds prolifically and can take over, dominating a meadow for a couple of years before settling down to coexist with its companions. Growing 24 in. (60 cm) high and doing well in sun or partial shade, it is easily raised from seed.

The perennial flax, *Linum perenne*, (zone 5–8) is a less robust beauty with fine stems, to 16 in. (40 cm) high, and shining blue flowers that open only in the morning. It must have very well-drained soil and little competition from other plants, so it is often grown in gravel rather than in a meadow. This is a short-lived perennial, and it is worth collecting seed in late summer to sow the following spring.

Malva moschata (zone 3–8), the musk mallow, tolerates fertile soils and grows well on alkaline soil. Its large, open, shining pink blooms look positively exotic. They are borne among deeply cut leaves on stems up to 24 in. (60 cm) high, over a long period all through summer.

The bright red field poppy, *Papaver rhoeas* (annual, zone 7–9), is a popular flower, but it will seed itself only in disturbed soil, and even then rarely performs the following season. *Papaver orientale* (oriental poppy) (zone 3–8) is a perennial and offers a showy scarlet alternative to the annual

Papaver orientale 'Beauty of Livermere'

poppy. Fading foliage after flowering, deemed a failing in the herbaceous border, is an advantage in the meadow, as it allows grasses to take over, and its tendency to collapse is somewhat overcome by the surrounding plants. Deep red *Papaver orientale* 'Beauty of Livermere' is a particularly good choice for its upright stems, 3 ft. (90 cm) high, and glowing garnet blooms, which are not too large. (See also page 148.)

The versatility of the cowslip, *Primula veris* (zone 5–7), has led to its adoption as a garden plant for almost any situation. Growing in sun or shade and on dry or damp soils, it is also happy in grass and a wonderful late spring flower for the meadow. It carries its scented, pale yellow flowers well above the crinkled leaf rosettes, on stems that grow to 10 in. (25 cm) high. Even in the wild it will hybridize with the closely related *Primula vulgaris* (primrose) and *Primula elatior* (oxlip). Plants can be divided after flowering, or seed can be collected and sown in the fall to over-winter outside.

Few flowers capture the spring and summer sunshine as effectively as the meadow buttercup, *Ranunculus acris* (zone 4–7). It also grows well in light shade. Although it may be considered a weed in the flower border, it is an essential in the wildflower meadow.

Silene dioica (red campion) (zone 6–8) is also happy in either light shade or full sun. Reaching 24 in. (60 cm) high, it has deep pink flowers, which appear from mid-spring onward; if stems are cut back after flowering it will produce another flush later on, in the fall.

The nectar-laden flowers of the clovers—species and varieties of *Trifolium* (zone 3–8)—are popular with bees and butterflies, and are a welcome addition to informal garden plantings. *Trifolium rubens*, a European native, is one of the largest: a clump-forming plant with many stems reaching 24 in. (60 cm). The large, pink or white flower heads appear in early summer. *Trifolium pratense* (common red clover) is easily grown from seed and is wonderful in a wildflower meadow or in rough grass in an orchard where the flowers will attract bees for pollination.

Trifolium pratense

GRASSES FOR WILDFLOWER MEADOWS

When starting a wildflower meadow from scratch, consult a reputable seed retailer and acquire a mixture of traditional meadow grasses, rather than using commercial lawn seed.

Galega officinalis • Lychnis flos-cuculi • Narcissus pseudonarcissus • Origanum vulgare • Saponaria officinalis •

Woodland settings

The dappled shade under the canopy of trees is the perfect setting for some of our loveliest herbaceous perennials. Enjoying the open soil beneath the leaf litter of the woodland floor, they emerge and bloom early, before the thickening leaf canopy steals the sunlight. In the garden, we can take advantage of the filtered light beneath trees and shrubs to create informal woodland plantings, using the charming unsophisticated species that originate in the natural habitat.

The beautiful blue-flowered *Corydalis flexuosa* (zone 5–8) prefers neutral to acid soil rich in leaf mold, so is ideal for growing beneath deciduous trees. The plant becomes dormant in summer, so will not suffer when the tree canopy deprives it of moisture. In late spring and early summer, tubular blue flowers are carried in graceful clusters above the fernlike foliage, which resembles that of *Dicentra*. About 12 in. (30 cm) high, this is a lovely plant to grow with lime green ferns under birch trees, where it can be left undisturbed to spread slowly. *Corydalis flexuosa* 'Purple Leaf' has purple foliage and sapphire blue flowers (see Good Companions, page 59).

The foxglove *Digitalis purpurea* (zone 4–8) is a biennial, forming a large rosette of broad oval, felted leaves in the first year and producing a majestic purplish-pink flower spike, 4 ft. (1.2 m) tall, in early summer of the second. It seeds freely and is an excellent plant to encourage where deer and rabbits are a

Corydalis flexuosa 'Purple Leaf'

Digitalis purpurea is a wonderful plant for any natural setting in the garden.

problem: These are well aware of the foxglove's toxic qualities and leave it untouched. The white-flowered *Digitalis purpurea* f. *albiflora* needs to be isolated from the purple species if white offspring are to be maintained. A garden cultivar, *Digitalis purpurea* 'Sutton's Apricot' has all the grace and charm of the species but with flowers of soft apricot pink; these look beautiful in a natural setting against tree bark.

Of the few evergreen woodland perennials, *Euphorbia amygdaloides* var. *robbiae* (Mrs. Robb's Bonnet) (zone 7–9) is one of the most useful. Spreading by underground stems, it produces heads of rounded leaves, crowned by lime green flowers that appear in early spring and last until early summer. Up to 16 in. (40 cm) high, this makes superb ground cover under large shrubs and tolerates sun as well as shade. In a woodland planting it provides evergreen interest at ground level throughout the year and competes with the vigorous growth of both periwinkle and ivy. (See also page 113.)

Euphorbia amygdaloides var. *robbiae*

Galium odoratum (sweet woodruff) (zone 5–7) is another delightful ground-cover plant for any shady spot under trees or shrubs. Its fine stems, 8 in. (20 cm) tall, quickly emerge in spring, clothed in whorls of bright green, narrow leaves. In late spring, clouds of tiny white flowers appear across the mats of foliage. It is a delightfully aromatic plant and can be gathered and

Lamium orvala

used to flavor white wine, or made into a refreshing cordial. Sweet woodruff looks lovely covering the ground around groups of the Lenten rose, *Helleborus* × *hybridus* (see pages 180–81), the fine foliage of the woodruff contrasting with the stiff, leathery hellebore leaves.

Lamium orvala (zone 4–8) belongs to the dead nettle family and has upright pinkish stems, 12 in. (30 cm) or more high, with toothed, medium green, slightly hairy leaves, well spaced in pairs; between them appear bruised pink, lipped flowers in mid- and late spring. It forms wide mats and is valuable ground cover, retaining its foliage well into late summer. (See Good Companions, below.) *Lamium galeobdolon* (zone 4–8), also known as yellow archangel, is similar, but more delicate in its habit, with silver-marked leaves and soft yellow flowers on fine stems. This is the perfect partner for English bluebells.

For those blessed with sandy, peaty, acid soil that remains moist in summer the blue poppies are a must in the light shade of trees. *Meconopsis* are among the most desirable of flowers—simple

Lamium galeobdolon

yet sophisticated, and heart-stoppingly beautiful. *Meconopsis betonicifolia* (Tibetan blue poppy) (zone 8–9) is a native of Tibet, Yunnan, and Burma and it grows in moist woods at high altitude, so likes cool conditions. It is easily raised from seed, forming a rosette of hairy leaves in its first year. Flower buds appear in the second year, but ideally these should be removed to encourage the formation of basal shoots that will establish the plant as a short-lived perennial. If buds are allowed to develop, the plant usually dies after flowering. Planting in groups will mean that at least some plants can

PLANTING HERBACEOUS PERENNIALS UNDER TREES

Fall is the best time to plant under deciduous trees. In winter and early spring, rain is able to penetrate and newly planted perennials have the opportunity to put down roots before the tree canopy thickens. If planted in spring, perennials will require regular and copious watering until their roots become established.

GOOD COMPANIONS

With its rich bronze metallic foliage, *Ajuga reptans* 'Atropurpurea' (1) (z. 4–7) sets off the crushed strawberry pink stems and flowers of *Lamium orvala* (2) (z. 4–8).

be left to flower, while on others the buds are taken off. The flower stems rise to 5 ft. (1.5 m) in summer, each with buds that open to four-petaled flowers varying from purplish blue to clear azure with golden stamens. *Meconopsis grandis* (Himalayan blue poppy) (zone 5–8) is similar but with longer, lighter green leaves. In its native Sikkim it is grown around shepherds' huts, where the seeds are used for oil. *Meconopsis × sheldonii* (zone 7–8), a hybrid of these two species, is shorter, at only 40 in. (1 m), and is easier to grow; it has given rise to some fine named cultivars. Not all meconopsis are shades of blue.

Meconopsis × sheldonii

Meconopsis cambrica

SPRING BULBS

Bulbs that flower in early spring are natural planting partners for woodland perennials under trees. They, too, are well prepared to produce their display before the leaf canopy thickens. Natural species and graceful, small-flowered hybrids are always the best choice. Large-flowered garden hybrids and strong colors look out of place in a natural woodland setting.

Some of the best are:

Anemone blanda (z. 5–8)
Cyclamen coum (z. 6–8)
Cyclamen repandum (z. 7–8)
Erythronium dens-canis (z. 4–8)
Erythronium californicum 'White Beauty' (and others) (z. 4–8)
Galanthus nivalis (and other snowdrops) (z. 4–8)
Narcissus 'February Gold' (z. 5–7)
Narcissus 'Hawera' (above) (z. 4–9)
Narcissus 'Peeping Tom' (z. 4–8)

Meconopsis cambrica (Welsh poppy) (zone 6–8) is normally yellow, and some orange forms occur, as do those with double flowers. It does not require acid soil but does prefer shade; thriving in conditions of low fertility, it does well naturalized in gravel, seeding itself freely. A long-lived plant with a deep, branched tap root, it has ferny foliage and upturned papery flowers, borne singly on fine 12 in. (30 cm) stems throughout summer. The bright blooms glow in the shade.

The various species of *Polygonatum* (Solomon's seal) (zone 4–7) are native to American, European, and Asian woodlands and hedgerows. They usually have gracefully arching stems of waxy foliage, which in late spring carry creamy, bell-shaped flowers tinged with green. After the flowers fade, the foliage persists until late summer. Up to 3 ft. (90 cm) high, they are effective in providing seasonal height among periwinkle and ivy, and follow the early spring display of snowdrops. (See also page 127.)

The British native primrose, *Primula vulgaris* (zone 6–7), is a charming plant, only 8 in. (20 cm) high, that found its way from woodland edge to cottage garden many years ago. Easy to grow, it thrives on both acid and alkaline soils;

Spigelia marilandica 'Wisley Jester'

where it is happy, it seeds freely, forming large colonies. Soft yellow blooms emerge from the rosette of bright green leaves in late winter and continue into late spring. A rare soft salmon form also occurs. (See Good Companions, right.)

Spigelia marilandica (zone 5–8) is a hardy, clump-forming woodland plant from the southeastern states, thriving in moist, fertile soil in semi-shade. Upright stems quickly rise to 12 in. (30 cm), clad in narrow, fresh green leaves, and the flowers appear at the stem tips from late spring onwards. Long, pointed red buds

GROWING UNDER TREES

Growing conditions can be improved beneath trees by selective thinning of the canopy. This is particularly effective with light-headed trees such as birch; careful thinning of the branches will allow cultivation to within 40 in. (1 m) or so of the trunks of mature trees. As an added bonus, thinning the lower branches makes attractive bark more visible in summer and winter.

OTHER PERENNIALS FOR WOODLAND *Actaea racemosa* • *Asarum europaeum* • *Campanula lactiflora* •

Toad lilies (Tricyrtis)

Toad lilies are interesting perennials originating from Japan, China, and Taiwan. They need moist, shaded woodland conditions to grow well. They are attractive early in the year as the shoots unfurl glossy, sometimes spotted leaves. By early fall, the stems reach 20–40 in. (0.5–1 m) tall, according to species. Flowers are produced singly or in clusters in the leaf axils or in clusters at the end of the stems: small and waxy, they are strikingly marked and spotted. Toad lilies form dense clumps and make effective ground cover. With their exotic appearance and subtle coloring, they are excellent for small, shaded gardens as well as for woodland settings. They associate well with ferns, hostas, heucheras, and other foliage plants. In time, plants can become congested, particularly in heavier soils, and will need to be lifted and divided.

OTHER GOOD TOAD LILIES

Tricyrtis hirta (z. 5–7) More relaxed in habit than *Tricyrtis formosana*, with arching stems. Bears white purple-spotted flowers in late summer and fall.

Tricyrtis 'Lilac Towers' (z. 4–8) Has stiff, upright stems and flowers similar to *Tricyrtis hirta*.

Tricyrtis formosana (z. 4–9) forms wide clumps of stems, up to 32 in. (80 cm) tall. The leaves are shining green with darker spots. Flowers are white with deep strawberry pink markings, and are borne in open clusters at the end of the stems in early fall. This is one of the easiest toad lilies to grow.

Uvularia grandiflora

open to reveal a creamy yellow interior; as the petals reflex, the flowers resemble tiny jester's hats. The Hillier selection of this spigelia was named 'Wisley Jester' (zone 5–8), after the British Royal Horticultural Society's Wisley Gardens, to celebrate the 2004 bicentennial.

Uvularia grandiflora (zone 5–9) is another North American woodland native, also known as merrybells. Oval to lance-shaped leaves unfold in mid- to late spring, revealing pendent, bell-shaped, pale to medium yellow flowers,

sometimes with a hint of green, each one made up of clearly separate, gently twisted petals. Related to Solomon's seal (see left), this slowly spreading herbaceous plant will thrive in a rich, moist site and will deliver rare spring color in deep or partial shade. Once

established, it can reach 24 in. (60 cm); its upright stems look stunning among ferns, *Tiarella,* and the pendulous sedge, *Carex pendula*. *Uvularia perfoliata* (zone 4–8) has more rounded, lance-shaped leaves and pale yellow flowers that mix well with bluebells.

GOOD COMPANIONS

Lime green fronds of the shuttlecock fern *Matteuccia struthiopteris* (1) (z. 2–7) rise above the sapphire flowers of *Corydalis flexuosa* 'Purple Leaf' (2) (z. 5–8).

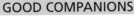
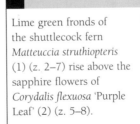

The soft yellow of the primrose *Primula vulgaris* (z. 6–7) is the perfect partner for *Anemone blanda* blue shades (z. 5–8). Truly the colors of spring, they are brighter and all the more welcome in the dappled shade of trees.

Campanula latifolia • Mertensia virginica • Phlox divaricata • Phlox stolonifera • Tiarella cordifolia • Trillium •

Shady sites

Nearly all gardens have some form of shade; it can be a problem or a blessing, depending on what you plant. As a rule the showiest flowers are not found in shade, but you will find interesting foliage. The lower light conditions intensify color and definition and plants are not scorched or bleached by high summer sunshine. Gardens with a high proportion of shade may not be the most colorful, but they can be wonderfully effective in a quieter way.

Arum italicum ssp. *italicum* 'Marmoratum'

Happy in partial shade or in sun, **Arum italicum** ssp. **italicum** 'Marmoratum' (formerly *Arum italicum* 'Pictum') (zone 5–8) grows from tuberous roots and forms a clump of arrow-shaped leaves 16 in. (40 cm) high. These are dark glossy green and attractively patterned with a tracery of silver veins. The plant is very early to emerge: it breaks through the soil in midwinter, and the leaves last until late spring. The greenish white spathes often go unnoticed, but they are followed by spikes of orange berries, which persist when the leaves die down. This is an excellent plant to combine with early spring bulbs and for early foliage interest among hostas.

Eranthis hyemalis carpets the ground under trees or shrubs from late winter to early spring.

WHAT WILL GROW IN PARTIAL SHADE?

As a general rule, areas of the garden that get a few hours of sunshine in the course of the day will support most plants, apart from those requiring an open, sunny position. There is always a certain amount of trial and error here, but it is never worth persevering with perennials in shade if they become drawn and weak, struggling toward the light. Plants like this are not happy; move them and fill the gap with something else.

OTHER GOOD PERENNIALS FOR DRY SHADE *Ajuga reptans* • *Alchemilla mollis* • *Brunnera macrophylla* •

FORMS OF SHADE

Shade comes in different forms: wet and dry, deep and light, total and partial. The amount of shade usually depends on the time of year and the position of the sun. Some areas may get several hours of sun in summer, but are in shade in winter, often because of the position of the house. For deciduous herbaceous perennials this is no problem if they have retreated below ground during the shady period. The periphery of areas of shade is usually described as light shade; here plants still get good light levels, from the side, even if they do not get much direct sunlight.

Moist shade supports a wide range of plants that look good for most of the season. Fewer plants can cope with the dry shade under trees and shrubs or at the base of a wall, although some woodland plants will perform early in the season while winter moisture is available in the soil. Indeed, many of the plants featured in Woodland settings (see pages 56–59) can be used in shady sites anywhere in the garden.

Convallaria majalis

Asarum europaeum

Asarums are low-growing woodland plants, well adapted to deep shade. The Japanese species often have beautiful marbled leaves but are too delicate for garden cultivation. The American and European natives are hardy characters useful for foliage ground cover in shady spots. Their flowers are insignificant and usually hidden beneath the leaves.

They grow from aromatic rhizomes, hence the common name "ginger." *Asarum caudatum* (zone 7–9), a native species, has heart-shaped, dark green leaves. *Asarum europaeum* (zone 5–7) has rounded, glossy, bright green leaves.

With bold, leathery, evergreen foliage and early spring flowers in white to deepest purple, **bergenias** are excellent plants for shade or partial shade. They will not succeed in dry sites and want fairly fertile soil, as well as adequate moisture. Most widely grown is pink-flowered *Bergenia cordifolia* (zone 4–8), to 16 in. (40 cm) high; it has been in cultivation since the 17th century and is very tolerant, surviving extremely cold conditions. (See also pages 110–11.)

Evoking memories of the cottage gardens of old, *Convallaria majalis* (lily of the valley) (zone 4–8) has earned its place among gardeners' favorites. It is found in much of the northern hemisphere, preferring deep to partial shade and happy in almost any soil, apart from heavy clay or marsh. The spreading rhizomes bear pairs of leathery, medium to dark green leaves, from which 8 in. (20 cm) stems of numerous pendent, waxy, white bell-shaped flowers arise in late spring. Sometimes flowers are followed by scarlet berries. Lily of the valley needs careful siting in the garden. It can be invasive, and will sometimes snub the original planting place, only to thrive elsewhere, in a site of its own choosing. It is useful to fill those narrow strips of redundant soil alongside paths and walls, and often thrives in full sun despite its preference for shade. Its dense foliage makes an effective weed control, perfect in a shrubby border. Plants acquired as dormant bare roots should be planted as soon as possible, with the rhizomes laid in shallow holes 1½ in. (4 cm) below the surface.

Although *Convallaria majalis* is most commonly found, there are a number of variations of note. Most flower at about 10 in. (25 cm) but the large flowers of

GROWING PERENNIALS IN DRY SHADE

Even plants that thrive in dry shade will still need care after planting until the roots become established. Cultivate the planting position well, and improve the soil by adding well-rotted compost or manure. Keep new plants watered thoroughly during the first growing season. A mulch of gravel or bark over the soil will help to conserve moisture, but this must be applied only when the soil is thoroughly moist. Some plants, such as *Tiarella, Galium,* and *Arum* will grow in quite dry conditions if given care while they become established.

Epimedium pinnatum • *Euphorbia amygdaloides* var. *robbiae* • *Linaria triornithophora* • *Vinca major* • *Vinca minor* •

Epimedium × rubrum

Geranium macrorrhizum

Lamium maculatum 'Beacon Silver'

of the best ground-cover plants for partial shade.

Geraniums are normally associated with dry soil and a sunny position. *Geranium phaeum* (zone 7–8), however, is often found naturalized in moist, shady sites. It has darkly marked foliage and long, fine stems, 24 in. (60 cm) high, which bear small, dark plum-purple flowers in early summer. This is not an arresting plant, but interesting to lighten patches of heavy foliage and add detail. *Geranium macrorrhizum* (zone 4–7), on the other hand, is good in dry shade and will form dense ground cover, 12in. (30cm) high, under a tree or at the base of a wall. In such a position it holds its foliage for much of the year, but will not display the autumn color that is a feature of the plant in full sun. Dainty pink or white flowers appear in late spring. The aromatic foliage is unattractive to animals, so it is a good choice where deer and rabbits are a problem.

The cultivars of *Lamium maculatum* (zone 4–7) are easy to grow in partial shade and make attractive low ground cover. These creeping members of the nettle family often have pleasing silver-marked leaves and white or pink flowers according to variety. **'White Nancy'** has silver leaves and pure white flowers; **'Beacon Silver'** has silvery green leaves

and pink-purple flowers (see also page 106). They will withstand quite dry conditions once established.

With its leathery, grasslike foliage and dense spikes of lilac-blue flowers borne in late summer and fall, *Liriope muscari* (lilyturf) (zone 6–9) is a splendid evergreen for shade. It grows only to 12 in. (30 cm) or so high, but eventually forms broad clumps and makes effective ground cover. A native of China and Japan, it is a woodland plant, preferring soil rich in organic matter. Although hardy, it is not tolerant of the coldest conditions, so the shelter of trees and shrubs is a blessing. (See Good Companions, right, and page 101).

Myrrhis odorata (sweet cicely) (zone 5–8) somewhat resembles Queen Anne's lace, but has wonderful ferny foliage that smells sweetly of aniseed and lasts throughout the season. The white lace-like flowers are produced over a long period from late spring to midsummer. It will grow to 4 ft. (1.2 m) tall and seeds itself where it is happy, but is never invasive. It likes a moist situation but will tolerate drier conditions, although growth is restricted here. This is a delightful plant to fill those shady gaps at the back of the border or to bring charm and interest to a neglected corner. It fits easily into any situation, rural or urban.

'Fortin's Giant' rise at least 12 in. (30 cm) above broader leaves. **'Flore Pleno'** has double white flowers, while those of var. *rosea* are larger and lilac-pink. The more rounded foliage of **'Albostriata'** is finely striped with gold along its length—simple yet stunning.

Epimediums (zone 5–8), also known as bishop's hat or barrenwort (see pages 112 and 114), are another excellent choice, requiring moist shade or partial shade with moderately fertile soil. Many are evergreen and make marvellous year-round ground cover with a carpet of richly hued foliage. *Epimedium × rubrum*, 12 in. (30 cm) high, with red-tinted young and mature leaves, is one

Myrrhis odorata

OTHER GOOD PERENNIALS FOR MOIST SHADE *Actaea simplex* • *Aspidistra elatior* 'Milky Way' •

There are few showy flowering perennials that succeed in shade. One of the loveliest is *Phlox stolonifera* (zone 5–8), a woodland native. It forms spreading mats of underground shoots that emerge from the soil in rosettes of leaves. In late spring and early summer, the scented flowers turn them into a colorful carpet. This is a hardy plant, 8–12 in. (20–30 cm) high, excellent for ground cover beneath deciduous trees, or for a scree bed that gets only a few hours of sun each day. It prefers neutral to acid, well-drained soil. The cultivar 'Pink Ridge' is strong pink, and 'Blue Ridge' is ice blue. *Phlox divaricata* (zone 3–7) has pinkish blue or white blooms; it thrives in similar conditions but has a lighter, more sprawling habit and is better suited to woodland.

Pulmonarias, or lungworts (see pages 106 and 115–16), bring interest

Phlox stolonifera 'Pink Ridge'

Pulmonaria 'Lewis Palmer'

to shady sites with both their early spring flowers and their exotically marked foliage, which can stay looking good for most of the year and rivals that of many hostas. They prefer moist shade; in drier conditions the foliage will deteriorate. *Pulmonaria longifolia* 'Bertram Anderson' (zone 3–8), 12 in. (30 cm) high, has long, narrow, well-spotted leaves and mauve-pink buds opening to rich blue flowers. *Pulmonaria* 'Lewis Palmer' (zone 2–8) is about the same height, with dark blue flowers held above narrow, dark green leaves, heavily blotched greenish white.

Most **symphytums** (comfreys) are tough plants, native to shady places. With its cream-variegated foliage and lilac-blue spring flowers, *Symphytum ×　uplandicum* 'Variegatum' (zone 5–7), up to 3 ft. (90 cm) tall, is very useful in moist shade. The green to gold markings on the dark green leaves of *Symphytum* 'Goldsmith' (zone 5–7) are best in early spring. Growing 10 in. (25 cm) high, with pink to pale blue flowers, it mixes well with blue-flowered bulbs (see Good Companions, left, and pages 116–17).

Many plants in the saxifrage family thrive in shade. *Tellima grandiflora* (fringe cups) (zone 6–8) is one of these—valuable for its clumps of green foliage and spikes of lime green flowers in late spring and early summer. It grows 24 in. (60 cm) high, flourishing in both moist and quite dry conditions, and is useful ground cover over spring bulbs.

Tolmiea menziesii (zone 6–9) is similar but even less showy. Known as the pickaback or piggyback plant, it produces offspring at the end of the leaf stalks. Its indestructible nature has led to its adoption as a houseplant. *Tolmiea menziesii* 'Taff's Gold', with yellow-marked foliage, brings welcome color to shady areas under shrubs and trees and among ferns. It grows 18 in. (45 cm) tall.

GOOD COMPANIONS

The green and gold variegated foliage of *Symphytum* 'Goldsmith' (1) (z. 5–7) is beautiful with sapphire blue *Muscari armeniacum* (2). (z. 3–8) Both will establish themselves firmly in a shady spot.

Phlox stolonifera 'Pink Ridge' (3) (z. 5–8) and *Ajuga reptans* 'Atropurpurea' (4) (z. 4–7): The phlox's vivid pink flowers shine out against the bronze metallic foliage and deep blue flowers of the ajuga.

The deep green, strap-like leaves of *Liriope muscari* (5) (z. 6–9) contrast well with the soft silver-gray variegation of the ivy *Hedera helix* 'Glacier' (6) (z. 4–9).

Galium odoratum • Hosta • Lamium galeobdolon • Ligularia 'The Rocket' • Petasites palmatus • Tiarella cordifolia •

Sunny sites

Silver, spiky, or aromatic foliage and bright flowers are often the livery of sun-loving plants. Natives of the Mediterranean, South Africa, California, Mexico, and other warm, dry regions, these perennials luxuriate in sunny situations and shun the cold and damp.

Agapanthus Headbourne hybrids

Many South African natives that enjoy full sun and good drainage must have plenty of moisture during the summer. **Agapanthus** (African blue lily) is a classic example. In their natural habitat these plants grow in moist, peaty soil, often in grassy and rocky sites. They have become naturalized across the world, from the sand dunes of the Scilly Isles, in Britain, to the rocky terraces of Madeira, Portugal. In gardens they fail to flower if they receive insufficient sun, or if their roots have too much freedom

Silver foliage and aromatic shrubs combine with sun-loving perennials in an open gravel garden.

PLANT ADAPTATIONS

Many herbaceous perennials are well adapted to dry, sunny situations, where they get a good baking in summer and water is often scarce. Some have developed fleshy or woody roots that store food and water. When conditions become too difficult, the parts above ground simply fade away, and those below the surface keep things ticking over until the following season. Other perennials have modified their leaves and stems in order to prevent water loss, perhaps with an insulating layer of hairs, or have developed thick, fleshy leaves that store water. In some, the foliage is aromatic, because of the presence of oil, another way of preventing desiccation.

or the soil is too rich. Agapanthus produce bold clumps of grasslike leaves and, in the summer, rounded heads of trumpet or tubular flowers in shades of blue or white. The **Headbourne hybrids** (zone 7–10) are still the best for garden cultivation. They were raised in the 1940s by the Hon. Lewis Palmer at Headbourne Worthy, near Winchester, in England. Some were selected and named, but they are usually offered as mixed shades of blue. They do not grow as tall as many agapanthus species and flower more freely in temperate climates. (See also pages 152–53.)

Silver-foliage perennials are a natural choice for sunny situations. *Anaphalis triplinervis* (zone 3–8) is a clump-forming, silver-leaved plant that bears flowers from late summer to early fall. Clustered at the top of stems 12 in. (30 cm) tall, these are small, white, and everlasting, and can be cut and dried. Anaphalis relish full sun and good drainage, but do not like to be too dry in summer. (See page 102.)

Artemisias, too, are valued for their silver leaves, but their flowers tend to be of little interest. Some artemisias are truly herbaceous and deciduous; others are partly woody. The ever-popular *Artemisia* 'Powis Castle' (zone 6–10) can grow into a substantial shrub, 40 in. (1 m) high, and lives longest in the poorest soil. *Artemisia pontica* (zone 4–8), from northern Europe to central Asia, is one of the hardiest species. It forms clumps of fine stems with delicately cut silver foliage (see Good Companions, page 67). *Artemisia schmidtiana* (zone 3–7), from Japan, is similar but more silvery with creeping stems; it forms a low mound of soft, hairlike foliage. *Artemisia alba* 'Canescens' (zone 6–8) has wiry stems and leaves that suit contemporary schemes. While these three reach 24 in. (60 cm) high, *Artemisia stelleriana* (zone 3–7) is more prostrate, and has

silver-white, lobed foliage; it loves sandy soil, so is useful near the coast. (See also pages 51, 91 and 102–105.)

Centranthus ruber (zone 4–8), the red valerian, is a native of the Mediterranean region, but is widely naturalized in parts of the United States and in northern Europe. It produces a tough, woody root and clings in rocky crevices and gaps in paving, walls, and sand dunes. The hollow stems, up to 40 in. (1 m) tall, carry light, evergreen leaves and clouds of red, pink ('**Roseus**') or white ('**Albus**') flowers from early summer onward. It is a good choice for inhospitable sunny sites where other plants struggle. Remove flower heads as they fade to prevent the downy, willow-like seeds from spreading.

Cosmos atrosanguineus (zone 7–10), known as the chocolate plant, grows from a tuber like that of a dahlia, and the flowers and foliage are not dissimilar, although this cosmos reaches

Cosmos atrosanguineus

only 24 in. (60 cm) high when in flower, in mid- to late summer. The blooms, 1½ in. (4 cm) across, are darkest maroon-crimson, with a rich scent of chocolate. A warm, sunny spot is essential, and it needs protecting in winter with a thick mulch of straw or bracken. It is late starting into growth, so mark its position carefully. It is a natural partner for warm pinks, oranges, reds, and yellows.

Dictamnus albus (zone 4–8), a member of the rue family, is a good example of a plant that survives dry conditions because of the presence of

CENTRANTHUS IN A BORDER

Although usually associated with the base of walls and gravel areas, *Centranthus ruber* (z. 4–8), the red valerian, is useful in the border. It looks especially attractive with peonies, its light flower heads contrasting well with the heavy, flamboyant peony blooms. It is also a good companion for the oriental poppy, *Papaver orientale* (z. 3–8): the valerian's strong stems and flower heads conceal the fading foliage of the poppy after it finishes flowering

aromatic oils in its foliage. A native of southern Europe, through Turkey into Asia, it grows wild in dry, rocky places. The erect stems, 32 in. (80 cm) high, bear pretty, fireflylike flowers in pink or white in early summer. *Dictamnus albus* var. *purpureus* (zone 4–8) has soft mauve-purple flowers with darker veining. On a hot, still evening, the

Dictamnus albus var. *purpureus*

whole plant can be set alight because of the oils vaporizing from the foliage. It will burn for a few seconds without sustaining harm. In the garden it likes a sunny, sheltered position. Avoid touching the foliage in warm weather: like rue, it is an irritant.

Echinops ritro

Echinops ritro (zone 6–7), the globe thistle, is a native of southern Europe to central Asia, where it is found in inhospitable, dry, stony places. The spiny, thistlelike leaves are green above and white beneath. Stiff stems, 40 in. (1 m) or more high, carry globe-shaped heads of steely blue flowers in late summer and fall. This is a superb garden plant, striking with both gray foliage subjects and the hot oranges and reds of late summer flowers (see Good Companions, right). It survives anywhere, in shade as well as sun, and is excellent for a dry bed against a wall.

Erigeron karvinskianus (zone 8–10) is also a pioneer of dry, hostile places. Formerly named *Erigeron mucronatus*, and originally from Mexico, it has

Erigeron karvinskianus

become naturalized in parts of the United States, southern Europe, and Britain. It colonizes places similar to those attracting valerian (see page 65), but is seen at its best in wall crevices, where the dainty, pink-tinged daisy flowers and wiry stems are the perfect contrast to the solidity of the stone. It is not very hardy but regenerates freely from seed.

Erigeron glaucus (zone 8–9) has larger daisy flowers and makes a low, dense clump of soft, dull green leaves reaching 12 in. (30 cm) tall. The flowers have bold centers and short raylike petals, which are normally soft mauve in color. They are produced over a long period from late spring to fall. *Erigeron glaucus* is widely distributed in the Pacific coastal area, where it thrives. A

Erigeron 'Dimity'

Erigeron 'Azurfee' (AZURE FAIRY)

number of showier garden varieties are derived from it. *Erigeron* 'Dimity' (zone 6–7) is compact, with pink, gold-centered flowers, orange-tinged in bud.

The taller erigerons are often confused with asters, to which they are closely related. They have green foliage and bright flowers with orange-yellow centers. They bloom in midsummer and need full sun. *Erigeron* 'Dignity' (zone 5–8), 18 in. (45 cm) high, has violet-blue flowers. 'Azure Fairy' (zone 5–8) is lilac-blue, while 'Darkest of All' is deep purple-blue; both reach 24 in. (60 cm).

The spiky metallic foliage and flowers of **eryngiums** tend to be associated with the coast because of the species *Eryngium maritimum* (zone 5–9), the sea holly. All eryngiums like full sun; some prefer dry conditions, and some demand moisture at their roots when growing. *Eryngium agavifolium* (zone 6–9) is a succulent-looking plant with upright rosettes of fleshy, toothed, evergreen leaves, and tall, thick stems up to 40 in. (1 m) high carrying greenish brown flowers in midsummer. It works well planted in gravel but is out of place in a mixed border. This species does not like to be too dry. Neither does the widely available *Eryngium variifolium* (zone 5–8), which produces leathery leaves and branching flower stems reaching 20 in. (50 cm) tall. Its flowers are spiky and metallic and a good contrast with the evergreen, silver-veined leaves. The hardy species

DRYING ERYNGIUMS

Eryngiums make excellent dried flowers for winter decoration and lend themselves to contemporary designs, as well as traditional arrangements. Cut the flowers in their prime, and hang them upside down in a warm place with good air circulation until dry; this can take two or three weeks. Once dry, the flowers will last for several seasons.

OTHER PERENNIALS FOR SUNNY SITES *Acanthus spinosus* • *Anthemis tinctoria* • *Baptisia australis* •

Eryngium maritimum

Eryngium bourgatii 'Oxford Blue'

Eryngium bourgatii (zone 3–8) tolerates much drier conditions, and grows to 20 in. (50 cm) when in flower in summer. The showy flower heads vary in color from stainless steel to rich blue. The flowers of the cultivar **'Oxford Blue'** are particularly spectacular. **Eryngium alpinum** (zone 4–8) is perhaps the most striking of all: Large flowers with a broad, spiky ruff are borne on stout stems, 40 in. (1 m) high, in early summer. It looks stunning at the front of the border, grouped with silver-foliage plants such as lavender and artemisia. This species does not like to be too dry. (See also page 103.)

Most herbaceous **geraniums** enjoy a sunny site. **Geranium macrorrhizum** (zone 4–7) is the most reliable for a dry, sunny spot; it is also good in shade (see page 62). **Geranium × magnificum** (zone 4–7), 24 in. (60 cm) or so high, with large blue flowers, is a fine plant. It likes good drainage and sunshine and will tolerate an exposed site. Its flowering season in early summer is short, but it is still worth growing.

Geranium ibericum (zone 6–8) from Turkey, is similar but blooms in mid- to late summer, so is good to plant with *Geranium × magnificum* for continuity of flower. **Geranium renardii** (zone 5–7) is a lovely foliage plant, its sage green leaves forming a neat mound 12 in. (30 cm) high. Prettily veined white flowers appear in midsummer. (See also pages 47–48, 91, 137 and 159.)

Limonium platyphyllum (zone 4–8), the sea lavender, is popular in coastal gardens. A tough plant with leathery, evergreen leaves, it can withstand very dry conditions. In summer, wiry, branched stems, 24 in. (60 cm) high, carry masses of starry, lavender-blue flowers, which last for several weeks and can be dried. **'Robert Butler'** and **'Violetta'** are two superior cultivars. All three are useful for gravel or scree, and mix well with silver-foliage plants.

Another natural partner for silver-leaved plants, **Nepeta × faassenii** (zone 3–9) makes a soft edging for hot, dry borders, particularly on alkaline soils. Growing to 12 in. (30 cm) in height, it has silvery foliage and lilac-blue flowers throughout summer (see page 69). It flows over the edge of paving in a low cloud and looks lovely with lime green *Alchemilla mollis* (see page 46).

(continued on page 69)

GOOD COMPANIONS

The soft gray leaves of *Artemisia pontica* (1) (z. 4–8) look lovely with *Allium cristophii* (2) (z. 4–10) and will do an excellent job concealing the allium's unsightly fading foliage.

The steely blue globes of *Echinops ritro* (3) (z. 6–7) contrast superbly with the fiery orange stars of *Crocosmia* 'Lucifer' (4) (z. 7–9)

For a striking color combination, try the bright blooms of *Verbena bonariensis* (5) (z. 8–9) floating above the rising torches of *Kniphofia* 'Samuel's Sensation' (6) (z. 6–9).

Eryngium planum • *Papaver orientale* • *Romneya coulteri* • *Scabiosa caucasica* • *Sisyrinchium striatum* •

Kniphofias

Commonly known as red hot pokers or torch lilies, kniphofias (zone 6–9) are not beautiful in isolation but when well planted can be some of the most striking subjects in the late summer and autumn garden. Towering above clumps of grasslike foliage, erect flower spikes provide strong vertical structure and contrast well with softer neighbors. They are useful to prolong interest in herbaceous plantings and look good with prairie plants and grasses. They are also striking against dark evergreens or the shining bark of trees such as *Prunus serrula* (zone 5–8). (See also pages 42 and 175.)

Natives of South Africa, kniphofias like fertile soil that does not dry out in summer; some simply will not flower if the soil is dry. They do, however, need a well-drained site and loathe cold, wet winters. Clumps should be divided in early spring every few years.

Kniphofia 'Ice Queen' is a statuesque plant, with towering blooms 4 ft. (1.2 m) high in mid- to late summer. The cool yellow flowers open from green buds and gradually fade to ivory as the season progresses.

Kniphofia **'Little Maid'** One of the more diminutive varieties. Has delicate spikes of creamy yellow flowers only 24 in. (60 cm) high, in late summer and early fall. It is excellent for a scree garden.

Kniphofia **'Royal Standard'** is the classic red hot poker, with large red and yellow flower spikes, 40 in. (1 m) high, in mid- to late summer. Another classic is *Kniphofia rooperi*, a vigorous species that flowers in autumn.

Kniphofia **'Samuel's Sensation'** is an excellent plant producing tall, bold spikes of warm orange-red with a hint of yellow at the base. The flower stems can reach 5 ft. (1.5 m) and appear from late summer onward. (See also Good Companions, page 67.)

OTHER GOOD KNIPHOFIAS

Kniphofia **'Bees' Sunset'** Blooms in midsummer, with rich orange flowers carried on mahogany stems 32 in. (80 cm) tall.

Kniphofia linearifolia Flowers in fall, with orange and yellow spikes 5 ft. (1.5 m) tall. The parent of many garden cultivars.

Kniphofia uvaria Grows 6 ft. (2 m) high, with red flowers, fading to yellow at the base of the spike, in the fall. The coarse, spiky leaves form a dense clump and are evergreen.

Tulbaghia violacea

Verbena rigida

Zauschneria californica

Nepeta 'Six Hills Giant' (zone 4–7) is a much taller plant, reaching up to 40 in. (1 m) high, with stronger stems and darker flowers. This is better towards the back of the border and grown with some support. (See also pages 42–43.)

Phlomis russeliana (zone 5–8) is a native of Turkey and is used to heat, but in its natural environment it often grows in woods or scrub, so will tolerate partial shade in dry conditions as well as full sun. It has large, sagelike leaves and whorls of yellow dead nettlelike flowers borne on stiff, upright, square stems in summer. It is not wholly deciduous, retaining whorls of foliage in winter. The dead flower heads are attractive if left on the plants during the early part of winter. *Phlomis samia* (zone 7–10), with soft pink flowers, is similar and enjoys the same conditions. *Phlomis tuberosa* (zone 5–8) is a deciduous species, overwintering by means of root tubers. A tough, easy plant to grow, it has green leaves and pink flowers.

Tulbaghias (zone 7–10) look like miniature agapanthus, with slender grassy foliage and pretty lilac or white flowers on fine stems. Members of the lily family, they are strongly aromatic with a musty garliclike odor. *Tulbaghia violacea* is reasonably hardy in a sunny, well-drained position. The variety 'Silver Lace' is particularly attractive, with its silver- and sage-striped leaves and violet-pink flowers in early summer and fall. Reaching only 20 in. (50 cm) high,

it is a good choice for the front of the border or planted into gravel.

Verbena rigida (zone 7–10) is a stiff, wiry perennial with aromatic foliage. The purple-magenta flowers, produced from midsummer to late fall, are striking and work well with silver foliage plants. (See page 152.) Growing from tuberous roots, it copes with dry soil and loves full sun. Only 20 in. (50 cm) high, *Verbena rigida* offers a more compact alternative to ethereal *Verbena bonariensis*, (zone 8–9) which can grow to 6 ft. (2 m) in height (see Good Companions, page 67, and see page 169).

Watsonias (zone 9–10) are members of the iris family and hail from South Africa. They grow from corms and make dense clumps similar in habit to crocosmias. They are hardy in mild zones in full sun and moisture-retentive

soil. *Watsonia pillansii* grows to less than 40 in. (1 m) tall, with spikes of funnel-shaped flowers in oranges, reds, and pinks. *Watsonia borbonica* may reach 5 ft. (1.5 m), and has clear pink flowers, arranged on only one side of the spike (not both, as in *Watsonia pillansii*). *Watsonia borbonica* ssp. *borbonica* 'Arderne's White' is pure white and easier to accommodate. All of these flower in summer.

Zauschneria californica (zone 6–8) also likes a warm position in full sun but must have excellent drainage. It is a low, sprawling plant with many stems and usually narrow leaves. The bright orange flowers are borne freely in late summer and fall. It will nestle at the base of a wall or soften the edge of paving or a raised bed. The cultivar 'Dublin' has excellent blazing orange-red flowers.

PLANTING PARTNERS

Dark lilac-blue *Nepeta* × *faassenii* (z. 3–9) mixes with the blooms of *Rosa gallica* var. *officinalis* (the red rose of Lancaster) (z. 6–8) at the peak of the season and extends it as the roses fade. Both *Rosa gallica* var. *officinalis and Rosa gallica* 'Versicolor' (known as Rosa mundi) (z. 6–8) are excellent choices where growing conditions are less than hospitable.

The scree garden

The scree or gravel garden is a new style of planting, particularly good for sunlovers that like their feet in fast-draining soil. Growing plants in a bed or border topped with gravel shows them off beautifully. The effect can be that of a meadow, run through with sweeps of color, but scree is also suitable for minimalistic schemes and provides the perfect setting for plants like phormiums, cistus, grasses, silver foliage subjects, alpines, and dwarf bulbs.

Scree is ideal for an informal planting of grasses and sun-loving perennials.

ADVANTAGES OF GRAVEL

Scree is found naturally in many areas of the world, where rocks near the surface have shattered to create a layer of stony debris. In the garden, a sunny, well-drained scree or gravel bed gives plants from the Mediterranean, Australasia, and South Africa the best chance of coping with the North American climate. Alpines, low perennials, and shrubs look better in this setting than in the false environment of a small rock garden.

Gravel shows off individual specimens to maximum advantage. It conserves moisture, but reflects light back onto the plants; and it prevents water splashes that spoil the lower foliage.

Gravel is low maintenance: there is no grass to cut. It is relatively inexpensive to install. A level site is not necessary: it is often more attractive if allowed to follow the natural contours of the land. A narrow scree bed alongside a path or a wall provides a pleasing solution to an awkward dry area.

Asphodeline lutea (yellow asphodel) (zone 6–9) has rosettes of blue-green, waved, grasslike leaves, from which the flower stems rise in spring, reaching 5 ft. (1.5 m) by the time the starry yellow flowers open. These fade to leave round green seedpods on ragged spikes. Asphodel looks awkward with other plants, but on well-drained scree in full sun it is striking. In larger sites it is

Diascias

Diascias have become popular plants for pots and hanging baskets. They grow quickly, flower profusely, and are easy to propagate from cuttings. Many lovely hybrids have been raised in recent years. Diascias originate from South Africa, where they grow in moist sites by streams and other damp places, often in semi-shade. They tend to be considered sun lovers because of the way they are grown. Of course in baskets and containers they get regularly watered, and, if overwintered in a greenhouse, they are protected from the worst of winter. When grown in scree beds with good, moisture-retentive soil under the gravel layer, they are rewarding plants with a very long flowering season.

Diascia rigescens (z. 7–9) has small spikes of strawberry pink flowers on a plant that forms a dense mat, about 12 in. (30 cm) high. It normally flowers during late spring and early summer, but in the right conditions can be in bloom for much longer.

Diascia fetcaniensis (z. 8–10) is one of the most reliable diascias. Up to 12 in. (30 cm) high, it has fine creeping stems of medium green leaves and dainty spikes of pink flowers in summer.

Diascia barberae 'Ruby Field' (z. 8–11/ann.), loose in habit and only 8 in. (20 cm) high, has plenty of large pretty, salmon red flowers in summer.

a perfect partner for the bold foliage of *Cynara cardunculus* (see page 102).

Many **dianthuses** revel in dry scree, especially on alkaline soil (see also pages 81 and 136). *Dianthus deltoides* (maiden pink) (zone 4–7) forms low mats of fine blue-green leaves that are transformed from midsummer onward with myriad bright perfect flowers, borne on upright stems 8 in. (20 cm) high. It has given rise to many excellent varieties, from white to the most vivid cerise and dark red. Easy to grow, and perfect for scree, the similarly sized *Dianthus gratianopolitanus* (zone 5–8) bears deep pink flowers with cut

Dierama pulcherrimum

petal edges and a delightful clove scent. It is also known as the cheddar pink.

Often plants grown in dry gardens prefer a moist soil but must have good drainage; this is particularly true of many South African natives such as dieramas. Grasslike perennials growing from bulbous bases, they are usually evergreen, so are treated as herbaceous plants and are not normally sold as dry bulbs. *Dierama pulcherrimum* (zone 4–8) is the most spectacular, with upright foliage to 24 in. (60 cm) long, and arching stems, more than 5 ft. (1.5 m) tall, with large silky, bell-shaped flowers that are papery at the base. This

THE GARDEN HOUSE

At The Garden House, Buckland Monachorum, in Devon, England, the traditional garden is integrated into the surrounding landscape using rolling scree beds planted in naturalistic styles. Here, drifts of *Dierama pulcherrimum* (wandflower) (z. 4–8) and *Campanula lactiflora* (milky bellflower) (z. 5–7) blur the boundaries of the scree. Both plants grow naturally in rather drier conditions, but scree planting provides excellent drainage at their feet, helping them to thrive even in the locally damp climate.

is the lovely feature that gained these plants the common name "wand-flower." As with all dieramas, they bloom from early to midsummer, and colors range from white through shades of pink to dark purple. *Dierama dracomontanum* (zone 8–9) is a charming little plant for the smaller scree garden and dances happily above sedums, thymes, and saxifrages. It grows to only 18 in. (45 cm) tall and has flowers in various shades of dark pink. *Dierama floriferum* (zone 8–9), too, grows only 18 in. (45 cm) high and has fine foliage and narrow bells of blue-mauve. Often mistaken for a grass, it is fun to plant with fescues and stipas.

The whorlflower, *Morina longifolia* (zone 6–9), is a native of the moist but steep slopes of the Himalayas. It has rosettes of aromatic, thistle-like foliage, 12 in. (30 cm) long, and in summer these give rise to tall stems, up to 24 in. (60 cm) high, of small white flowers

Morina longifolia

COLOR WITH BULBS

Dwarf bulbs are shown at their best on scree, when they can get lost elsewhere in the garden. Choose those with fine leaves or those that die down quickly to prevent the fading foliage spoiling the effect.

A few of the best bulbs for scree:

Crocus chrysanthus 'Ladykiller' (z. 3–8)
Crocus tommasinianus
'Whitewell Purple' (z. 3–8)
Cyclamen coum (above) (z. 6–8)
Iris reticulata (z. 5–8)
Narcissus 'Hawera' (z. 4–9)
Tulipa linifolia Batalinii Group
'Bright Gem' (z. 4–8)
Tulipa dasystemon (z. 4–8)

that become pink with age. A scree bed with good soil that does not get too dry is the best place for it in the garden.

Platycodon grandiflorus (balloon flower) (zone 4–8), a member of the campanula family from Japan and China, enjoys similar conditions. Its thick roots compete with grass on moist but well-drained slopes. The glaucous foliage, carried on wiry stems 24 in. (60 cm) high, is particularly fine. Large, bell-shaped blue flowers top the stems in late summer. The species is rarely grown but a number of hybrids are available: **'Mariesii'** is blue and early flowering; **'Albus'** is white; and **'Apoyama'** is deep mauve. The beauty of the plant is lost among other perennials in a border; in a scree bed it can be shown off to advantage.

The lovely **roscoeas** also thrive in moist but well-drained soil, but they enjoy fairly cool conditions and benefit from the shade cast by their neighbors. Rather orchidlike in flower, most are dwarf and upright, producing succulent stems that emerge in spring from fleshy roots. *Roscoea cautleyoides* (zone 7–8) has soft yellow flowers and *Roscoea purpurea* (zone 6–9) is rich purple. Both bloom in early summer.

ESTABLISHING A SCREE BED

An open, sunny site is best for a scree bed and allows cultivation of the widest range of plants. It is essential to rid the site of perennial weeds before establishing the bed.

Ensure good drainage by digging in coarse grit and improve water retention by adding plenty of well-rotted, organic manure or compost. On poorly drained sites raise planting areas into mounds.

Top the soil with at least 3 in. (7 cm) of washed pea gravel. Larger stones, pebbles or slate scree can be added on the surface to enhance the scheme.

Roscoea purpurea

Sedums (zone 4–8) are versatile plants, in spite of their succulent appearance. (See also pages 97 and 176.) The ice plant, *Sedum spectabile*, is widely grown in mixed plantings and is useful for its clumps of sea green foliage, 18 in. (45 cm) high, and its flattened heads of pink flowers in late summer. *Sedum spectabile* 'Iceberg' has large heads of white flowers and paler leaves. The large flower heads of the slightly taller *Sedum* **'Autumn Joy'** ('Herbstfreude') turn from dark pink to chestnut as fall moves into winter. They are a favorite haunt of butterflies in late summer. These sedums suit scree planting on sandy soil, so long as they have adequate moisture in summer. They contribute bold form among grasses and softer perennials.

OTHER GOOD PERENNIALS FOR SCREE *Centranthus ruber* • *Crambe maritima* • *Erigeron karvinskianus* •

Sedum telephium ssp. maximum 'Atropurpureum'

Sedum telephium ssp. maximum 'Atropurpureum' (zone 3–8), a solid plant with a few erect stems up to 20 in. (50 cm) tall, has pinkish red flower heads and deep wine purple foliage; it contrasts well with the fine foliage of *Festuca glauca* (blue fescue) (zone 4–8). **Sedum 'Ruby Glow'** (zone 4–8) is the perfect candidate for scree, with its sprawling stems of very gray foliage and deep purple-red flowers in late summer.

More prostrate sedums are ideal for carpet planting with thymes in dry areas—bringing a feeling of space, the equivalent of a lawn, to a larger scree bed. Good varieties include **Sedum cauticola 'Lidakense'** (zone 5–9), forming a mat of blue-gray leaves on fine stems with deep pink flowers, and bright yellow **Sedum spathulifolium 'Cape Blanco'** (zone 5–9), which has rounded, succulent gray leaves with a white bloom. Both flower in summer.

SCREE GARDENS ON WET SITES

Gardeners with wet sites or heavy clay are not precluded from enjoying this style of planting. Adding organic matter and sharp grit works wonders on even the heaviest soil. Raising the planting areas into mounds keeps the plants' feet out of the damp.

SELF-SEEDERS

Gravel provides the perfect medium for self-seeding subjects to germinate next year's plants. Grasses such as **Festuca glauca** (blue fescue) (zone 4–8) and the feather grass **Stipa tenuissima** (zone 7–9) seed themselves liberally. They need only a little judicious thinning. Annuals like California poppy, *Eschscholzia,* with shimmering blooms of brilliant orange, create a sensational summer display and are often perennial in mild zones. When planted with low silver foliage shrubs and early-flowering helianthemums they prolong the season of interest. Or try them with purple-pink geraniums such as *Geranium cinereum* 'Ballerina' (see page 137) or *Geranium sanguineum* (see page 159).

Sisyrinchiums are excellent in scree and seed freely. *Sisyrinchium striatum* (zone 7–9), with its summer spikes of pale creamy yellow flowers 24 in. (60 cm) high, can be overpowering in small areas but is valuable for the sharp lines of its gray-green, irislike leaves. The cultivar 'Aunt May' (see page 97) is less vigorous, to 18 in. (45 cm) high, and has leaves striped cream and green. The smaller, grasslike species, to about 6 in. (15 cm) high, provide strong tufts of foliage and brightly colored flowers. *Sisyrinchium angustifolium* (blue-eyed grass) (zone 3–7) produces its

SCREE IN SMALL SPACES

Scree is a good alternative to a lawn in a small garden, where a patch of grass can be difficult to maintain and only rarely looks its best. A landscape of planting into gravel creates a soft sense of space that is easily cared for and can look attractive all year round.

violet flowers from late spring until fall. The cultivar *Sisyrinchium idahoense* **var. bellum** 'Rocky Point' (zone 7–8) is excellent, with large blue flowers borne over a long period in summer. *Sisyrinchium californicum* (zone 10–11), the yellow-eyed grass, bears yellow flowers in late spring. These are useful perennials when allowed to seed and drift between other subjects, although some thinning may be required to prevent invasion.

Stipa tenuissima with red crocosmias and white achilleas, in a creative planting by Alan Bloom.

Eucomis bicolor • Gentiana • Rhodohypoxis • Saponaria ocymoides • Saxifraga • Sempervivum • Silene schafta •

Wet conditions

Some of the most spectacular and arresting herbaceous plants are those that will grow on wet or waterlogged soil. All tend to have lush stems and foliage; with a plentiful supply of water at their feet they are able to grow to greater proportions than their cousins on dry ground. Whether you want to create a planting area around a pond or beside a stream, or turn a poorly drained patch of ground into a bog garden, there is a wealth of plant material from which to choose.

Aruncus dioicus

Aruncus dioicus (goatsbeard) (zone 4–7) is a handsome plant 6 ft. (2 m) tall, with fernlike foliage and light, airy creamy white blooms in early and mid-summer. It likes moist, peaty soil and needs semi-shade; otherwise the flowers quickly fade to brown. It is often mistaken for astilbe, but the habit of its leaves and flowers is more open and wiry. It is perhaps better than astilbe in a naturalistic setting. (See Good Companions, page 79).

Like goatsbeard, **astilbes** (zone 5–8) are plants for moist, peaty soil in semi-shade. Their fernlike foliage contrasts well with other heavier subjects, and their feathery plumes of flowers appear as colorful see-through clouds when planted at the water's edge. They may be 24 in. (60 cm) to over 40 in. (1 m) in height, and they flower from late spring

Some of the most beautiful herbaceous perennials grow in wet soil alongside water, as at Le Clos du Coudray, Normandy, France.

SUCCESS WITH ASTILBES

Astilbes need lifting and dividing every three to five years if they are to maintain vigor; otherwise, the rhizomes become woody with age and the plants become overcrowded and deteriorate.

Buy astilbes as pot-grown plants, and get them into the ground in early spring when the new foliage is emerging. Choose named varieties. Plants sold as dry rhizomes rarely give the best performance.

MARWOOD HILL GARDENS

The National Collections of astilbe and *Iris ensata* are held at Marwood Hill Gardens, Barnstaple, Devon, in England. The work of the late Dr. Jimmy Smart, the gardens are filled with an abundance of plant material in a beautiful naturalistic setting. The lakes and bog garden contain a wide range of perennials that enjoy wet conditions.

GOOD VARIETIES OF ASTILBE

Astilbe 'Bressingham Beauty' (z. 5–8) Grows to 40 in. (1 m) and has broad, drooping panicles in deep pink.

Astilbe 'Cattleya' (z. 5–8) 3 ft. (90 cm) tall, produces broad, angular plumes of orchid pink.

Astilbe chinensis var. *pumila* (z. 5–7) Only 16 in. (40 cm) tall, with narrow, upright pink panicles.

Astilbe 'Deutschland' (z. 5–8) One of the most widely planted, grows 20 in. (50 cm) tall, with white panicles.

Astilbe 'Fanal' (z. 5–8) 24 in. (60 cm) high and early flowering, with dense, glowing red plumes.

Astilbe 'Jo Ophorst' (z. 5–8) 3 ft. (90 cm) tall, produces stiff, upright panicles of deep mauve-pink.

Astilbe 'Weisse Gloria' (z. 5–8) 24 in. (60cm) tall, has early white flowers.

into midsummer, depending on variety. In shades from white through pink to deepest red, they mix well with white and purple irises. Astilbes are at their best planted in groups or drifts; they rarely look impressive as solitary plants. The dwarf varieties are useful to lighten the effect of hostas and bergenias.

Caltha palustris (zone 3–7), a native of parts of North America, Britain and other northern temperate regions, is commonly known as the kingcup or marsh marigold. It has dark stems, 18 in. (45 cm) high, clad in kidney-shaped, toothed, medium green leaves. Large, golden yellow, buttercup-like flowers appear in early spring. The double form *Caltha palustris* 'Flore Pleno' seldom exceeds 10 in. (25 cm) high, with flowers that resemble marigolds. It needs a rich, moist soil, preferably in full sun, and is often seen in boggy ground at the edge of a pond. Although it can be grown in water, in a planting container, it will not tolerate having its feet submerged for more than a month or two at a time.

A member of the saxifrage family, *Darmera peltata* (zone 7–8) has round, veined leaves up to 24 in. (60 cm) across; these are the main feature of the plant, rather than the pinkish flower heads that emerge first. It prefers moist conditions in semi-shade. The dwarf *Darmera peltata* 'Nana' is useful beneath the vast leaves of gunnera (see Good Companions, page 79)

Houttuynia cordata (zone 6–10) is an excellent low ground-cover plant for wet sites in sun or shade. Its creeping rhizomes will wend their way between moisture-loving ferns and hostas. The stems can grow to 12 in. (30 cm) tall, with heart-shaped velvet green leaves and white flowers in summer. The foliage smells unpleasant if disturbed. There is a double-flowered form and some colorful variegated cultivars. *Houttuynia cordata* 'Chameleon':

Iris sibirica 'Flight of Butterflies'

with leaves of gold, red, orange, and green, it is striking when planted imaginatively with other boldly colored foliage. (See also page 100.)

The most difficult sites are those that are wet in winter and dry in summer; here, few plants can thrive. *Iris spuria* (zone 6–8) is an exception, since it grows naturally in these conditions in full sun, which it needs to flower well. It also tolerates alkaline and saline sites. Its lilac blooms, on stems 3 ft. (90 cm) tall, appear in early summer. Many superb cultivars have been raised in the U.S.

Most irises fall into two groups: those that like an open, sunny site and good drainage and those that like their feet wet. *Iris sibirica* (zone 4–8) is one of the more adaptable; it relishes wet conditions, but is also content in normal soil so long as it does not dry out. It will grow and bloom happily in full sun or semi-shade. The fine vertical foliage looks good for longer than that of its sun-loving relatives, and the dainty blue flowers, carried high on slender stems, 40 in. (1 m) tall, are a delight in early summer. The sapphire blue *Iris sibirica* 'Flight of Butterflies' looks appealing when planted in drifts with moisture-loving ferns. (See also pages 140–41.)

The yellow flag, *Iris pseudacorus* (zone 5–8), with its bright blooms in early spring, is too vigorous for most gardens, but *Iris pseudacorus* 'Variegata' is worth considering. Growing 40 in (1 m) tall in sun or semi-shade, it has creamy yellow striped, sword-shaped foliage.

Iris setosa (zone 2–7) likes wet, peaty soil; it has striking rich purple flowers in early summer, and grows 30 in. (80 cm) high. *Iris laevigata* (zone 5–8) has bluish purple blooms in early summer, on stems of a similar height. *Iris ensata* (zone 5–8), from Japan (see Good Companions, below), has produced many beautiful cultivars, including the large-flowered **Kaempferi hybrids**, which sometimes involve hybridization with *Iris laevigata*. These elegant plants have large, flattened blooms, in white, pink, and lavender to deep purple, in early summer. They like wet soil, or shallow water, and prefer drier conditions in winter. They can also be grown in planting containers in a pond, removed in winter and plunged into the ground, then returned to the pond in spring. They seem to survive happily in wet conditions, so long as they have full sun; they do not flower well in shade.

Liatris spicata

Liatris spicata (zone 2–8) is a tall, upright perennial with vivid, light purple flowers in stiff bottlebrush spikes, which open from the top downward. It flowers from midsummer to fall. The plant grows from cormlike rhizomes, which look as if they require a dry site; in fact, it needs waterside planting in the sun, though it tends to rot if wet in winter.

Ligularias (zone 3–8) offer colorful flowers and fine foliage in mid- to late summer. They enjoy moist soil in sun or semi-shade. The various cultivars of *Ligularia dentata* have bold, rounded leaves with dark stems and undersides.

Ligularia 'The Rocket'

Lobelia 'Queen Victoria'

Ligularia dentata 'Desdemona' has strong stems carrying clusters of rich orange, daisylike flowers in summer. The newer variety *Ligularia dentata* 'Britt-Marie Crawford' has superb dark wine purple foliage (see page 87). These are not plants to grow where slugs and snails are a problem; these pests would soon devour the young foliage. *Ligularia* 'The Rocket' is very different in appearance. Its black stems, to 6 ft. (2 m) tall, bear triangular, toothed leaves and slender spikes of tiny yellow flowers. A good see-through plant, it is well placed at the water's edge and offers strong but light vertical interest among hostas and rodgersias.

Lobelia 'Queen Victoria' (zone 8–9) has a long season of interest. Clumps of rich red-purple leaves emerge in spring,

GOOD COMPANIONS

With its upright shoots and orange-red bracts, *Euphorbia griffithii* 'Fireglow' (1) (z. 5–7) is about 12 in. (30 cm) high when *Iris sibirica* 'Ego' (2) (z. 4–8) blooms. The velvety, deep blue iris flowers flutter above the glowing heads of the euphorbia.

Rich blue *Iris ensata* (z. 5–8) looks stunning when planted against the golden explosion of a clump of *Carex elata* 'Aurea' (z. 5–9). When the iris flowers fade, the upright foliage still works well with the flowing leaves of the grass.

contrasting well with fresh green ferns. As summer progresses, the flower stems develop, reaching upward to 40 in. (1 m) or more. Finally the brilliant scarlet flowers open up against the dark plum purple stems—a spectacular color combination. It thrives in moist soil, in sun or semi-shade, but is not for cold zones. In more severe climates choose *Lobelia cardinalis* (zone 3–7), which has flowers of a similar color but without the dark red foliage.

Lythrum salicaria (purple loosestrife) (zone 4–8) is an upright perennial, up to 5 ft. (1.5 m) tall, with slender spikes of purple-pink flowers from early summer. The crepe-paper flowers are crowded in close whorls up the spikes. An easy plant to grow, in sun or partial shade, it provides continuity of color, coming into its own just as the spring flowers fade. 'Blush' has more subtle pale pink flowers; **'Firecandle'** ('Feuerkerze') is an iridescent pinkish red. *Lythrum virgatum* (zone 3–9) is more compact but still stunning, with some fine named cultivars: **'Dropmore Purple'** and **'Rose Queen'** need no further description beyond 'vibrant'; **'The Rocket'** has erect stems of deep pink flowers.

Many **primulas** enjoy a moist site, often originating from wet mountain meadows and streamsides in cool areas. They are mostly hardy plants, easy to grow in the right conditions. *Primula denticulata* (zone 5–7), also known as the drumstick primula, is among the most tolerant of drier soils. Its large drumstick-like flower heads appear in spring, on stems up to 16 in. (40 cm) tall, as the foliage is in its infancy. Colors range from white through pink and mauve to deep red-purple. It grows in sun or semi-shade. *Primula vialii* (zone 5–8) is often mistaken for a hardy orchid, because of its narrow, pointed, mauve flower heads showily tipped with crimson in late spring. Growing to about 24 in. (60 cm) tall, it prefers moist but

Primula vialii

Primula pulverulenta

Primula florindae

Primula japonica varieties

well-drained soil in semi-shade. In boggy conditions it needs planting on a mound. The loveliest of the pastel-colored forms, *Primula alpicola* (zone 4–8) needs a wetter site and prefers shade. Its drooping clusters of creamy flowers, liberally dusted with a waxy, silver farina, appear at the top of elegant 24 in. (60 cm) stems in spring. *Primula florindae* (zone 6–7) is one of the largest primulas, with bold green foliage and tall stems up to 40 in. (1 m) high, topped in spring to early summer, by a shower of bright yellow flowers trimmed with silver farina around the base. It is easy to grow in sun or semi-shade and mixes well with some of the heavier foliage plants of the bog garden.

The **Candelabra primulas** (zone 5–7) include many species and hybrids with whorls of flowers spaced at intervals up slender stems 12–30 in. (30–75 cm) tall. They vary in origin, but generally they enjoy wet, peaty soil in semi-shade. These are truly the highlights of the late spring bog garden, the

brilliance and delicacy of their blooms being second to none. The flowers of *Primula bulleyana* (zone 6–7) are red in bud, opening to orange. *Primula beesiana* (zone 5–7) is carmine with yellow eyes; *Primula pulverulenta* (zone 6–7) is red with dark eyes. *Primula japonica* (zone 5–7) has given rise to many named hybrids including the wonderful **'Miller's Crimson'** and **'Postford White'**. One of the easiest to

---

MAKING MORE OF CANDELABRA PRIMULAS

Candelabra primulas happily cross-pollinate and hybridize. They prefer a little space between the plants, which should be kept free from weeds. After flowering, leave some of the seed heads to develop and ripen. Seed allowed to fall onto the moist ground between the plants usually germinates successfully to produce plenty more young plants. Leave these *in situ,* and transplant them the following spring. The hybrids will be variable and exciting.

Trollius chinensis

Rheum palmatum 'Atrosanguineum'

full sun but tolerates semi-shade. It is a good choice for a sheltered courtyard garden. (See Good Companions, right.)

FOLIAGE DRAMA

Big, bold foliage is a feature of bog gardens, and *Gunnera manicata* (zone 7–10) has the biggest and boldest of all (see Good Companions, right). In rich, moist soil, in sun or shade, this Brazilian beauty reaches 10 ft. (3 m) in height with leaves 6 ft. (2 m) across. It is the ultimate in natural vegetable architecture. It is, however, not beyond cultivation in the smaller garden; it will survive in a large barrel of wet soil, the restricted space naturally limiting its growth. In cold areas, provide winter protection in the form of a frost cover or dry mulch; traditionally the leaves are cut in the fall and upturned on the crown of the plant.

Rheum palmatum (zone 5–7) gives the same foliage drama, but on a lesser scale and with more color. This is the best choice for smaller gardens. Many rheums have reddish stems and veins in the foliage: *Rheum palmatum* 'Atrosanguineum' is one of the most colorful with deep red-purple emerging leaves and deep plum undersides to the mature foliage. The stately rhubarb

flower stems can reach 6–10 ft. (2–3 m) tall, with myriad tiny flowers developing pinkish seeds. Removing these early prevents the flowers and seeds from dropping all over the foliage. Some claim that removing the flower spike prevents the early demise of the foliage; probably the most important factor is maintaining enough moisture at the roots. Rheums like plenty of well-rotted manure around the roots each year to maintain the richness of the soil. Enjoying sun or semi-shade, they are hardier than gunneras and a better choice for colder areas.

On a still smaller scale, but no less impressive, *Rodgersia aesculifolia* (zone 4–8) offers the finest foliage in the bog garden, reaching about 40 in. (1 m).

grow is *Primula prolifera* (zone 4–8), with white or yellow flowers. Candelabra primulas look their best planted in drifts of different colors; their clashing hues work to create a shaft of shimmering colored light against the lush foliage of their neighbors.

Candelabra primulas in orange and purple make good planting partners for *Trollius* × *cultorum* hybrids (zone 5–7), moisture-loving plants that grow in sun or partial shade, producing luminous globelike flowers, resembling huge buttercups, above attractive divided leaves. Flower color varies, from the pale greenish yellow of 'Alabaster' and the lovely pale yellow 'Lemon Queen' to the rich orange of 'Fireglobe' ('Feuertroll'). Although the hybrids are striking, *Trollius chinensis* (zone 5–8), from China, is unsurpassed for color. The upward-facing, open cups are brilliant orange-yellow, with upright, narrow petals. All flower in late spring or early summer, on 30 in. (70 cm) stems.

There is, however, no more exotically beautiful herbaceous perennial than *Zantedeschia aethiopica* (zone 9–11), familiar to most as the arum lily. Although often grown as a sunroom or conservatory plant, it is reasonably hardy in open ground, in a sheltered position, or with the added insulation of shallow water. Given a moist site and fertile soil, it grows to 40 in. (1 m) high, with glorious white blooms in spring and lush green foliage that stays looking good throughout the season. It flowers best in

Gunnera manicata

OTHER PERENNIALS FOR WET CONDITIONS *Cardamine pratensis* • *Euphorbia palustris* • *Mimulus ringens* •

Rodgersia aesculifolia

GRASSES AS PLANTING PARTNERS

There are many grasses, sedges, and rushes that thrive in moist conditions. These are useful to lighten the heavy foliage that is typical of many moisture-loving perennials. The golden and variegated types bring summer-long color and relief to heavy green leaves.

A few of the best:

Carex elata 'Aurea' (see page 76) (z. 5–9)
Carex oshimensis 'Evergold' (z. 5–9)
Glyceria maxima var. *variegata* (right) (z. 5–8)
Imperata cylindrica 'Rubra' (z. 6–9)
Scirpus sylvaticus (z. 6–9)

The dense, astilbelike flower heads are of secondary importance to the leaves, which are deep green-bronze and rigid, resembling those of horse chestnut. They last well into the fall, turning a richer red-bronze as the season progresses (see Good Companions, right). Rodgersias grow in sun or semi-shade and prefer moist, peaty soil but will tolerate drier conditions.

Lysichiton americanus

By midsummer, the yellow skunk cabbage, **Lysichiton americanus** (zone 6–7), has leaves like a huge romaine lettuce: great elliptical shields, up to 5 ft. (1.5 m) tall, of fresh green that catch the light and contrast with heavier subjects such as gunnera and rheum. The flowers, waxy yellow and arumlike, with a musky smell, appear first in early spring. A native species, it is hardy and easy to grow in the bog garden. White-flowered **Lysichiton camtschatcensis** (zone 7–9), from Asia, has similar requirements for moisture and neutral to acid soil. It is a smaller plant and smells sweeter, but is less often seen in gardens.

GOOD COMPANIONS

The light, variegated foliage of *Cornus alba* 'Sibirica Variegata' (1) (z. 2–8) contrasts with the bold leaves of *Rodgersia aesculifolia* (2) (z. 4–8). Both take on reddish tones as fall approaches.

Try setting the light, wiry form of goatsbeard, *Aruncus dioicus* (3) (z. 4–7), against the bold foliage and white flowers of the arum lily, *Zantedeschia aethiopica* (4) (z. 9–11).

The rounded leaves of *Darmera peltata* 'Nana' (5) (z. 4–8) reflect the vast umbrellas of *Gunnera manicata* (6) (z. 7–10) and provide low interest under its canopy.

GROWING MOISTURE-LOVERS IN DRY GARDENS

Gardeners with dry soil can achieve wet, boggy conditions by lining a shallow, basin-shaped hole, 24 in. (60 cm) deep, with butyl pond liner and filling it with rich loamy soil. It is essential to have an overflow pipe or drainage holes in the liner to prevent continual waterlogging in winter. Moisture-loving plants such as primulas, irises, and other, not too vigorous perennials will grow happily in this mini bog garden. It is also an excellent way to give new purpose to a leaking pond.

Persicaria bistorta • *Pontederia cordata* • *Ranunculus aconitifolius* • *Sagittaria latifolia* • *Sarracenia* • *Thalictrum* •

Alkaline soil and clay

Alkaline soil and clay are often seen as problem substrates by those who garden on them. Alkaline soil, such as that found in the Southwest, the Great Plains and parts of the Rocky Mountains, tends to be dry and low in nutrients; clay is wet, heavy, and difficult to work. In fact, both soil types can provide the perfect conditions for plants that are adapted to them.

A perennial border on alkaline soil, at Bramdean House, Hampshire, in England.

PERENNIALS FOR ALKALINE SOIL

Most popular border perennials are unfussy when it comes to soil. The majority enjoy free-draining conditions and only moderate fertility; too much moisture and highly fertile soils can lead to soft, lush growth that will need some form of support and may be produced at the expense of flowers. For most perennials, therefore, alkaline soils are almost ideal, needing only the addition of organic material to increase retention of water and nutrients. Many plants actually prefer alkaline conditions, and soils derived from limestone are by nature alkaline, to a greater or lesser degree (see page 19).

Clematises are usually thought of as climbers that retain flexible, woody stems during the dormant season. There are, however, several species that grow as herbaceous perennials, producing a clump of often lax stems and dying down to ground level in winter.

THE IRRIGATION PROBLEM

Summer drought is the main problem on alkaline soils, hence the need for irrigation and the addition of organic matter to improve water retention. When plants are in maximum growth and flower, they are quickly put under stress if there is a lack of water at the roots. For example, although achilleas tolerate drought, they do not enjoy a sudden dry spell after a moist period, and respond with wilting foliage.

OTHER GOOD PERENNIALS FOR ALKALINE SOIL *Acanthus • Achillea • Asphodeline lutea • Campanula lactiflora •*

Clematis × diversifolia 'Hendersonii'

Dianthus 'Doris'

Clematises prefer alkaline soils; adding lime to the soil often helps them to succeed where conditions are acid.

Clematis tubulosa (zone 5–9) is shrublike in growth with sprawling stems up to 40 in. (1 m) high that need support. *Clematis tubulosa* 'Wyevale' is the best cultivar, with starry bell-shaped flowers in late summer. These are a pretty shade of blue and scented. *Clematis integrifolia* (zone 3–8) is often shorter but more sprawling. The indigo blue flowers are borne above the foliage on dainty crooked stems from early summer right through to fall. They resemble those of *Clematis alpina* (zone 4–8), but are narrower and more pointed, and are followed by attractive silky seed heads. A popular hybrid of *Clematis integrifolia* is **Clematis × diversifolia** 'Hendersonii' (zone 3–9), with deep blue flowers.

Clematis recta (zone 3–8) blooms in early to midsummer, producing a mass of starry cream flowers on a lax plant with fine stems 3 ft. (90 cm) high. The flowers are fragrant and are lovely in semi-shade. *Clematis recta* 'Purpurea' has the advantage of wine-colored foliage, an attractive contrast to the silky seed heads that follow the flowers.

Dianthuses are wonderful plants for alkaline conditions and will thrive on shallow limestone soils. They are very tolerant of drought, but deeply resent wet and soggy conditions. Cultivated since Roman times, they include myriad species and cultivars, from small alpine pinks to tall, large-flowered border carnations. (See also page 136.)

The old-fashioned garden pinks, with fine, grayish green evergreen foliage, flower early in summer and are prized for their fragrance. *Dianthus* 'Mrs. Sinkins' (zone 5–10) is one of the best known, with sweetly scented white flowers. Growing 8 in. (20 cm) high, it is often planted by the edge of a path and mixes well with gray foliage plants.

The modern garden pinks, with blue-gray evergreen foliage, flower over a long period, from early summer until early fall, producing long-lasting, weather-resistant, scented blooms. Most grow to about 12 in. (30 cm). Many are the result of crossing old-fashioned garden pinks with perpetual-flowering carnations, and are often known as hybrids of *Dianthus × allwoodii* (zone 3–9), after the nursery where some of them were raised. *Dianthus* 'Doris' (zone 3–9), a lovely soft salmon with a deeper salmon eye, is popular. It is an excellent cut flower and an easy color to mix with blue and silver partners. *Dianthus* 'Diane' (zone 4–9) is a deeper salmon orange variety of similar quality.

Gypsophila paniculata (baby's breath) (zone 4–8) is one of our most familiar cut flowers. Its fine stems and clouds of tiny blooms are the perfect accompaniment to roses, sweet peas, and other summer flowers. It grows from a large tuberous tap root and has traditionally been sold as a bare root in the dormant season. Gypsophilas are also valuable border plants: they rarely need support, and have a long flowering season from early to late summer. They are ideal to partner bold, large blooms such as those of poppy or peony and introduce a light ethereal look when combined with silver and blue subjects. Gypsophilas need alkaline soil if they are to thrive, and must have full sun; they do not enjoy wet conditions. *Gypsophila paniculata* 'Bristol Fairy' is the most reliable, producing a cloud of tiny, double white flowers on stems up to 40 in. (1 m) high. *Gypsophila* 'Rosy Veil', which is also known as

---

MAKING MORE OF PINKS

Garden pinks are easily propagated from cuttings, taken in summer. Root nonflowering side shoots in loam-based soil mix with added sharp sand for good drainage, and keep them in a cold frame. Once rooted, they should be potted individually and left in the frame until spring, when they can be planted out. Pinks deteriorate after a few years, so make sure you have young stock coming on as replacements.

Centranthus • *Euphorbia characias* • *Lychnis* • *Salvia × superba* • *Verbascum* • *Verbena bonariensis* •

Potentilla 'Gibson's Scarlet'

Potentilla 'Gloire de Nancy'

'Rosenschleier', is a more spreading plant, reaching up to 40 in. (1 m) across, but only 24 in. (60 cm) high. The double white flowers turn pale pink with age.

The herbaceous forms of *Potentilla* (zone 5–8) are some of our brightest and prettiest perennials, with an informal wildflower character. They are plants for full sun and are useful at the front of a border with companions such as alchemilla (lady's mantle). The hybrids of *Potentilla atrosanguinea* are among the most vivid. Most grow to about 16 in. (40 cm) high, with strawberry-like leaves and buttercup flowers all summer. *Potentilla* 'Gibson's Scarlet' has single, brilliant scarlet flowers with dark centers. 'William Rollison' is semi-double with orange-red petals, gold on the reverse. 'Gloire de Nancy' is similar but orange-brown and red. All these will mix well with achilleas, dahlias, and crocosmias in a border with a hot color scheme.

Potentilla nepalensis (zone 5–8) offers some softer colors. The cultivars grow taller, often to 24 in. (60 cm), with heavily toothed leaves and branched stems carrying profuse flowers throughout the summer. 'Miss Willmott' is the most popular, with strawberry pink flowers with darker centers.

Most species of **scabious** are native to limestone grassland, so they are not a good choice for heavy, wet clay.

Scabiosa atropurpurea is regarded as an annual or biennial, although some cultivars can be grown as short-lived perennials on well-drained soil. Cultivars commonly sold as the Chile series have enjoyed recent popularity. These are tall plants with slender stems to 3 ft. (90 cm) high, producing pincushion flowers with small outer petals throughout summer. 'Chile Black' is the deep garnet, black and velvety; 'Chili Pepper' has rather larger, flatter flowers of soft red; and 'Chili Sauce' has ruffled purple flowers with a delicate white edge to the petals. These are wonderful plants to provide deep highlights in a border and they are good for cutting. In all cases some support will be needed.

Scabiosa caucasica cultivars (zone 4–9) are the familiar scabious of the cottage garden, in bloom from early summer onwards. Forming a low clump of divided leaves, the plants give rise to stems 24 in. (60 cm) or more high, each of which carries a large round, frilled flower with a pincushion center. Open and sparse in character, these are detail plants rather than ones to make a bold impact; they are, however, superb as cut flowers. 'Clive Greaves' is a lovely shade of lavender-blue. 'Stäfa' is much darker with a central cluster of florets in inky blue, a color more intense in the striking 'Blue Lace'. 'Miss Willmott' has large, tissuelike white flowers.

Hybrids of *Scabiosa columbaria* (zone 5–9), the small scabious, are more compact at 12 in. (30 cm) high and flower more freely throughout the summer. *Scabiosa columbaria* ssp. *ochroleuca* is a charming plant, very tolerant of dry conditions. With gray-green leaves and small greenish yellow flowers, it is a delightful companion to the pale yellow foxglove *Digitalis lutea* (zone 5–8). *Scabiosa* 'Butterfly Blue' (zone 5–9) has been one of the most popular perennials of recent years. A compact plant with pretty cut foliage, it produces masses of lilac-blue flowers from late spring until mid-autumn. The related scabious, 'Pink Mist' (zone 5–9), is similar in habit but has attractive mauve-pink flowers.

Scabiosa atropurpurea 'Chile Black'

Scabiosa caucasica 'Clive Greaves'

OTHER GOOD PERENNIALS FOR CLAY *Astrantia major* • *Brunnera macrophylla* • *Campanula glomerata* •

PERENNIALS FOR CLAY

Most popular perennials grow well on clay soils, which are usually fertile and hold water well. However, clay soils can be difficult and heavy to work and will bake hard in summer if water is short. They are often alkaline, as a result of being dressed regularly with lime, which helps to break up sticky clay.

Perennial weeds are nearly impossible to eradicate on clay soils, especially between herbaceous perennials. If you try to dig out goutweed, bindweed, docks, and thistles, the fleshy roots quickly snap in the heavy clay, leaving numerous fragments to regrow.

Routine tasks like lifting and dividing clumps of perennials are more arduous on clay soils. Imagine lifting a large clump of hemerocallis (daylilies) from heavy clay in winter, then attempting to divide it and replant.

The planting of pot-grown subjects may be difficult, too. Sticky, wet clay soil is not easy to replace around the roots of a newly planted perennial without damaging emerging shoots; they are not as resilient as those of a woody shrub.

As a rule of thumb, plants with strong root systems and deep tap roots will do well on clay. Because clay soils are often wet, many perennials that thrive in boggy conditions succeed here,

Filipendula rubra 'Venusta'

A perennial border brimming with color at Hadspen Garden, on alkaline clay, Somerset, England.

providing there is adequate moisture in summer (see pages 74–79).

Many of the prairie subjects do well on clay so long as they do not become too dry in summer. *Aster* (zone 2–8) and *Solidago* (zone 3–9) are both certain winners on clay soils, hence their widespread use in gardens for many years. *Filipendula rubra* 'Venusta' (zone 2–8) is another useful prairie native, its statuesque form and astilbe-like flower heads mixing well with shrubs and other perennials. (See also pages 50–53.)

Campanula latiloba (zone 5–7), with its tall spikes of open bell-shaped flowers in late summer, is easy to grow on clay, in sun or partial shade. There are some lovely cultivars including the pale mauve 'Hidcote Amethyst', 'Alba', which has white flowers, and the blue 'Highcliffe Variety'.

The early-flowering yellow daisy *Doronicum orientale* 'Magnificum' (zone 3–7) is also good on clay, but needs a partially shaded site.

Hemerocallis (daylilies) (zone 4 –10) are at their best in sun, and they, too, do well on clay, enjoying its fertility and reveling in the damp conditions on wet sites (see pages 138–39).

With its pretty, fernlike leaves and mauve, gypsophila-like flower heads, *Thalictrum aquilegiifolium* (zone 5–8) provides foliage interest all summer as well as a good display of flowers. It is easy to grow in either full sun or partial shade, and succeeds in all but waterlogged ground. (See also page 49.)

OVERCOMING THE PROBLEM OF CLAY SOIL

Plants enjoying good drainage and dry conditions are not usually a natural choice for clay soils, although they may succeed if planted on top of the clay. Add sharp grit to the soil beforehand, and plant on a mound rather than in a dip. This will prevent water from collecting at the crown of the plant and causing it to rot.

Geranium himalayense • *Lamium galeobdolon* • *Physostegia virginiana* • *Rudbeckia* • *Symphytum caucasicum* •

FOLIAGE

Herbaceous perennials provide us with some of the most dramatic, colorful, and textural foliage in the garden. From the large, bold leaves of many waterside subjects to the soft silver of sun lovers, long-lasting foliage effects come from perennials and grasses in the lower layers of the planting picture. Those that are grown especially for their colored foliage have become some of the most popular plants in our gardens. The number of available hosta and heuchera cultivars increases every year, each new variety welcomed for its contribution to the leafy garden scene.

RIGHT: A variety of foliage forms: hostas, grasses, and phormiums

Purple and plum foliage

Perennials blessed with purple and plum foliage are good mixers; they get along with their colorful neighbors and work with them to produce a dramatic effect. Punctuating the mass of greenery, plants with warm wine tones in their leaves are striking alongside companions with silver or golden yellow foliage, while their rich notes bring flowers of many colors to life.

PURPLE AND PLUM FOLIAGE FOR SEMI-SHADE

Plants with purple foliage need good light to achieve the best leaf color. In heavy shade plum tones can be muddy; dark green predominates and red-purple pigments fade. However, a number of purple-foliage subjects prefer a site in semi-shade rather than a dry position in full sun.

Actaea simplex **Atropurpurea Group** (zone 3–8) enjoy fertile, somewhat moist soil in partial shade. Formerly known as *Cimicifuga*, these choice perennials take a little time to make an impact in the border. Container-grown plants can take a few seasons before their black stems reach over 40 in. (1 m) high and the large elegant, fernlike leaves spread to 12 in. (30 cm) or more in length. White bottlebrush flower heads rise above the leaves in the fall. The cultivar **'Brunette'** has foliage of a wonderful burgundy-black color: both sophisticated and dramatic. Although the plant grows tall, to 5 ft. (1.5 m) or so, it rarely requires support. (See Good Companions, right.)

Ground-hugging **ajugas** (bugle) (zone 4–7) enjoy similar conditions. Purple-leaved forms are useful foliage plants that remain evergreen in all but the coldest areas. *Ajuga reptans* **'Atropurpurea'** (see page 118) forms rosettes of shining purple foliage, each

Fringed and feathered—*Tulipa* 'Black Parrot' amid the purple foliage of *Anthriscus sylvestris* 'Ravenswing'.

strongly veined leaf up to 4 in. (10 cm) long. *Ajuga reptans* **'Burgundy Glow'** is the darkest, with oblong rounded leaves of rich wine red, deep green beneath. The much larger, dark, bronzed leaves of *Ajuga reptans* **'Catlin's Giant'** (see page 119) are excellent with golden hostas.

PURPLE GROUND COVER

Purple bugles make excellent ground cover. They are ideal on slopes and banks and are particularly effective in gravel. The shining purple plantlets are easily transplanted to bring evergreen interest to winter pots and containers.

Ligularia dentata 'Britt-Marie Crawford'

Persicaria microcephala 'Red Dragon'

For a selection of **heucheras** grown for their colored foliage, see pages 88–89.

Ligularias (zone 3–8) contribute architectural structure, bold foliage, and stunning flowers (see page 76). An old favorite, the attractive *Ligularia dentata* 'Desdemona' has rounded leaves of rich chocolate and green, which make a perfect setting for the large orange, daisy flowers (see Good Companions, below right). *Ligularia dentata* 'Britt-Marie Crawford' is one of the finest for foliage. This herbaceous perennial forms a clump of dark purple, glossy, rounded leaves 12 in. (30 cm) or so across, with undersides of an equally gorgeous dark red. The 12 in. (30 cm) leaf stalks are a similar color. Flower stems over 40 in. (1 m) high carry starry medium yellow flowers in summer.

The dark reddish brown, sprawling stems of *Persicaria microcephala* 'Red Dragon' (zone 5–8) are clothed in spectacular broad, oval leaves. Centered on the red spine of each leaf is a dark chocolate brown heart marked with a silver flash against margins of purple and green. From midsummer each stem carries a spray of tiny white flowers. On moist, fertile soil in semi-shade, the plant will grow more than 40 in. (1 m) high by the end of the season. The stems and foliage are knocked to the ground by the first frost.

A number of **primulas** are blessed with bronze and chocolate foliage. The

Primula Wanda Group (zone 3–8) are widely cultivated as spring bedding plants for their jewel-like flower colors and their rich, dark foliage. *Primula* Cowichan (zone 6–8) series, the winter-blooming polyanthus, have similar coloring (see page 182). *Primula* 'Guinevere' (zone 5–9) bears clusters of yellow-eyed purple-pink polyanthus flowers above an evergreen rosette of chocolate and red, bronzed leaves. All these primulas make delightful partners for the purple-leaved bugles, planted in partial shade.

Commonly called the bloody dock, *Rumex sanguineus* var. *sanguineus* (zone 6–9) is an attractive form of the pernicious weed. Very hardy and robust,

it has a rosette of broad, lance-shaped, dark green leaves to 6 in. (15 cm) long. Each leaf has a dark red midrib, which appears to bleed into the veins, forming an elaborate pattern. In summer, erect stems, to 3 ft. (90 cm) high, bear many tiny, delicate, star-shaped green flowers, which mature through red-orange to dark brown. Like its relatives, this dock will grow anywhere; to prevent it from spreading, cut and dispose of the flowering stems before the seeds fall.

Rumex sanguineus var. sanguineus

GOOD COMPANIONS

Ligularia dentata 'Desdemona' (1) (z. 3–8) contrasts with the fresh yellow foliage of *Cornus alba* 'Aurea' (2). (z. 2–8) The cornus provides red stems when the ligularia dies down in winter.

Actaea simplex Atropurpurea Group 'Brunette' (3) (z. 3–8) with *Acer palmatum* 'Fireglow' (4): the dark leaves of the actaea complement the acer's flame-red autumn shades.

Heucheras

Predominantly native to North America, heucheras were originally cultivated for their flowers: showers of tiny blooms borne on fine, graceful stems for long periods in the summer (see page 140). Today, few other plants have such popular appeal for the beauty of their foliage; and no other dark-leaved perennial delivers such a variety of tones. A steady stream of new selections reach our gardens every year, and heucheras are now almost as common as hostas.

The rounded to heart-shaped, semi-evergreen or evergreen leaves are carried on either short and stocky or long and airy stalks, forming a clump of foliage 4–12 in. (10–30 cm) high. The leaves vary in size and texture, and the color ranges from handsome shades of green through red to deep burgundy; many exhibit fine variegation in white, silver, or bronze. (For heucheras with golden yellow foliage, see page 93.)

Robust and easy to grow, these perennials thrive in moist, well-drained, neutral soil. Although extremely hardy, they resent waterlogged conditions, especially in the winter months. Heucheras with dark leaves excel in full sun, the strong light intensifying the color of the foliage; in warmer climates, however, they appreciate a little shade. Even in the coldest areas, heucheras maintain a superb show of foliage throughout the year; regular feeding in the growing season enhances both quality and color. Heucheras are also excellent for permanent or seasonal planting in pots and containers.

Mature plants develop thick, woody stems at the base and benefit from pruning. In late spring, cut back old growth by half; this may appear extreme, but new stems soon appear. The removed shoots can be used as cuttings to produce more stock.

Seed can be collected in mid- to late summer. Sow immediately in a tray of moist soil mix for seeds; cover lightly and place in a cool, shady situation. The seed germinates in spring; the offspring are variable but may be uniquely different.

Heuchera 'Plum Pudding' (z. 4–8), with shiny plum-burgundy foliage, is a popular purple heuchera. Reaching 12 in. (30 cm) tall, it is an essential in winter containers with *Primula* 'Wanda' (z. 3–8) and early purple crocuses. As spring progresses, the deep purple leaves contrast with the sulfur-yellow bracts of *Euphorbia polychroma* (z. 5–8), and later with the foamy lime green flowers of *Alchemilla mollis* (lady's mantle) (z. 4–7).

Heucheras are especially attractive to vine weevil, the larvae feeding voraciously on the roots through fall and into spring. Biological control in the form of beneficial nematodes can be used in early fall, or a suitable systemic insecticide can be applied in fall or spring.

Heuchera 'Amethyst Myst' (z. 4–8) forms a clump of impressive dark purple, glossy foliage reaching 12 in. (30 cm) in height. The waved, heart-shaped leaves are partially divided and burnished silver pink. They look fantastic intermingled with the finely cut silver foliage of *Artemisia* 'Powis Castle' (z. 6–10).

Heuchera micrantha var. *diversifolia* 'Palace Purple' (z. 4–7) was the original purple heuchera and is the parent of many cultivars. It produces fine, dark stems up to 24 in. (60 cm) tall, bearing large, glossy, dark red leaves with jagged margins. It is usually sold as a seed-raised selection, and the foliage color is variable and can be muddy.

Heuchera 'Licorice' (z. 4–8) has dark, ruffled leaves and is outstanding planted with the golden yellow foliage of *Lysimachia nummularia* 'Aurea' (z. 5–7). Height 12 in. (30 cm).

OTHER GOOD HEUCHERAS

Heuchera 'Cascade Dawn' (z. 4–8) Dark leaves burnished with lavender-silver, and with rich purple veins. Height 12 in. (30 cm).

Heuchera 'Chocolate Ruffles' (z. 4–8) Forms a tight clump of rich red-brown leaves with ruffled margins. Height 12 in. (30 cm).

Heuchera 'Chocolate Veil' (z. 4–8) Black and purple leaves, traced with silver. Height 12 in. (30 cm).

Heuchera 'Obsidian' (z. 4–8) A newcomer, with rounded, dark purple, almost black leaves; one of the darkest. Height 10 in. (25 cm).

Heuchera 'Purple Petticoats' (z. 4–8) A neat mound of dramatically ruffled, glossy, dark purple leaves. Height 12 in. (30 cm).

Heuchera 'Velvet Night' (z. 4–8) Luxuriant leaves, 6in. (15cm) across, slate black burnished silvery purple. Height 16 in. (40 cm).

Heuchera 'Can-can' (z. 4–8) has ruffled red-purple leaves, lightly burnished silver, forming a neat clump 8in. (20 cm) high and 12 in. (30 cm) across. It is striking against the small silver-centered, nettlelike leaves of *Lamium maculatum* 'Album' (z. 4–7).

PURPLE AND PLUM FOLIAGE FOR SUNNY POSITIONS

Purple foliage usually becomes richer and redder in full sun, the red pigments masking the underlying green of the leaves. Perennials with purple foliage are useful to bring depth and substance to bright summer-flowering plants. They mix particularly well with the pinks, mauves, and blues of the midsummer border and are the perfect foil for hot reds, oranges, and yellows. They are successful partners for silver foliage plants that also favor sunny situations.

Anthriscus sylvestris 'Ravenswing'

Anthriscus sylvestris (cow parsley) is a common sight along hedgerows and verges in Britain in late spring. A froth of lacy white flowers that suddenly appear above the grass is a sign that summer is on the way. *Anthriscus sylvestris* 'Ravenswing' (zone 7–10) has burgundy-purple fernlike foliage and flower stems, and the same white filigree flower heads. It does well on dry soil in full sun, reaching 3 ft. (90 cm) tall. A short-lived perennial, it is easily raised from freshly sown seed; leave the seedlings to mature so that those with the best foliage color can be selected. (See page 86.)

The imposing *Eupatorium rugosum* 'Chocolate' (zone 5–8) forms a clump of stiff brown stems to 40 in. (1 m) high, with deep chocolate and purple, nettle-like leaves, and produces insignificant heads of gray-white blooms in early fall.

Eupatorium rugosum 'Chocolate'

It likes moist soil and will grow in semi-shade, although the color is better in sun. It is notoriously slow to get going at the beginning of the season, not making any impact in the border before late summer. Plant it alongside early performing perennials such as achilleas.

The purple-leaved **euphorbias** are stunning when the lime green flowers open in early spring and contrast with the velvety wine-colored leaves. Sadly, these are often marred by mildew in damp, crowded conditions. To avoid problems, give plants an open position, and use a preventive fungicidal spray in dry weather in winter. *Euphorbia amygdaloides* 'Purpurea' (zone 7–9) grows 12 in. (30 cm) tall, with red-

Foeniculum vulgare 'Purpureum'

purple foliage and lime green flowers. *Euphorbia dulcis* 'Chameleon' (zone 5–7) forms a clump of upright stems, 12 in. (30 cm) high, clad in velvety purple leaves. The more recent cultivar *Euphorbia* 'Blackbird' (zone 6–9), up to 18 in. (45 cm) high, is even darker and promises greater disease resistance.

Foeniculum vulgare 'Purpureum' (bronze fennel) (zone 5–8) is a great mixer and a wonderful see-through plant. Its feathery foliage is ornate and tactile, with a delicious aniseed aroma. Very hardy in all but the wettest soils, fennel emerges in early spring; by mid-spring its feathery bronze foliage is the

CONTAINING FENNEL

The aromatic seeds of bronze fennel (*Foeniculum vulgare* 'Purpureum') (z. 5–8) are easily germinated and frequently come true to type. On light, sandy soils the plants seed profusely, and the deep-rooted seedlings can be troublesome. Remove the flowers as they fade to prevent seeds from developing.

perfect partner for tall, elegant tulips. Its new growth throughout spring and summer is a rich, deep bronze before maturing to bronzed green. Over 5 ft. (1.5 m) tall, it bears airy heads of tiny yellow flowers in midsummer.

All **gauras** (zone 6–9) have curiously spotted foliage, their deep green leaves often blotched with chocolate. Some forms are blessed with red-purple foliage, particularly those with pink

Gaura lindheimeri 'In the Pink'

OTHER PERENNIALS WITH PURPLE AND PLUM FOLIAGE *Aster laterifolius* 'Prince' • *Canna* TROPICANNA • *Dahlia* 'Bishop of Llandaff' • *Heuchera* 'Regina' • *Lobelia cardinalis* • *Lobelia* 'Queen Victoria' •

flowers. *Gaura lindheimeri* 'In the Pink' (zone 6–9) has a long flowering season from midsummer to late fall. It is a good choice for the front of a border or a container. If winter wet is avoided, this hardy perennial will produce many medium pink, starry flowers above compact, bushy growth 12 in. (30 cm) high. The foliage is dark green and bronzed; the new growth deep purple-red.

There is no denying the rich beauty of purple-leaved **geraniums**. *Geranium pratense* (zone 4–7), the meadow cranesbill, has provided some desirable cultivars with the magical combination of divided purple and chocolate leaves and blue-purple flowers in early summer. *Geranium pratense* **Midnight Reiter strain** is a little gem of a plant, rarely growing to more than 8 in.

Geranium pratense Midnight Reiter strain

(20 cm) high. The foliage stays close to the ground so is better against gravel than bare earth. Other selections include **'Purple Heron'** and **Victor Reiter Junior strain**. These are beautiful, but can be temperamental. They enjoy sun but do not like to be too dry, preferring reasonably moist soil that is moderately fertile. Plants for detail rather than impact, they need careful positioning to avoid being lost in the border.

Geranium phaeum **'Samobor'** (zone 7–8) is easier and grows up to 24 in. (60 cm) in height. Each stunning leaf boasts a dark purple-black broken circle at its center and can reach over 4 in. (10 cm) across. The violet-purple flowers are relatively insignificant.

Geranium phaeum 'Samobor'

Lychnis × *arkwrightii* **'Vesuvius'** (zone 6–8) boasts a divine combination of foliage and flower color. Star-shaped flowers in vivid scarlet-orange are carried in small clusters above dark red-brown leaves, on similarly colored, softly hairy stems, 18 in. (45 cm) high.

Of all the purple-leaved perennials *Lysimachia ciliata* **'Firecracker'** (zone 5–8) is perhaps the most useful. Its new foliage is a sumptuous chocolate brown and matures to wine red as its stems reach 40 in. (1 m) or more. Growing in sun or light shade on any soil, this plant is an excellent mixer and is a natural addition to many plantings. (See Good Companions, below.)

Although *Sedum telephium* ssp. *maximum* **'Atropurpureum'** (zone 3–8) is not a pretty plant, it could be

Lysimachia ciliata 'Firecracker'

described as handsome. Its stiff stems, clad in succulent, deep wine purple leaves, form an upright clump to 20 in. (50 cm) high. Loose heads of tiny pinkish red flowers appear in late summer. (See Good Companions, below, and see page 73.) When fully grown, the plant may become top-heavy; to prevent this, cut stems back by half in early summer.

KEEPING 'FIRECRACKER' LOOKING GOOD

The starry yellow flowers of *Lysimachia ciliata* 'Firecracker' (z. 5–8) are stunning against the foliage but if they do not suit the color scheme, cut the plant back to one-third of its height in midsummer. New shoots are produced, and the purple foliage effect is preserved.

GOOD COMPANIONS

The deep plum-colored new shoots of *Lysimachia ciliata* 'Firecracker' (1) (z. 5–8) are stunning among the vivid lime green spring flowers of *Euphorbia cyparissias* 'Fens Ruby' (2) (z. 4–8).

The heavy purple foliage of *Sedum telephium* ssp. *maximum* 'Atropurpureum' (3) (z. 3–8) contrasts with the soft silver of *Artemisia stelleriana* 'Boughton Silver' (4) (z. 3–7).

Ophiopogon planiscapus 'Nigrescens' • *Pennisetum setaceum* 'Rubrum' • *Penstemon digitalis* 'Husker Red' • *Ranunculus ficaria* 'Brazen Hussy' • *Rheum palmatum* 'Atrosanguineum' • *Tiarella* 'Spring Symphony' •

Yellow and gold foliage

Bright and sunny, demanding attention and attracting the eye, yellow can be a dominant color; it can also be uplifting and invigorating to other colors. Yellow can be soft and soothing or acidic and aggressive. When it comes to foliage, gold and yellow fulfill all these roles in the garden. Yellow leaves glow brightly in sunshine and mellow to soft lime green in shade. Most gold-foliage plants are at their best in spring and early summer and again in late summer and fall; the intense sunlight of midsummer can scorch and bleach some golden favorites.

The striking form and foliage of *Dicentra spectabilis* 'Gold Heart' make a stunning setting for the heart-shaped, deep pink flowers, borne from late spring into early summer.

Agastache rugosa 'Golden Jubilee'

Gold-foliage shrubs, both evergreen and deciduous, are plentiful and popular; while herbaceous plants offer fewer yellow-leaved options, those that exist provide bright relief to the predominant green in the border and the often drab leaves of many perennials.

A dead nettle-like plant that comes reliably true from seed, *Agastache rugosa* 'Golden Jubilee' (z. 8–10) emerges from a winter-dormant crown to form upright 28 in. (70 cm) stems of golden yellow leaves; above these rise spires of tubular lavender-blue flowers from midsummer onward. A sun-loving prairie native, it combines well with grasses, rudbeckias, and echinaceas.

Some perennials with golden foliage display their most brilliant color in early spring and summer when the new leaves unfurl. Few come close to the flaming orange-red of the emerging shoots of *Dicentra spectabilis* 'Gold Heart' (z. 4–7), with foliage that

92

OTHER PERENNIALS WITH YELLOW AND GOLD FOLIAGE *Campanula garganica* 'Dickson's Gold' • *Carex elata* 'Aurea' • *Milium effusum* 'Aureum' • *Phormium* 'Yellow Wave' • *Physostegia virginiana* 'Olympic Gold' •

matures to golden yellow. The arching pink-red stems, reaching 24 in. (60 cm) high, carry both the golden leaves and the deep pink "bleeding heart" flowers (see Good Companions, page 95). A plant for fertile, moist, free-draining soil, this beauty dislikes the bright sun of midsummer, which speeds it into early dormancy, a trait typical of the species.

In the shade, the unusual *Farfugium japonicum* 'Aureomaculatum' (zone 6–9) has distinctive glossy, dark green, kidney-shaped leaves splashed with irregular yellow spots. The leaves have an almost reptilian quality and contrast well with the lighter foliage of shade-loving ferns. Borne on long, slender stalks, they form a clump, above which yellow heads of flowers on stems 24 in. (60 cm) high bloom from early to late fall. In areas of severe frost, a dry winter mulch of bark or bracken is needed.

Filipendula ulmaria 'Aurea' (zone 2–8), the golden meadowsweet, is happy in sun or partial shade and thrives in wetter soils. A hardy herbaceous perennial, 24 in. (60 cm) high, it forms a clump of textured medium yellow leaves that mature to creamy yellow then green, as heads of tiny, fluffy, creamy white flowers arrive in midsummer.

Geranium × *oxonianum* 'Spring Fling' (zone 4–8) stands out in the border in early spring: the new palmate leaves are bright yellow, flecked pinkish red. By midsummer the foliage matures to pale green and is joined by white flowers with dark pink veining. Growing to 24 in. (60 cm) high, it enjoys well-drained soil, in sun or semi-shade.

The ever popular *Geranium* 'Ann Folkard' (zone 5–7) combines magenta black-eyed blooms and lime green foliage, which takes on stronger yellow tones in sun. A rampant grower, 24 in. (60 cm) high, it makes marvelous ground cover in semi-shade.

Heucheras (zone 4–8) are usually associated with purple foliage (see

Geranium 'Ann Folkard'

pages 88–89), but there is an increasing number of golden yellow varieties. More than mere novelties, these eye-catching foliage plants are particularly useful in pots and containers and to contrast with their purple cousins. The golden-leaved heucheras are more compact plants, with foliage mostly around 8 in. (20 cm) high. The waved evergreen leaves of the gorgeous *Heuchera* 'Amber Waves' are rich golden bronze with orange tones maturing to medium ocher yellow

as summer progresses. When young, 'Amber Waves' can be slow to get going; but once established, it thrives in moist soil shaded from midday sun.

A more uniform golden orange is found in the foliage of *Heuchera* 'Marmalade', with new growth and the undersides of the leaves flushed pink. *Heuchera* 'Crème Brûlée' is robust and compact in habit, with ruffled, creamy gold foliage flushed orange. *Heuchera*

Heuchera 'Amber Waves'

Humulus lupulus 'Aureus'

'Key Lime Pie' produces refreshing, shiny bright green leaves that become flushed with pale lemon in strong sun. The lovely × *Heucherella* 'Gold Strike' (zone 4–8) has reliably golden leaves with a distinct red-brown flush broadly coloring the center of each leaf.

For a selection of **hostas** with yellow and gold foliage, see page 94.

Herbaceous perennials come in many forms. *Humulus lupulus* 'Aureus' (golden hop) (zone 5–8) is grown for its rapidly climbing, twining stems of coarse, bright yellow leaves, which look even brighter in strong sun. It will put on 15 ft. (5 m) of growth in a season before dying back to the ground in the fall. Care should be taken in positioning such (continued on page 95)

USING YELLOW LEAVES

Yellow foliage works best when combined with other yellow-leaved plants and yellow, white, or blue flowers diluted with sufficient green. An occasional yellow plant in a border will always look out of place, since it will attract the eye, often to the exclusion of all else. Yellow foliage is particularly useful when combined with yellow-variegated leaves to lighten semi-shade.

Pleioblastus viridistriatus • *Saxifraga* 'Cloth of Gold' • *Smyrnium perfoliatum* • *Symphytum* 'Goldsmith' •
Symphytum ibericum 'All Gold' • *Tanacetum parthenium* 'Aureum' • *Tradescantia* Andersoniana Group 'Sweet Kate' •

Yellow and gold hostas

Of all perennials, hostas provide the greatest variety of yellow leaves, offering shades of creamy yellow and pale lemon gold in the form of both solid colors and attractive variegation. Most excel in semi-shade, and especially enjoy the dappled shade from trees; in full sun the foliage can become bleached and lackluster.

The original hosta species reached cultivation in the late 18th century from their native habitats in Korea, China, Japan, and eastern Russia. Virtually unrivaled success in hybridization has brought us the range we know today.

In fertile, moist, free-draining soil, these hardy herbaceous perennials form neat clumps of rounded, oval or heart-shaped leaves, which vary from 4 in. (10 cm) to over 20 in. (50 cm) in length. Attractive tubular, lilylike flowers of white and shades of pink to lilac grace upright stems from early to late summer.

Slugs and snails are the major problem, but they can be kept at bay with barriers, baits, and cultivation techniques. Grow hostas away from damaging winds, which scorch and break the succulent leaves.

Hosta fortunei var. *albopicta* (z. 4–8) is a very popular hosta, with soft golden yellow leaves irregularly edged in green. In early spring the color is strong and eye-catching; it fades as the season progresses and as stems of mauve-white flowers appear above the foliage in midsummer. Best in semi-shade, it grows 18 in. (45 cm) high and 24 in. (60 cm) across.

OTHER YELLOW AND GOLD HOSTAS

Hosta 'Golden Prayers' (z. 4–8) Bright golden yellow leaves, with lavender-blue flowers just above the foliage in midsummer. Grows 18 in. (45 cm) high, 24 in. (60 cm) across.

Hosta 'Piedmont Gold' (z. 4–8) Grows 20 in. (50 cm) high, 40 in. (1 m) wide. Deeply veined blue-green leaves flushed sulfur yellow. Pale lavender flowers in midsummer.

Hosta 'Zounds' (z. 4–8) Large, veined and puckered leaves of soft gold tinged blue-green. Grows 16 in. (40 cm) high and 3 ft. (90 cm) across. Pale lavender flowers rise above the foliage in late summer.

Hosta 'August Moon' (z. 4–8) grows to 20 in. (50 cm) high and 28 in. (70 cm) across. Its gently cupped leaves are initially pale green, maturing to soft golden yellow. Stems of lilac-white flowers rise above the foliage in midsummer. Tough and reliable, it produces the best leaf color when grown in full sun.

Hosta 'Sum and Substance' (z. 4–8) is a big, bold hosta, 32 in. (80 cm) high with a spread of 5 ft. (1.5 m). Massive heart-shaped leaves are glossy, yellow-green, gently puckered with age. Palest lavender flowers appear just above the foliage in late summer.

a vigorous plant; it will soon sprawl over its neighbors, adventurous shoots emerging far from the main plant. In the right place, it will create dramatic effect.

Lysimachia nummularia (creeping Jenny) (zone 5–7) forms a carpet of stems with rounded leaves, excellent for evergreen ground cover. *Lysimachia nummularia* 'Aurea' has bright golden yellow foliage in sun, more lime yellow in shade. It is delightful trailing over the edge of a pot or in a hanging basket.

Favored by butterflies, *Origanum vulgare* 'Aureum' (zone 5–8), the golden wild marjoram, is wonderfully

Stachys byzantina 'Primrose Heron'

Valeriana phu 'Aurea'

GOLDEN COVER

Lysimachia nummularia 'Aurea' (z. 5–7) is useful to bring the effect of golden foliage to ground level. Try planting it beneath a gold-leaved tree or shrub like *Catalpa bignonioides* 'Aurea' (z. 5–9) or *Ptelea trifoliata* 'Aurea' (z. 3–9) for a carpet of summer sunshine.

---

versatile. Stems 24 in. (60 cm) high bear rounded, pale to golden yellow, aromatic leaves, which can be used for cooking in the same way as those of the green species. Clusters of rosy pink, tubular flowers are produced in late summer. Extremely hot sunshine may scorch the foliage; if this occurs, cut the plant back and it will produce another flush of growth. When the flowers have faded in fall, cut the plant back to the ground to leave a mat of golden foliage that may persist through the winter. Origanum is a perennial that thrives on poor soil in a sunny position and is successful on alkaline soil.

Commonly known as lamb's ears, *Stachys byzantina* (zone 4–8) has long been a garden favorite (see page 105). The cultivar *Stachys byzantina* 'Primrose Heron' has silver-felted leaves flushed lemon yellow, the color becoming more prevalent in full sun (see Good Companions, below). Above the leaves, woolly stems 18 in. (45 cm) high

carry small pink-purple flowers; these are best removed to preserve the effect of the foliage. Like the species, 'Primrose Heron' must have free-draining soil, but with adequate moisture. Drought can reduce the vigor of the plant and increase its susceptibility to mildew.

The foliage of the golden valerian, *Valeriana phu* 'Aurea' (zone 4–8), is full of springtime promise. It appears above ground early in the season and is the brightest of yellows. The leaves, 8in. (20cm) long, are divided into well-defined leaflets that age from yellow through lime green to mid-green. Airy

heads of tiny white flowers form on slender stems over 40in. (1m) high; although not showy, these bring light relief to the border and offer a white alternative to the rich lilac-purple of *Verbena bonariensis* (zone 8–9). Golden valerian is an easy plant to grow, thriving on most soils.

Veronica prostrata 'Trehane' (zone 5–8) is a low-growing, mat-forming plant. The foliage is lime yellow in shade and a bright golden yellow in full sun, and it creates a striking background for the 6in. (15cm) spikes of inky-blue flowers that appear in early summer.

GOOD COMPANIONS

Stachys byzantina 'Primrose Heron' (1) (z. 4–8) with *Heuchera* 'Can-can' (2) (z. 4–8): the soft, silvery lemon foliage of the stachys contrasts with the waved, red-purple heuchera.

The pink and green blooms of *Tulipa* 'Fantasy' (3) (z. 4–8) pick up on the pink stems and flowers of *Dicentra spectabilis* 'Gold Heart' (4) (z. 4–7) and contrast with its golden foliage.

Variegated foliage

Plants with variegated foliage have a special appeal; perhaps because these plants rarely occur in nature, gardeners identify them as theirs to cultivate. They are easy to accommodate, as most have some green in the leaves, providing a link with surrounding plants. Variegated shrubs are among the favorite garden plants; variegated perennials are less common but no less valuable.

The architectural form of the species *Euphorbia characias* is further accentuated in the cream-variegated foliage of *Euphorbia characias* 'Silver Swan'.

Erysimum linifolium 'Variegatum'

VARIEGATED PERENNIALS FOR DRY, SUNNY SITES

Erysimum linifolium 'Variegatum' (zone 7–8) is a form of perennial wall-flower. A bushy, woody-based plant, it grows to 24 in. (60 cm) high, with pale stems clothed in narrow evergreen leaves conspicuously edged in creamy white. These are a striking contrast to the purple-pink flowers in late spring and summer. Like other perennial wall-flowers, it is short-lived, and new plants should be started from cuttings every few years. These are usually taken in late summer and rooted in a cold frame; take plenty, since they are not so easy to root as the green-leaved varieties.

There have been several variegated forms of *Euphorbia characias* introduced over the years; often sulky plants, they are slow-growing and unreliable. Not so *Euphorbia characias* 'Silver Swan' (zone 8–9): a magnificent evergreen, it has stout stems forming an elegant, upright bush to 3 ft. (90 cm) high, with eye-catching foliage. The narrow leaves are blue-green broadly edged in creamy white, presenting a vivid picture all year in a sunny site on well-drained soil. The late spring flowers are creamy white and usually go unseen against the foliage. Prune out flowered stems to ground level in summer to allow new stems to develop. This is a wonderful plant in the winter garden, especially when it is set close to the white stems of birch (*Betula*) (zone 4–9), the white-suffused leaves of *Prunus laurocerasus* 'Castlewellan' (zone 6–8), or the silver foliage of *Pittosporum* 'Garnettii' (zone 9–10).

There are variegated forms of iris for wet and dry conditions. *Iris pallida* (zone 6–8), from rocky limestone hills around the Adriatic, forms spreading clumps of pale gray-blue leaves that remain in good condition throughout the season, even after the fragrant, pale lilac-blue flowers have faded. Variegated forms are more often seen than the species, with fans of sword-shaped leaves up to 24 in. (60 cm) high. The variegation is bold: broad creamy white

OTHER VARIEGATED PERENNIALS FOR DRY, SUNNY SITES *Arabis alpina* ssp. *caucasica* 'Variegata' •

Iris pallida 'Variegata'

stripes in the case of **Iris pallida 'Variegata'** (zone 6–8), the most widely grown form (see also page 152.)

Although they are really sub-shrubs, the variegated forms of common sage, *Salvia officinalis* (zone 5–10), are often sold with herbaceous perennials (see page 166). *Salvia officinalis* **'Icterina'**, with golden-variegated foliage, and *Salvia officinalis* **'Tricolor'**, with white- and purple-variegated leaves, are much less vigorous than the green and purple sages and need full sun and good drainage to succeed.

Sedum erythrostictum (zone 3–10) has upright stems of gray-green foliage,

with heads of green-white flowers in late summer and fall. The variegated forms include **'Mediovariegatum'**, which has bold creamy yellow centers to the leaves, and **'Frosty Morn'**, with clear white markings (see page 176). *Sedum sieboldii* **'Mediovariegatum'** (zone 6–8) has trailing stems 6 in. (15 cm) long bearing blue-green, coin-like leaves, creamy yellow in the center and often flushed bright pink; heads of pink flowers form in late summer.

The fans of soft, swordlike leaves of *Sisyrinchium striatum* (zone 7–9) are hardy and evergreen in free-draining ground. The variegated *Sisyrinchium striatum* **'Aunt May'** has creamy white striped leaves in fans reaching 16 in. (40 cm); the stems of pale lemon flowers rise just above the leaves in early summer. The variegated form is more compact and less invasive than the green form, but is a little less hardy.

Tulbaghia violacea **'Silver Lace'** (zone 7–10) forms expanding clumps of gray-green, narrow, fleshy, grasslike leaves, striped silver-white. From early summer, slender 20 in. (50 cm) stems are each topped in a cluster of lilac-pink blooms, which open to six-pointed stars; these have a gentle, sweet fragrance best enjoyed at dusk. The foliage has a

strong aroma when disturbed, hence the common name "society garlic." The aromatic foliage has its uses, some species being cultivated as snake repellents. Dry soil in winter is essential, so a position at the foot of a sunny wall or in a well-drained scree bed is ideal.

VARIEGATED PERENNIALS FOR MOISTER SOIL

Few plants will grow in any soil in both sun and full shade. *Aegopodium podagraria* **'Variegatum'** (zone 4–8), however, is an exception and thrives on neglect, providing valuable ground cover in otherwise barren areas of the garden. Up to 12 in. (30 cm) high, it has leaves made up of three or more toothed leaflets, which are olive-green edged and splashed in creamy white. In *(continued on page 100)*

PATHS AND POTS

Aegopodium podagraria 'Variegatum' (z. 4–8) makes an attractive path edging if contained by tiles pushed vertically into the ground to create a narrow border along the path. It also looks good in a pot. It will quickly fill a container, producing a mass of bright, pest-proof foliage that will stay looking good throughout the season, especially if flower stems are removed.

WHAT IS VARIEGATION?

Variegation is often caused by mutation: a change to the genetic information in the plant's growing point. The pigments of variegated leaves are unevenly dispersed, resulting in white, cream, or yellow spots, splashes, streaks, stripes and, most commonly, leaf centers or margins, against the original green leaf color. The areas of the leaf that are not green lack chlorophyll, which the plant uses to manufacture food for growth. Variegated plants are therefore often less vigorous than their green counterparts.

Sisyrinchium striatum 'Aunt May'

Aegopodium podagraria 'Variegatum'

Aubrieta 'Argenteovariegata' • *Iris foetidissima* 'Variegata' • *Ophiopogon jaburan* 'Vittatus' •

Variegated hostas

Hostas (zone 4–8) offer an outstanding range of variegated leaves: every combination of silver and green, blue and yellow has been selected and developed by the hybridists to create a phenomenal choice of cultivars.

Rounded, oval, or heart-shaped leaves range from less than 4 in. (10 cm) long to 20 in. (50 cm) or more, ample surface to show off the variegation. The smaller, delicate varieties are more for the collector and the enthusiast; all gardeners can grow and appreciate the more substantial cultivars. Tubular flowers in white or shades of pink to lilac are borne in early to late summer.

Hostas thrive in fertile, moist, free-draining soil. They are often thought of as plants for shade, but many do best in a sunny spot. While too much shade may limit color development, strong sun can damage some variegation. As a rule, shadier positions result in larger leaves and fewer flowers; sunnier sites produce more compact plants with small leaves and more flowers.

Variegated hostas have many uses. In mixed borders their foliage color helps to reinforce a color scheme,

Hosta 'Patriot' (z. 4–8) is perhaps the boldest and showiest of the variegated hostas. Strong, narrow, heart-shaped leaves form large open rosettes up to 18 in. (45 cm) high and 30 in. (75 cm) across. The leaves are rich dark green, with broad white margins overlapping the green and streaking the center with gray-green. Stems of lilac flowers stand well above the foliage in midsummer. A superb variety for a pot and outstanding in the border, it is normally recommended for light shade but will withstand a reasonable amount of full sun.

and their bold leaves provide contrast and a focal point in the planting. They are useful in shady situations to lighten the dark green of shade-loving subjects. They make excellent planting partners for early-flowering bulbs, their lush foliage covering the ground when the spring display of the bulbs is over.

Hostas are also striking subjects for pots, the ideal place to grow them in gardens plagued by slugs and snails. Copper tape placed around the pot or a copper-impregnated mat beneath it will help defend emerging shoots and succulent leaves from attack.

Hosta 'June' (z. 4–8) has elegant leaves, broad and lance-shaped, forming a fairly upright clump 20 in. (50 cm) high and the same across. Each leaf is soft yellow with an irregular blue-green margin, suffusing the center with soft blue-green and yellow. Lilac flowers appear in mid- to late summer on tall stems, above the foliage. Excellent for a pot and for cutting, it succeeds in light shade but needs a reasonable amount of sun to develop the best color.

OTHER VARIEGATED HOSTAS

Hosta 'Cherry Berry' (z. 4–8) Compact, at 10 in. (25 cm) high and 16 in. (40 cm) wide. Narrow, dark, glossy green leaves with a cream center. Red-flushed stems and violet-mauve blooms.

Hosta fortunei var. aureomarginata (z. 4–8) Large, deeply veined, dark green leaves with golden yellow edges ageing to cream. Reaches 18 in. (45 cm) high and 24 in. (60 cm) across. Pale lavender flowers, well above the foliage.

Hosta 'Francee' (z. 4–8) Large, spreading and 24 in. (60 cm) high and 3 ft. (90 cm) across. Foliage is late but matures to narrow, heart-shaped leaves of rich green with white margins. Bears lavender flowers well above the foliage.

Hosta 'Revolution' (z. 4–8) Medium-sized, 12 in. (30 cm) high and 24 in. (60 cm) wide. Dark green leaves with white markings. Pale lilac flowers.

Hosta 'Wide Brim' (z. 4–8) grows 24 in. (60 cm) high and 3 ft. (90 cm) across. Its large, puckered, heart-shaped leaves are rich green with an irregular creamy margin overlapping the green, resulting in green-yellow shades toward the center. White flowers in midsummer rise above the foliage on sleek stems. Excellent for large containers, for borders in light shade, and for cutting.

Hosta 'Gold Standard' (z. 4–8) is one of the most popular hostas. It emerges in late spring, the leaves unfurling sage green, becoming light yellow as they mature, and fading to cream with a dark green margin. It is a large spreading plant, 20 in. (50 cm) high by 3 ft. (90 cm) across. Lilac flowers are borne in midsummer, held well above the leaves. Despite its popularity, it is not the easiest to grow; dappled shade is ideal, allowing the gold color to develop, without the leaves becoming scorched.

Hosta 'Frances Williams' (z. 4–8) is very large, reaching 24 in. (60 cm) high and 40 in. (1 m) across. The large, thick, puckered leaves are rounded and gently cupped and of a dusky blue-green with pale creamy yellow margins. Lavender flowers appear in midsummer on thick, leafy stems the same height as the leaves. Does best in shade.

Armoracia rusticana 'Variegata'

early summer, lacy white flower heads appear on tall green stems. This is the variegated form of bishop's weed; a weed cursed by many gardeners; but it is less invasive and is a very useful plant.

Armoracia rusticana 'Variegata', (zone 4–8) the variegated horseradish, is an underused perennial with lush green foliage dramatically marked in cream and white. It forms a vigorous clump of leaves to a height of 24 in. (60 cm) and multiplies readily. It grows anywhere but gives its best performance in an open position on deep, moist, fertile soil. It can bring interest to the edge of the vegetable garden; the long taproot can be used for culinary purposes in the same way as that of the green form.

Striking in spring, *Astrantia major* 'Sunningdale Variegated' (zone 5–8) forms a rounded clump, 8 in. (20 cm)

Astrantia major 'Sunningdale Variegated'

high, of large, deeply divided, dark green leaves, marked in creamy white. The variegation ages to pale green in summer, as the delicate, pincushion-like flower heads, framed in pale pink bracts, appear on 16 in. (40 cm) stems.

Houttuynia cordata 'Chameleon' (zone 6–10) is a robust, spreading ground-cover plant with brightly variegated foliage. It has numerous red stems, to 12 in. (30 cm) high, and heart-shaped leaves of green, flame, and gold. Small white flowers in summer are of secondary importance. This houttuynia likes moist soil and will grow happily in partial shade, although full sun brings

the most intense leaf color. It makes a colorful subject for a container. The stems and leaves are knocked back to the ground with the first frost. The plant's worst quality is an unpleasant aroma given off when the foliage is disturbed. A number of other selections are available, among them 'Pied Piper' and 'Flame', both of which have brighter foliage of red and orange with green and cream variegation (see Good Companions, below).

Iris ensata 'Variegata' (zone 5–8) must have constant moisture. The narrow, upright sword-like leaves, 3 ft. (90 cm) high, are striped in white or creamy yellow. Large purple blooms are a stunning contrast to the bright foliage

Houttuynia cordata 'Flame'

GOOD COMPANIONS

The bright colors of candelabra primulas (1) (z. 5–7) are striking with the emerging flame-colored shoots of *Houttuynia cordata* 'Flame' (2) (z. 6–10).

The striped, grasslike foliage of *Liriope muscari* 'John Burch' (3) (z. 6–9) mixes well with the similarly variegated but differently shaped leaves of *Euonymus fortunei* 'Silver Queen' (4) (z. 5–8).

OTHER GOOD VARIEGATED PERENNIALS FOR MOISTER SOIL *Oenanthe javanica* 'Flamingo' •

in early summer. *Iris pseudacorus* **'Variegata'** (zone 5–8) is more tolerant of drier situations. Its creamy yellow striped leaves usually fade to green from midsummer onward. Small yellow flowers are produced in spring.

Growing 20 in. (50 cm) high, *Kalimeris yomena* **'Shogun'** (zone 6–9) is ideal mid-border, covering the unsightly stems of taller herbaceous perennials. It emerges from the ground with creamy shoots in late spring. The blue-mauve flowers in midsummer resemble those of aster, a close relative, yet its dark green and cream foliage is refreshingly unique.

Liriope muscari (lilyturf) (zone 6–9) forms a clump of broad, grassy, dark green leaves from which appear short, dense spikes of small lilac-blue flowers in late summer and fall. Variegated forms can offer light foliage interest in the shade of trees. *Liriope muscari* **'John Burch'** (see Good Companions, left) has creamy yellow striped leaves, 12 in. (30 cm) long. Although it tolerates drought, it grows best on fairly moist, slightly acid soil.

Moist soil and light shade are ideal conditions for the variegated forms of the loosestrife *Lysimachia punctata* (zone 4–8). The cultivar **'Alexander'** has upright stems 30 in. (75 cm) high, densely clothed in green leaves edged with creamy white. **'Golden Alexander'** has leaves with margins of golden yellow. Both have the starry yellow flowers of the species in early summer (see page 144), although both are at their best before the flowers, when the leafy, upright shoots provide a contrast to the bold foliage of hostas.

The variegated **mints** are not only ornamental but deliciously aromatic culinary herbs of popular appeal. They are happy in poor, moist soils and are easy to grow. They are propagated by root cuttings, usually taken in fall, or by layering the stems in summer.

Liriope muscari 'John Burch'

Mentha × *gracilis* **'Variegata'** (zone 3–8), the ginger mint, has upright, red-tinted stems, up to 12 in. (30 cm) high, bearing oval, medium green leaves marked with bright yellow. The stems bear small lilac flowers in summer.

Mentha suaveolens **'Variegata'** (pineapple mint) (zone 7–10) has a pineapple scent. Its vigorous stems are clothed in small, oval to rounded, hairy gray-green leaves, with irregular creamy streaks, tips, and margins. Tiny, tubular pink or white flowers form short, dense spires on 20 in. (50 cm) stems.

Persicaria virginiana **'Painter's Palette'** (zone 4–8) prefers moist soil in semi-shade and shelter, where wind will not damage the foliage. It forms stems 24 in. (60 cm) high of green leaves marked with cream, each with a brown central zone and flushes of salmon pink.

Persicaria virginiana 'Painter's Palette'

A native of England and parts of western Europe, *Scrophularia auriculata* (zone 6–9) is found in woods and meadows and along river banks, where it thrives in rich, moist soil. With small brown flowers, the species is not worth growing, but the variegated form *Scrophularia auriculata* **'Variegata'** deserves a place. A good companion for hostas, ligularias, and sedges, it has tall, square red stems, nearly 40 in. (1 m) high, carrying toothed, wrinkled medium green leaves, boldly edged and splashed in creamy white.

Symphytums grow well on any soil and make excellent ground cover (see pages 116–17). The variegated forms are tough plants that will often succeed where choicer subjects may struggle. *Symphytum* **'Goldsmith'** (zone 5–7) successfully colonizes moist shade: its carpet of tumbling, early spring foliage illuminates the ground, despite the thickening tree canopy. A hardy perennial, growing from rhizomes, it produces crinkled, coarse, lanceolate leaves of dark green with thick, irregular variegation of lime green to bright gold. Stems 10 in. (25 cm) high, bear clusters of pendent tubular, pink to pale blue flowers in mid-spring. *Symphytum* × *uplandicum* **'Variegatum'** (zone 5–7), up to 3 ft. (90 cm) tall, is popular for the creamy white margins of its leaves. Unfortunately, it tends to revert to plain green unless happy in its situation.

CONTROLLING MINT

Variegated mints can be as invasive as the culinary types grown in the herb garden. Although their habit of running between other plants, throwing up random stems in the border, can be attractive, it may become overpowering. Contain clumps by planting in large pots sunk into the soil. The mints will also enjoy any additional moisture trapped by the containers.

Silver and blue foliage

Gray and blue are marvelous foils for other colors. Light, ethereal silver is a natural choice with the blue, pink, and purple flowers of sun-loving plants. It is also a ravishing contrast with deep red blooms. Blue-green foliage works as a bond between other colors, in the same way that blue flowers can provide that all-important link. As a contrast to the predominant green of most gardens, silver or blue foliage attracts the eye and draws attention to highlights in the border.

Anaphalis triplinervis

The dramatic silver foliage of *Cynara cardunculus* adds architectural impact to any border.

SILVER AND BLUE SUN-LOVERS

Anaphalis triplinervis (zone 3–8) thrives in full sun, so long as it has enough moisture in summer. A clump-forming plant, it is grown both for its neat, narrow silver leaves and for its tiny white, everlasting flowers, borne in clusters at the end of the stems.

Most silver-leaved perennials and shrubs are plants for sunny sites and soils with good drainage. They often hail from dry Mediterranean climates, the silver of their leaves a way of reflecting light and preventing water loss. Most silver shrubs have finely cut foliage; for broader silver leaves, the gardener needs to look to herbaceous perennials. Some have adapted to climatic conditions by covering their foliage with fine silver hairs, which create a microclimate over the surface, thereby preventing desiccation. Others have developed thick, leathery leaves with a reflective surface. These crave lots of light, and sit well among the reflective stones of scree or alongside walls and paved areas.

Many sun-loving sub-shrubs native to Mediterranean regions have silvery foliage: *Lotus hirsutus* (zone 8–10), *Helichrysum italicum* (zone 8–10, *Convolvulus cneorum* (zone 8–10), *Santolina chamaecyparissus* (zone 6–9), and many lavenders, for example. These are often offered alongside herbaceous perennials and have as much in common with them as they do with woody shrubs. *Artemisia* 'Powis Castle' (zone 6–10), with fine filigree silver leaves, is classified both as a shrub and as an herbaceous perennial. Although partly woody, it is often knocked back by half in winter, then sprouts from the woody base of the plant in spring. (See Good Companions, below, and see page 65.)

Eryngiums (see pages 66–67) are prized for the silver-blue metallic beauty of both their flowers and their foliage. Strikingly spiky plants, they are drought-resistant and contrast dramatically with the lush foliage of their neighbors. Contemporary in character, they are favored in modern garden design and floral art. The species can vary considerably in their silver and blue coloring, which is also affected by its situation.

The well-known biennial *Eryngium giganteum* (Miss Willmott's ghost) (zone 4–7) is reliable for the silver-white

Eryngium giganteum

of its flowers and foliage. Although the plant dies after flowering in summer, it readily self-seeds, especially on dry soils. The lovely *Eryngium* **'Jos Eijking'** (zone 4–8) is of similar size, reaching 24 in. (60 cm), but is a perennial, with silver-blue foliage and wonderful metallic-

blue flowers from mid- to late summer. It looks superb with artemisias and santolinas, its blue stars shining out from a cloud of silver-gray.

Helleborus argutifolius **'Silver Lace'** (zone 6–8) is more compact than the species. It grows to 12 in. (30 cm), and has bold ice green foliage with a silvery sheen. By late winter the domed plant is crowned with a loose head of lime green flowers. It prefers an open site on well-drained soil and mixes well with *Fritillaria meleagris* (zone 4–8).

Helleborus argutifolius 'Silver Lace'

Lychnis coronaria (zone 4–8) produces splendid white rosettes of soft, felted leaves and white-woolly flower stems, 20 in. (50 cm) high, carrying vivid magenta blooms in summer—a great contrast, but not ideal as a silver foliage plant because the flowers always steal the show. *Lychnis coronaria* **'Alba'**, with white flowers, is a superb mixer and will excel in white or silver schemes.

Salvia argentea (zone 5–8) is prized for its large white-woolly leaves. These are produced in a basal clump in the first season, before being upstaged in the second summer by the candelabra-like flower stem, which can reach 40 in. (1 m) high. The flowers are gray-white, sadly not a pretty combination with the white-woolly stems. This is a plant for a dry, well-drained position in full sun. A wet summer can reduce the leaves to a soggy mess on the soil surface.

SEASONAL SILVER PLANTS

In cooler zones, some herbaceous perennials are treated as annuals and used to contribute silver-gray foliage to seasonal planting schemes in the border and in containers. *Senecio cineraria* 'Silver Dust' (z. 8–10) is widely planted, and has attractively divided silver-gray leaves. *Tanacetum haradjanii* (z. 7–10) has curiously cut, fernlike leaves. *Tanacetum ptarmiciflorum* 'Silver Feather' (z. 8–9) is a useful, bushy plant with finely cut foliage. All grow to around 12 in. (30 cm) if kept in trim by removing the unattractive yellow daisy flowers before they open. All will overwinter in a sheltered, dry situation, but the plants often lose vigor and are slow to recover the following year, so it is best to replace them with new stock.

GOOD COMPANIONS

The softly divided foliage of *Artemisia* 'Powis Castle' (1) (z. 6–10) forms the perfect backdrop for the shining metallic blue blooms of *Eryngium alpinum* (2) (z. 4–8).

Stachys byzantina 'Silver Carpet' (3) (z. 4–8) and *Acaena microphylla* 'Copper Carpet' (z. 6–7) (4) is an ideal combination for edging a path in a sunny position.

BOLD, DRAMATIC SILVER

Cynara cardunculus (zone 6–9), the cardoon, is one of the most dramatic herbaceous perennials. The leaves, up to 40 in. (1 m) long, arch gracefully from the ground, dissected, sharply toothed, and silver-gray, especially when young (see page 102). Vast branched flower stems arise as summer progresses: silver-gray and also carrying foliage, they may grow 10 ft. (3 m) high. The large, spiny, thistlelike flower heads develop from buds at the top of the stems; as the heads mature they open to reveal purple-red bristly bracts. Once the flowers are at their peak, in late summer, the plant starts to deteriorate. At this point the flowering stems should be cut to ground level. New leaves will quickly appear, developing rapidly to full size; they will normally persist without damage throughout the winter in all but the coldest conditions.

Cynara cardunculus Scolymus Group (zone 6–9) is the globe artichoke, prized for its edible flower parts. It varies in its foliage color; some selections are quite blue and, like the species, can be used for dramatic effect.

Cynaras like deep, well-drained soil in full sun. They make a bold statement in

Macleaya microcarpa 'Kelway's Coral Plume'

the border but will also stand alone as architectural specimens.

Few herbaceous perennials have the stature of *Macleaya cordata* (plume poppy) (zone 4–8) and *Macleaya microcarpa* 'Kelway's Coral Plume' (zone 3–9). Spreading underground rhizomes throw up fleshy shoots that grow quickly to stems 6 ft. (2 m) or more high. These carry large, lobed leaves, gray-green above and silver-gray beneath, that resemble the pieces of a jigsaw. When disturbed by the wind

they flutter silver in the border. Light airy heads of small, tubular, pale coral flowers are borne at the tops of the stems in late summer. Macleayas are easily grown in sun or partial shade and look dramatic against dark evergreens. They rarely stay in the original planting position, and can be invasive.

Many **verbascums** (zone 6–8) are similar to *Salvia argentea* (see page 103) in their life cycle. *Verbascum thapsus* (Aaron's rod) produces a felty rosette in the first year, then a strong spike, 5 ft. (1.5 m) tall, of yellow flowers in the summer of the second, before the plant dies. It is, however, perennial in the garden because it so freely self-seeds, resulting in large numbers of seedlings in the following autumn and spring. Although impressive in flower, it is at its loveliest as a gray rosette, especially in winter when etched with frost.

Verbascum bombyciferum is an architectural plant, one of the most stunning in the border. In summer, its white-woolly 6 ft. (2 m) stems emerge from a rosette of large, silvery-gray leaves and bear closely packed, bright yellow flowers. *Verbascum olympicum* is similarly handsome: a long-lived, imposing perennial with tall, branched stems of yellow summer flowers rising from silver-gray leaf rosettes.

LIGHT, ETHEREAL SILVER

Artemisia absinthium 'Lambrook Silver' (zone 3–7) is a woody-based plant with finely cut, silver-gray foliage, somewhat broader and more parsleylike than *Artemisia* 'Powis Castle' (see Good Companions, page 103). In midsummer, 30 in. (75 cm) stems develop, with a mass of creamy yellow flowers. These tend to look dirty against the clean silver leaves and should be cut off. This preserves the quality of the foliage and encourages new growth, maintaining a bush of around 24 in. (60 cm).

Verbascum bombyciferum

OTHER PERENNIALS WITH SILVER AND BLUE FOLIAGE *Achillea clypeolata* • *Asphodeline lutea* •

Artemisia ludoviciana (zone 4–8) is a useful plant to introduce shots of silver among other perennials and shrubs. The upright stems, 24 in. (60 cm) high, of willowlike, toothed silver leaves are almost self-supporting in sunny, dry sites, needing only a little help from neighboring plants. The cultivars **'Silver Queen'** and **'Valerie Finnis'** (see page 51) are excellent, the latter increasingly used as a companion for summer-flowering annuals such as *Salvia farinacea* and *Salvia viridis* var. *comata*. Both artemisias are effective in herbaceous planting to add substance to *Nepeta × faassenii* (see page 67).

For frothy effect, *Artemisia pontica* (zone 4–8), *Artemisia alba* **'Canescens'** (zone 6–8), and *Artemisia schmidtiana* (zone 3–7) are unbeatable.

Artemisia ludoviciana 'Silver Queen'

Reaching 24 in. (60 cm) tall, these are the best silver clouds for planting among alliums, to disguise their fading leaves. *Artemisia schmidtiana* **'Nana'** usually reaches only 8 in. (20 cm). It is the finest, silkiest, and most silver of them all.

GARDEN ARCHITECTURE

Bold silver and blue leaves are the perfect partners for architectural stone in the garden. Statues, urns, balustrades, steps, and walls are a natural setting for the strong form and sympathetic tones of silver and blue, which can link the stone with the surrounding planting.

SILVER CARPETS

Artemisia stelleriana **'Boughton Silver'** (zone 3–7) is much heavier in character than other artemisias. It is a rosette-forming plant with divided, felted foliage, spreading by runners to form broad mats. It is not particularly

Artemisia stelleriana 'Boughton Silver'

elegant, but it is useful in a gravel area and especially good in a coastal garden.

Stachys byzantina (*Stachys lanata*), or lamb's ears (zone 4–8), is the ultimate evergreen, silver, mat-forming plant. Producing a series of rosettes of oval, pointed, heavily felted leaves, it is commonly seen at the front of borders, especially alongside paving. Small purple flowers are carried in woolly 16 in. (40 cm) spikes in summer. These can be cut back to preserve the quality of the foliage. *Stachys byzantina* was a favorite

of Gertrude Jekyll, who planted it widely. It associates well with old roses, dianthuses, and *Viola cornuta*.

There are several named cultivars, of which the best known and most useful is perhaps *Stachys byzantina* **'Silver Carpet'** (see Good Companions, page 103), which does not flower. *Stachys byzantina* **'Cotton Boll'** does produces flower spikes, but with woolly bobbles up the stems rather than flowers: an attractive novelty and good for cutting.

In a sunny situation with well-drained soil, *Veronica spicata* ssp. *incana* forms a mat of silver foliage, and in summer produces 12 in. (30 cm) spikes of sapphire blue flowers that shine out against the gray of the leaves. There are a number of forms: **'Silver Carpet'** lives up to its name.

STACHYS BYZANTINA AND MILDEW

Mildew is the scourge of this excellent ground-cover plant, usually disfiguring the foliage in midsummer. The woolly leaves do not take kindly to being sprayed, so prevention is better than cure. The risk of infection is increased by drought and overcrowding. Keep plants free from competitive neighbors and water them regularly.

Stachys byzantina

Cerastium tomentosum • Crambe maritima • Festuca glauca • Helichrysum petiolare • Leucophyta brownii •

SILVER IN THE SHADOWS

Some silver-leaved plants will grow in full or partial shade. These provide shining relief from the heavy greens, which also thrive in such conditions, and complement the white variegation of shrubs such as *Vinca minor* 'Argenteovariegata' (zone 5–8), *Euonymus fortunei* 'Emerald Gaiety' (zone 5–8), and *Osmanthus heterophyllus* 'Variegatus' (zone 6–9).

Shade-loving silver plants do not have woolly leaves; instead, they have reflective markings or marbling on the leaf surface. In the case of *Brunnera macrophylla* **'Jack Frost'** (zone 5–8) the foliage appears metallic silver,

Brunnera macrophylla 'Jack Frost'

etched and veined in medium green. Sprays of bright blue forget-me-not flowers form in early spring. The plant is deciduous, but the heart-shaped leaves are still perfect at the onset of winter, forming a mound of bold silver 8in. (20cm) high. They look dramatic beneath the deep plum foliage of *Acer palmatum* 'Bloodgood' (zone 6–8).

A number of the lower-growing **dicentras** have attractive blue-green leaves and create a silvery effect against deep green foliage. *Dicentra eximia* **'Snowdrift'** (zone 5–7) has fine fernlike foliage of blue-green and white flowers in late spring to early summer. It forms splendid light ground cover at a height

Dicentra 'Langtrees'

of 10in. (25cm). *Dicentra* **'Langtrees'** (zone 4–8) is popular, with low silver-gray leaves and dainty white flowers.

Heuchera **'Mint Frost'** (zone 4–8) makes a change from the popular purple heucheras. Its fresh green leaves are overlaid with silver, making a striking mound of foliage 8 in. (20 cm) high. The coloring resembles that of *Lamium maculatum* 'Beacon Silver' but is softer. The deep red leaves of *Heuchera* **'Silver Scrolls'** (zone 4–8) are similarly mottled silver (see Good Companions, below).

Lamiums often have silver markings on their foliage and are particularly useful on sites with poor soil. *Lamium maculatum* **'Beacon Silver'** (zone 4–7) has superb silver-green foliage with just a narrow margin and veins of darker

green. From a distance the overall effect is of a mat of silver, studded in summer with pink-purple flowers. (See Good Companions, below, and see page 62.)

Mertensia virginica (zone 3–7), the Virginia bluebell, is a woodland plant with smooth gray leaves and sprays of tubular violet-blue flowers in spring. Up to 16 in. (40 cm) high, it mixes well with pulmonarias and dicentras.

The silver-spotted foliage of the **pulmonarias** (lungwort) has earned them their names both botanical and colloquial. The wonderful *Pulmonaria* **'Margery Fish'** (zone 4–8), 12 in. (30 cm) tall, has leaves overlaid with silver-green, which look lovely with lilac-blue and mauve-pink spring flowers. (See also pages 63 and 115–16.)

Heuchera 'Mint Frost'

GOOD COMPANIONS

Hosta 'Fragrant Blue' (1) (z. 4–8) with *Dicentra* 'Langtrees' (2) (z. 4–8): The large, bold leaves of the hosta set off the fern-like, silver-blue foliage of the dicentra and its pearly white flowers.

The silvery wine red leaves of *Heuchera* 'Silver Scrolls' (3) (z. 4–8) contrast with the silver and green foliage and purple flowers of *Lamium maculatum* 'Beacon Silver' (4) (z. 4–7).

Blue hostas

Hostas with blue leaves are mostly plants for semi-shade, where the sun cannot bleach or scorch the exquisite foliage. They offer some of the most stunning leaves in the garden: beautiful in their own right but also dramatic partners to other leaves and flowers. Many bloom in mid- to late summer, producing stems of tubular flowers in white and shades of pink to lilac.

They make excellent subjects for pots, their waxy blue-green hues associating well with both the matte earth tones of terracotta and the shinier oriental glazes. Although still at risk from slugs and snails, blue-leaved hostas seem to suffer less damage than other hostas.

When planting in groups, give each plant plenty of room to grow. Light foliage subjects such as dicentras are perfect partners, contrasting well with the boldness of the hosta leaves.

There are innumerable named hosta varieties, often having only minor differences between them. Such

Hosta 'Fragrant Blue', at 8 in. (20 cm) high and 12 in. (30 cm) across, is one of the smaller hostas, with small, smooth, heart-shaped leaves of blue-green. Fragrant, pale lavender flowers are carried on leafy stems in midsummer.

subtleties are really of concern only to collectors: Simply choose varieties of a good color with a leaf shape that you find pleasing.

Hosta 'Blue Umbrellas' (z. 4–8) is the best blue variety for a sunny site, with plenty of moisture. The large, leathery leaves are curved on stiff stalks. Height 24 in. (60 cm), spread 40 in. (1 m). Very pale lilac flowers in midsummer.

OTHER BLUE HOSTAS

Hosta 'Blue Angel' (z. 4–8) Faster-growing than *Hosta sieboldiana* var. *elegans* and has better flowers.

Hosta 'Blue Moon' (z. 4–8) Slender heart-shaped leaves of a wonderful blue. Height and spread 10 in. (25 cm).

Hosta 'Silvery Slugproof' (z. 4–8) Resistant to slugs and snails. Grows 16 in. (40 cm) high, 1 m (40 in)

Hosta 'Halcyon' (z. 4–8) has elegant blue leaves and grayish lavender flowers rising above them in mid-summer. The blue is most intense in shade where, in moist soil, the plant will reach 20 in. (50 cm) high, 40 in. (1 m) across. The pointed leaves are narrow on young plants, wider on more mature specimens. Excellent for a pot.

Hosta 'Blue Wedgwood' (z. 4–8) is a smaller hosta reaching 12 in. (30 cm) in height by 24 in. (60 cm) across. The wavy-edged, pointed leaves are intense blue-green. Pale lavender flowers are carried on straight stems above the foliage in midsummer.

Hosta sieboldiana var. *elegans* (z. 4–8) is the classic big blue hosta, with large, cupped, corrugated, silver-blue leaves. In midsummer, pale lilac flowers are borne in silver-blue spikes, rarely higher than the leaves. Height is 24 in. (60 cm), spread 40 in. (1 m). *Hosta* 'Big Daddy' (z. 4–8) is similar but with rounded, more cupped leaves.

SEASONS

Summer is the season for herbaceous perennials: As the flowering shrubs complete their spring display, perennials take on the star role. Making the most of the leafy backdrop of their woody neighbors, they fill the garden with a pageant of color. As the heat of summer dies away, autumn flowers begin to shine in the warm light. Later on, their faded remains are decorated with frost and snow, an effect surpassed only by the clear beauty of delicate winter flowers—until the ground awakens in a carpet of fresh spring foliage and bright new blooms.

RIGHT: Penstemons, bronze fennel, and lilies in a summer garden

Early spring

As winter releases its grip, the garden becomes a place full of promise, with fresh shoots, unfurling leaves, and jewel-like flowers. Early spring is a time for preparation: soil conditioning, planting, and division are just some of the early annual tasks. Plans for a new or refurbished border can now take the first steps toward becoming reality. Any committed gardener will agree: The anticipation and creation of a new garden feature is one of the greatest pleasures.

The green shoots of herbaceous perennials appear among the fading leaves and flowers of spring bulbs at East Lambrook Manor, Somerset, in England.

Bergenias (elephant's ears) produce evergreen rosettes of large rounded, leathery, glossy leaves. The foliage of most varieties takes on some kind of winter coloring, from subtle bronzing and reddening on the upper surface, to bold ruby red on the underside. As spring approaches, stems in shades of light green to dark red carry clusters of bell- or funnel-shaped flowers, which may be white, pale pink, rose pink, salmon pink, or almost red.

Originating from central and eastern Asia, bergenias are found in moist woods, meadows, and moorland. They are hardy perennials, most tough enough to endure the Siberian winters. The plants spread slowly to form dense ground cover that suppresses all but the most determined weeds. They are truly useful garden plants, thriving in both sun and shade, although a site in full sun certainly improves flower quantity and quality. (See also page 61.)

Bergenia ciliata (zone 5–7), a distinctive Himalayan beauty, has large, rounded, densely hairy leaves, 14 in. (35 cm) long, and short red stems, 10 in. (25 cm) high, bearing tight clusters of white or sometimes pink-blushed flowers in spring. Although very hardy, it behaves as a deciduous plant in exposed areas, and a sheltered position brings the bonus of glorious burnished winter foliage.

Gertrude Jekyll praised *Bergenia cordifolia* 'Purpurea' (zone 4–8) for its

Bergenia purpurascens

Bergenia 'Silberlicht' (SILVERLIGHT)

Brunnera macrophylla

Brunnera macrophylla 'Dawson's White'

beauty in both winter and summer. Its rounded to heart-shaped, fleshy, deep green leaves, to 12 in. (30 cm) long, are gently puckered, with purple tints in fall and winter. Magenta flowers on tall red

A SELECTION OF GOOD BERGENIA HYBRIDS

All do well in moist soil in sun or shade. Flowers are produced from early to late spring.

Bergenia 'Evening Bells' ('Abendglocken') (z. 4–8) Large, glossy green leaves, reddening in autumn, and semidouble crimson flowers.

Bergenia 'Evening Glow' ('Abendglut') (z. 4–8) Medium to dark green leaves, Ruby red beneath. Semidouble magenta-crimson flowers.

Bergenia 'Bressingham White' (z. 4–8) Broad, deep green leaves and pure white flowers.

Bergenia 'Bressingham Ruby' (z. 4–8) Foliage colors in winter to glowing red-purple with copper tints. Red-purple flowers.

Bergenia 'Morning Red' ('Morgenröte') (z. 4–8) Deep green leaves and deep carmine-pink flowers; often blooms again in midsummer.

Bergenia 'Silverlight' ('Silberlicht') (above center) (z. 4–8) Gently scalloped medium green leaves. White flowers age to pink.

Bergenia 'Winter Fairy Tales' ('Wintermärchen') (z. 4–8) Deep green leaves with red undersides, bronzed in winter. Dark pink-red flowers.

stems, up to 24 in. (60 cm) high, appear in late winter to early spring. (See Good Companions, page 117.)

Bergenia purpurascens (zone 4–8) produces narrow leaves, 4–10 in. (10–25 cm) long, which are held more upright than most; they are deep green above and purple-red on the undersides. In autumn the upper surface becomes dark beet red, the underside rich mahogany. In mid- and late spring, rich brown-red stems, 18 in. (45 cm) high, bear nodding purple-red flowers.

Brunneras (zone 4–8), members of the borage family, are native to eastern Europe, where they grow in light woodland and scrub. In the garden they are excellent at the edge of a border or as ground cover; they are also useful in containers in shade, perhaps at the base of a Japanese maple (*Acer*). The pretty blue flowers offer a perennial alternative to the much-loved biennial forget-me-nots (*Myosotis*). They look wonderful against a backdrop of dark foliage, such

PROTECTING BERGENIAS FROM VINE-WEEVIL

Bergenias can be prone to attack by vine weevil. Problems are indicated by notching around the leaf edge, and eventually the plant collapses as the roots are destroyed by vine weevil larvae. Treat in fall and early spring with a suitable systemic insecticide, or use a biological control.

as a privet or laurel hedge, and are delightful beneath shrubs with silver foliage such as *Elaeagnus* 'Quicksilver'.

Brunneras prefer moist but well-drained soil, and will tolerate full sun as long as air movement is good. The variegated forms dislike being baked: The leaf margins are prone to browning when plants are dry.

Brunnera macrophylla has dark green foliage and a profusion of bright blue flowers, on stems 18 in. (45 cm) high, from early spring onwards. It is a tougher character than the variegated forms. **'Dawson's White'** brightens the spring garden with its heart-shaped medium green leaves, generously edged with white. Delicate stems of sky blue flowers contrast with the foliage. **'Hadspen Cream'** is similar but widely thought superior. **'Jack Frost'** has become the brunnera of choice for designers and gardeners alike. Its large heart-shaped leaves look metallic silver with a network of medium green veins,

111

and they make a stunning canvas for its sky blue flowers (see page 106). **'Langtrees'** (zone 4–8) is a very good ground-cover plant for shade. It has dark green leaves, heavily spotted silver-gray, and the same sky blue flowers.

Doronicum plantagineum

Epimedium × versicolor 'Sulphureum'

MAINTENANCE OF BRUNNERAS

Shoots of some variegated varieties may occasionally revert to green; these should be removed by cutting them off at the base. With brunneras grown for their foliage, remove the flower stems as they fade. This presents a sharper foliage effect, which will stay looking good throughout summer and well into fall.

The cheerful daisy flowers of leopard's bane or **doronicums** are a delight in the spring garden, rivaling the display of many summer-flowering daisylike plants. Native to Europe, southwest Asia, and Siberia, they are found in woodland, scrub, meadows, heath-lands, and rocky habitats; in the garden they do best in moist, well-drained, humus-rich soil, in sun or partial shade. Slowly spreading or clump-forming plants growing from rhizomes or tubers, they have medium green, oval, pointed leaves, often toothed and heart-shaped at the base. The yellow flowers, with slightly darker centers, are carried on branched stems, either singly or in clusters. They last well as cut flowers.

Doronicum **'Miss Mason'** (zone 4–8) is the best single-flowered cultivar, producing golden yellow blooms on 18 in. (45 cm) stems with bright green leaves. This is a good choice to set against the shiny copper bark of *Prunus serrula* (zone 5–8). A rare, taller cultivar, growing to 3 ft. (90 cm) high, *Doronicum* × *excelsum* **'Harpur Crewe'** (zone 4–8) gives an outstanding display, with large yellow flowers borne three or more on a stem. *Doronicum plantagineum* (zone 4–8), a native of

Europe, also produces a good show of large, golden yellow flower heads, on stems up to 32 in. (80 cm) high. The foliage dies back soon after flowering, which makes this a good species for naturalizing in grass. A dwarf cultivar, with a tidy, compact habit, *Doronicum* **'Little Leo'** (zone 3–7) is less than 12 in. (30 cm) tall; it is ideal to plant with forget-me-nots (*Myosotis*) and dwarf spring bulbs. *Doronicum orientale* **'Spring Beauty'** ('Frühlingspracht') reaches 24 in. (60 cm); its double flowers are bright and sunny, but it lacks the charm of the single varieties.

Epimediums (also known as bishop's hat and barrenwort) (zone 5–8) are undemanding treasures and deserve more attention. Clump-forming, hardy perennials, no more than 12 in. (30 cm)

in height, they may be deciduous, semi-evergreen, or fully evergreen. Their pointed, heart-shaped, fresh green leaves mature to bronzed leathery shields with gently spined margins. Early spring sees the arrival of slender stems of pendulous, starlike flowers in white, lilac, pink, red, purple, or yellow. The flowers resemble those of berberis, which belong to the same family.

Their native habitat is the scrub and woodland of East Asia and parts of the Mediterranean. In the garden they thrive in rich, moist, well-drained soil, enjoying the dappled shade of shrubs or trees. Plant container-grown plants in spring; they quickly become established and soon spread, forming excellent ground cover. Seedlings often arise in the most (continued on page 114)

GOOD COMPANIONS

The evergreen *Epimedium* × *versicolor* 'Sulphureum' (1) (z. 5–8) with its copper-bronzed foliage, mixes well with grasses and spring bulbs such as English bluebells (*Hyacinthoides non-scripta*) (z. 5–8) and *Anemone blanda* (2) (z. 5–8), and is effective beneath trees with attractive bark such as the black birch, *Betula nigra* (3) (z. 4–9).

Euphorbias

Euphorbia is a fascinating genus, containing a variety of plants ranging from cacti and poinsettias to some favorite hardy perennials. Herbaceous euphorbias are often thought of as plants for shade, but most prefer an open site and a reasonable amount of sun. Many hail from Mediterranean regions, so they enjoy good drainage and resent being waterlogged.

At home in traditional planting schemes as well as in contemporary settings, euphorbias work well with other bold foliage plants, such as phormiums, and look good in gravel and among paving. Some of the smaller forms make excellent ground cover; larger evergreen varieties are excellent for providing structure in a planting and can fulfill the role played by evergreen shrubs. All contribute to the spring garden with their fresh green-yellow flower heads, which last until early summer. (See also pages 57, 90, 96 and 122.)

All euphorbias contain a milky sap that can irritate the skin and eyes. Take great care when handling the plant, particularly when cutting the stems.

Euphorbia characias ssp. *wulfenii* 'Lambrook Gold' (above left) (z. 8–9) and 'John Tomlinson' (above right) (z. 8–9) are large, evergreen, yellow-flowered forms, 4 ft. (1.2 m) high.

Euphorbia polychroma (z. 5–8) is lower growing than most, at 18 in. (45 cm), and makes a stunning rounded plant with fresh green leaves and a profusion of yellow flower heads. Deciduous.

Euphorbia characias (z. 8–9) has a neat, shrublike habit up to 4 ft. (1.2 m) high, its many stout stems clothed with narrow, gray-green, often bluish, evergreen leaves. In early spring large, bold flower heads appear, made up of cuplike bracts in varying shades of yellow-green, with purple-brown or black nectar glands at the center.

Euphorbia palustris (z. 5–8) has tall, slender stems, 40 in. (1 m) or more high, clad in deciduous, oblong, lance-shaped pale green leaves and bearing heads of golden yellow flowers. It likes a moist site.

OTHER GOOD EUPHORBIAS

Euphorbia characias ssp. *characias* 'Humpty Dumpty' (z. 8–9) Very compact and dense, only 18 in. (45 cm) tall.

Euphorbia characias ssp. *wulfenii* (z. 8–9) Often confused with the species (see below left), but taller, with larger flower heads of a more reliable yellow-green.

Euphorbia cyparissias 'Fens Ruby' (z. 4–8) Fine stems of feathery, glaucous purple deciduous foliage and green-yellow flowers. 8 in. (20 cm) high. (See page 117.)

Euphorbia × martini (z. 7–10) Pretty yellow-green flowers and evergreen purple-tinged foliage. Compact and 24–30 in. (60–75 cm) high.

Euphorbia myrsinites (z. 5–9) Prostrate, with evergreen blue-green leaves on sprawling stems. Yellow-green flower heads. Needs sun and good drainage.

Helleborus argutifolius

SOME GOOD EPIMEDIUMS

Epimedium grandiflorum 'Crimson Beauty' (z. 5–8) Deep red buds opening to crimson flowers. Deciduous, fresh green foliage.

Epimedium grandiflorum 'Rose Queen' (z. 5–8) Large pink flowers. Deciduous green foliage.

Epimedium × rubrum (see page 62) (z. 5–8) Semi-evergreen leaves are red when young and old; tiny crimson and yellow flowers. One of the best foliage plants for ground cover.

Epimedium × versicolor 'Sulphureum' (see page 112) (z. 5–8) Yellow flowers and copper-red evergreen foliage.

Epimedium × versicolor 'Versicolor' (z. 5–8) Light to dark pink flowers with yellow centers and coppery evergreen foliage.

Epimedium × youngianum 'Niveum' (z. 5–8) Pendent, pure white flowers. Bronzed deciduous foliage.

Epimedium × youngianum 'Yenomoto' (z. 5–8) Similar to 'Niveum' but has larger flowers and green deciduous leaves.

unlikely of places, flourishing in small pockets of soil in paving and at the foot of a wall or steps. (See also page 62.)

Hellebores do much to lift our spirits in the darkest days of the year, but they are by no means confined to the winter months. The many beautiful forms of *Helleborus × hybridus* (zone 5–8), the Lenten rose (see pages 180–81), continue their lavish display into early spring. Alongside them other outstanding hellebores begin to perform.

Helleborus argutifolius (formerly known as *Helleborus corsicus*) (zone 6–8) has handsome, stout, bushy stems clad in evergreen, leathery, dark green leaves. Each is divided into three segments, gently edged with spines and exhibiting a faint network of pale green veins. In early spring of the second year, stems 40 in. (1 m) tall are topped with

slightly pendent, cup-shaped flowers in the palest green, lasting for a number of weeks. Rather shrublike in habit, this Mediterranean beauty is very useful for a mixed border, or it can be used as a specimen plant in gravel or alongside paving. (See also page 103.)

Helleborus foetidus (zone 6–8) is a native of southern Europe and Britain, and is also known as the stinking hellebore because of the odor given off by the foliage when bruised. Even so, its dark, glossy, deeply divided, evergreen leaves have long ensured its popular use in gardens. *Helleborus foetidus* grows to 32 in. (80 cm). Flowers start arriving at the end of winter, borne at the top of mature stems: clusters of pendent, bell-shaped, pale green blooms usually delicately tipped with purple.

Helleborus lividus (zone 8–9) is another Mediterranean beauty, native to Majorca; it is somewhat less hardy than

GROWING SPRING-FLOWERING HELLEBORES

All early spring hellebores should be sited in full sun or light shade, avoiding icy cold winds, and in free-draining, neutral to alkaline soil. Cut out the flowered stems as they deteriorate to allow fresh foliage to come through.

Helleborus foetidus

Helleborus argutifolius, so in cold areas will need protection from frost. Stems of purple-green are clothed in leathery silvery green leaves, each with three oblong-elliptic leaflets, lightly toothed. All have fine creamy white veins, and the leaf stalks have a pink-purple flush, which extends through the main veins beneath. In early spring of the plant's second year, purplish-green stalks, 18 in. (45 cm) high, bear clusters of bowl-shaped creamy green flowers, lightly flushed with pink or purple.

Helleborus × sternii (zone 6–9) is a hybrid between *Helleborus argutifolius* and *Helleborus lividus,* with many of its parents' attributes. A seed-raised plant, it may sometimes look more like one parent than the other, but it is always relatively dwarf, seldom exceeding 16 in. (40 cm) tall. Two reliable strains are

Omphalodes cappadocica 'Starry Eyes'

Pulmonaria 'Roy Davidson'

Pulmonaria saccharata 'Leopard'

Blackthorn Group (zone 6–9), with purple stems, clearly veined gray-green leaves, and flowers suffused purple-pink; and **'Boughton Beauty'** (zone 6–9), which has pink-red stems, medium green leaves with cream veins, and flowers that are green inside and satin pink-red to purple outside. Both are in full flower in early spring.

Omphalodes (navelwort) are little-known, yet fantastic garden plants. Once established in rich, moist soil, these hardy evergreens will give a long period of bloom from early spring. Hard frosts may damage the foliage, although their preference for a shady site affords enough protection in all but extreme conditions. Be prepared to fend off slugs and snails looking for an early meal.

A favored species is *Omphalodes cappadocica* (zone 6–8), a Turkish woodland native that forms a spreading clump just over 8 in. (20 cm) high. The slender, dark red-brown stems carry numerous small, five-petaled, inky blue forget-me-not flowers. **'Alba'** is pure white, while the popular **'Cherry Ingram'** has larger flowers in rich, deep blue. **'Starry Eyes'** is a similar shade, but each petal boasts a fine white margin.

Pulmonarias (lungwort) are hardy perennials originating from Europe and Asia, where they are found growing freely on mountains, in woodland, and at streamsides. As garden plants, they have many attributes: attractive foliage, wonderful early spring flowers, and the ability to thrive in relatively poor soil in sun or shade. Of the many varieties and cultivars, virtually all are evergreen and some shed their leaves only just before flowering, after which they soon regrow. Many have ornately marked foliage, which may be flashed, spotted, or variegated with silver-white. (See also page 106.) Seldom bothered by slugs or snails, they present a real alternative to dwarf hostas for foliage effect. None grows to more than about 12 in. (30 cm) high, and all have numerous

---

OTHER GOOD PULMONARIAS

Pulmonaria 'Lewis Palmer' (z. 2–8) See page 63.

Pulmonaria longifolia 'Ankum' (z. 3–8) Long-lasting mauve-blue flowers throughout spring.

Pulmonaria 'Opal' (z. 5–8) Medium green, silver-centered leaves that show off pearly-blue flowers.

Pulmonaria 'Roy Davidson' (top right) (z. 4–8) Pale ice blue flowers above strongly spotted foliage.

Pulmonaria 'Victorian Brooch' (z. 4–8) Magenta-coral flowers and white-spotted, medium green foliage.

---

delicate, funnel-shaped flowers, which may be white, pink, red, violet, or purple to deep blue, some displaying both pink and blue flowers in the same cluster.

Pulmonaria saccharata (zone 2–8) is the best known of those with dual-colored blooms. The fine old cultivar **'Mrs. Moon'** has felty leaves heavily spotted with silver-white and pink and blue flowers. **'Leopard'** is a pink variety, with flowers of a crushed strawberry shade and well-spotted leaves.

Pulmonaria **'Sissinghurst White'** (zone 4–8) is the only widely grown form derived from common lungwort, *Pulmonaria officinalis*. Its pure white bells brighten a shady spot, and the fresh green, white-spotted leaves complement the pale blue of *Chionodoxa luciliae* (glory of the snow) (zone 5–8) and *Anemone blanda* (zone 5–8).

Pulsatilla vulgaris

Pulmonaria longifolia (zone 3–8), widespread in western Europe, is a reliably tough plant with narrower, white-spotted leaves and usually blue flowers. It is more tolerant of drought than other pulmonarias. The cultivar *Pulmonaria longifolia* 'Bertram Anderson' is taller, with long, narrow leaves and a wealth of rich blue flowers.

In most gardens the pasque flower, *Pulsatilla vulgaris* (zone 5–7), is grown as an alpine: a sunny, free-draining site is the key to success. Like most plants from mountain regions, pulsatillas are hardy but hate the wet of winter. On heavy soil dig in plenty of gravel, grit, or sand before planting; alternatively grow pulsatillas in a raised alpine scree bed or in a container.

The emerging foliage is covered in fine silvery white hair and unfolds to medium green, fernlike, feathery leaves. In spring, short stems bear individual, gently nodding, bell-shaped flowers of silky texture, often purple-blue, but sometimes white or red, with vibrant golden yellow-orange stamens. These are followed by long-lasting, rounded, fluffy white seed heads. Several named cultivars exist, all growing to about 8 in. (20 cm) high.

Pulsatilla alpina, the alpine pasque flower, forms a clump of finely divided medium green foliage, above which

short stems, 10 in. (25 cm) high, bear showy, cup-shaped white flowers. The species grows in alkaline conditions while *Pulsatilla alpina* ssp. *apiifolia* (zone 5–7), with yellow flowers, grows on acid soil. Flowers and stems have soft, silky hair. *Pulsatilla halleri* is slightly later to flower, with erect, silky bells of lilac to lavender-blue on 8 in. (20 cm) stems.

Pulsatilla patens (zone 4–7) is the eastern pasque flower of Russian Siberia. In North America, this species is celebrated as the prairie crocus, floral emblem of both Manitoba and South Dakota. Here it is found in mountains,

although it makes its full impact in the vast plains, where its upright, cupped flowers, on stems only 6 in. (15 cm) high, create a sea of blue-purple (occasionally white), followed by a carpet of fluffy white seed heads.

Symphytums (zone 5–7), or comfreys, can be found in a range of habitats, from Europe to North Africa and Asia. Fairly coarse plants growing from rhizomes, they have large, crinkled, deciduous foliage and usually branched, leafy stems topped with clusters of pendent, tubular flowers. They often start to flower in early spring and go on into summer; some may bloom again in autumn if cut back after the first flush. Symphytums grow well on any moist soil, and the thick carpet of foliage thrives in shady situations, keeping weeds to a minimum. They are excellent for ground cover under rhododendrons, and the rich reddish brown foliage of *Lysimachia ciliata* 'Firecracker' (see page 91) (zone 5–8) is an attractive planting partner where soil is not too dry.

Symphytum caucasicum has oval to lance-shaped, deeply veined leaves, medium green in color. A tough, reliable ground-cover plant, 24 in. (60 cm) high, it often goes unnoticed until spring,

Symphytum caucasicum

when it produces tight clusters of tubular flowers in an intensely bright ink blue—a stunning shade, which rivals that of anchusas and delphiniums.

Symphytum ibericum (zone 5–7), 16 in. (40 cm) high, has creamy yellow flowers, opening from red-tipped buds. The popular symphytums 'Hidcote Blue' and 'Hidcote Pink', originating from Hidcote Manor in Gloucestershire, may be hybrids of this species. The hybrid *Symphytum × uplandicum* (zone 5–7) is distinctive in habit, with upright, well-branched stems, up to 6 ft. (2 m) high, clad in coarse, lance-shaped leaves. In late spring, clusters of pink-violet buds open to lilac-blue tubular flowers. (See also pages 63 and 101.)

Members of the lily family, **trilliums** are spectacular spring-flowering plants, from woodland and scrub in North America, the western Himalayas and northeast Asia. The name *trillium*, from the Latin for "three," refers to the fact that the leaves, petals, and sepals are all borne in groups of three.

Trillium erectum (birthroot) (zone 4–7) has stems up to 20 in. (50 cm) high, each with three oval, glossy, medium green leaves. A short, arching stalk bears an outward-facing, cupped, deep red-purple flower, occasionally white or yellow, with incurved petals.

Trillium grandiflorum

Trillium ovatum (zone 5–8) also grows to 20 in. (50 cm), its stems topped with three rounded medium green leaves, below a loosely cupped flower. The pure white, oval petals open fully to reveal medium yellow stamens in the center. *Trillium grandiflorum* (zone 5–7), known as wake robin, is similar, except that the large white petals have wavy edges and fade to pale pink with age. It is also slightly shorter, at 16 in. (40 cm).

Trillium luteum (zone 5–8), too, has stems of up to 16 in. (40 cm) tall, each proudly holding three medium green leaves strongly marbled with pale green-white. The upward-facing flowers have narrow, pale yellow petals, sometimes bronze-green, and are sweetly scented. *Trillium sessile* (toadshade) (zone 5–7) is similar in habit and leaf markings, but shorter, at only 12 in. (30 cm), with red-maroon, narrow-petaled flowers.

GROWING TRILLIUMS

If trilliums are purchased as dormant plants, the rhizomes should be checked to make sure they are firm and healthy. Ideally buy in early spring, when the first flush of growth is visible. They require cool deep or partial shade, provided by large shrubs or small trees, and humus-rich, moist but well-drained soil, preferably neutral to acid. Once established, trilliums perform well, but try to avoid disturbing them.

GOOD COMPANIONS

The vivid greenish yellow flowers of *Euphorbia cyparissias* 'Fens Ruby' (1) (z. 4–8) stand out sharply against the velvety foliage of the purple sage, *Salvia officinalis* 'Purpurascens' (2) (z. 5–10).

The large, glossy purple leaves of *Bergenia purpurascens* (3) (z. 4–8) contrast with the soft, woolly gray foliage of *Stachys byzantina* (4) (z. 4–8).

Late spring

As the days lengthen, colors intensify in the garden. Plants grow quickly in the warmer temperatures, and leaves unfurl from the pale acid green of early spring toward the full emerald shades of summer. Spring-flowering trees and shrubs are laden with blossom, and tulips and wallflowers color pots and borders. Herbaceous perennials fill out to cover the bare soil; suddenly all those empty spaces in the borders seem to be occupied.

The lime green flowers and foliage of *Smyrnium perfoliatum* are the perfect foil for the elegant glowing blooms of *Tulipa* 'Ballerina'.

Ajuga genevensis (blue bugleweed) (zone 4–7) forms a spreading clump of strong medium green, oblong-rounded foliage, with stems 12 in. (30 cm) tall carrying whorls of dark blue flowers. Its height lends it to naturalistic combinations with grasses, ferns, and primulas.

Ajuga pyramidalis (zone 4–7) forms a rosette of spreading, dark green foliage and produces spires of tightly packed, violet-blue to deep blue flowers on 8 in. (20 cm) stems. Pink- or white-flowered forms also occur naturally.

Ajuga reptans (zone 4–7) has spreading, spoon-shaped, dark green foliage, with 6 in. (15 cm) spikes of blue flowers. The species is invasive, but the cultivars are less badly behaved. Some have fancy, winter-hardy foliage, the most common being the deep bronze *Ajuga reptans* 'Atropurpurea' (see also page 86), cream-splashed *Ajuga reptans* 'Variegata', and

Commonly known as bugle, **ajugas** are grown mainly for the metallic beauty of their often evergreen foliage, but the showy flowers are a delight in spring. Carried on spikes 2–6 in. (5–15 cm) high, the tiers of tubular, two-lipped blooms may be medium to dark blue, purple, pink, or white. Ajugas' natural habitats are varied: hedgerows, woodland clearings, young coppice, scrub, and meadows, all areas where moisture-retentive, slightly acid soil is found.

Ajuga reptans 'Atropurpurea'

Ajuga reptans 'Catlin's Giant'

Anchusa azurea 'Loddon Royalist'

Anthemis tinctoria 'E.C. Buxton'

Anthemis tinctoria 'Sauce Hollandaise'

bronze, red, and cream *Ajuga reptans* 'Multicolor'. The less ostentatious foliage of *Ajuga reptans* 'John Pierpoint' is glossy medium green, which serves as a fine backdrop to the larger, pure white flowers. The same can be said of *Ajuga* 'Little Court Pink', a medium pink form.

Ajuga reptans 'Catlin's Giant' (zone 4–7) is large enough to mix with the big boys of the border. In its preferred conditions of rich, moist soil and partial shade, the lush, rounded, glossy leaves of bronzed purple can be 6 in. (15 cm) long. Tightly packed spikes of dark blue flowers bring its height to above 8 in. (20 cm).

The flowers of **anchusas** (zone 4–8) provide one of the most stunning blues in the late spring border. Native to Europe, Africa, and Asia, they thrive in a moist but well-drained, sunny site. The best garden species is *Anchusa azurea*, an herbaceous perennial of exceptional flower power, sadly often found to be short-lived; but it can be propagated from basal shoot or root cuttings. In favorable conditions, it will perform for a number of years, forming a rosette of narrow, lance-shaped, hairy, medium green leaves and branching stems, up to 5 ft. (1.5 m) high, with many cuplike, vibrant ink blue flowers, which become blue-purple. *Anchusa azurea* 'Loddon Royalist' is the most prized variety, with equally vibrant deep blue flowers borne on sturdy, self-supporting stems 3 ft. (90 cm) tall. *Anchusa azurea* 'Opal' is similar, but has powder blue flowers.

The delightful bright daisy flowers of *Anthemis* radiate their own sunshine from late spring until late summer. Mixing well with Mediterranean companions, such as lavender, rosemary, and thyme, they are sun-loving perennials similar in their requirements to salvias and many of the herbaceous geraniums. Anthemis fare best in free-draining, fertile soil; they dislike winter wetness. Many varieties are excellent for cutting.

Anthemis tinctoria (zone 2–8) has a number of cultivars, all with fernlike foliage, which varies from medium to dark green, some with downy gray undersides and all flowering at 24–32 in. (60–80 cm). By late spring, *Anthemis tinctoria* 'E. C. Buxton' is giving a sensational show, the flower heads having soft yellow petals around golden yellow, buttonlike centers. A popular variety is *Anthemis tinctoria* 'Sauce Hollandaise', with pale cream-white flowers. Much bolder in color are *Anthemis* 'Beauty of Grallagh', which is golden orange, and the pure gold *Anthemis* 'Grallagh Gold'.

Anthemis sancti-johannis (zone 3–7), native to southwest Bulgaria, is a short-lived perennial, often used as annual bedding. Borne on stems 24–36 in. (60–90 cm) tall, the golden flower heads of short petals make an impact. It has produced a number of hybrids with *Anthemis tinctoria*.

The diminutive *Anthemis punctata* ssp. *cupaniana*, only 12 in. (30 cm) tall,

BLUE, WHITE, AND SILVER COMBINATIONS

Blue and white flowers are always an appealing combination in the garden. Being among the bluest of them all, anchusas are natural planting partners. *Anchusa azurea* (z. 4–8) mixes well with the white willowherb, *Epilobium angustifolium* 'Album' (see page 133), and the pale lilac of perennial honesty, *Lunaria rediviva* (see page 126). It creates a cool, refreshing mix with the silver of *Artemisia ludoviciana* 'Valerie Finnis' (see page 51) or the multi-stems of hard-pruned *Eucalyptus gunnii* (z. 8–10).

Columbines (Aquilegia)

Commonly known as columbine or granny's bonnet, aquilegias are familiar perennials from the crowded borders of the cottage garden. The British native *Aquilegia vulgaris* (zone 4–8), an old favorite of English gardens, was joined by species from North America and Europe in the 17th century, and many years of close association have produced many hybrids.

From a rosette of deciduous foliage come long-stalked, medium green or blue-green leaves, each made up of three leaflets. In late spring and early summer, fine stems, up to 40 in. (1 m) high and sometimes branched, carry clusters of teardrop buds opening into bell-shaped flowers, which in some forms have spurs. Single-colored or bicolored blooms of white, pink, red, blue to purple, and even yellow and orange can be found in many combinations.

In the wild, aquilegias are found in damp woodland, marshes, and meadows; in the garden, they thrive in rich, moist, free-draining soil in full sun or partial shade. On heavy, wet soils, plants can be shorter-lived, often failing in winter. On light, well-

Aquilegia vulgaris is still widely cultivated in English gardens, and numerous selections and hybrids have arisen over the years.

drained soils, aquilegias can seed themselves too freely. Removing the flower stems once the blooms have faded prevents seeding and encourages new leaf growth.

Garden aquilegias can produce muddy-colored offspring, and these are worth weeding out. Grow named hybrids in isolation, to prevent dilution of colors in the population.

Aquilegia vulgaris hybrids, (z. 4–8) growing up to 40 in. (1 m) high, with a reliably robust constitution, are the most popular of aquilegias. *Aquilegia vulgaris* 'Nivea' (right) (z. 4–8) has erect stems of olive green foliage carrying stunning, pure white flowers. *Aquilegia vulgaris* var. *stellata* 'Nora Barlow' (z. 4–8) has large, spurless, pom-pom flowers in pale greenish white and red. *Aquilegia vulgaris* Vervaeneana Group (z. 4–8) have yellow-variegated leaves and blue-mauve or pink flowers.

Aquilegia McKana Group, (z. 3–9) up to 28 in. (70 cm) tall, have bright bicolored flowers in shades of blue, yellow, red, and white. These are short-lived perennials, but they will self-seed. Often used as early summer bedding.

Aquilegia alpina (alpine columbine) (z. 5–7) has compact foliage and stems 12 in. (30 cm) tall carrying numerous ink blue flowers, often tipped with white.

OTHER GOOD AQUILEGIAS

Aquilegia canadensis (z. 4–8) Lemon yellow and scarlet flowers and dark fern-like foliage. 24 in. (60 cm) tall.

Aquilegia caerulea (z. 4–8) White and blue flowers on 24 in. (60 cm) stems. Hardy.

Aquilegia flabellata (z. 5–7) Compact habit, at 12 in. (30 cm) high. Blue to purple petals tipped creamy white. Needs a moist, shady site.

Aquilegia longissima (z. 4–8) Yellow flowers on 24 in. (60 cm) stems. Short-lived but readily self-seeds.

is worthy of special note. Its simple, long-lasting flower heads of white petals and golden yellow centers set off the fine silvery foliage. It is good for a dry, sunny wall or alongside paving. (See Good Companions, page 126.)

Cerinthe major 'Purpurascens' (zone 5–9) is a distinctive plant. Its fleshy growth is often a glaucous powdery blue. Branched stems are clad in spoon-shaped leaves, lightly spotted white, and bear unusual purple-mauve, tubular flowers, sometimes tipped in white or yellow, from spring all through summer. The clustered flowers are swathed in gentle folds of purple-flushed bracts that look almost iridescent. (See Good Companions, page 126.)

Found on clifftops, scrub, and waste-land in the Mediterranean, cerinthes will grow in poor, free-draining garden soil. The bluish foliage of *Cerinthe major* 'Purpurascens' is more intense in plants that are carefully neglected. Grown as an annual, a biennial, or a short-lived perennial, it is surprisingly hardy and reliably sets seed that germinate freely in the vicinity of the parent plant. It is an excellent mixer, combining superbly with purple foliage plants such as

Dicentra spectabilis 'Alba'

Cerinthe major 'Purpurascens'

heucheras and adding depth to silver planting. If buying seed, choose a named variety; the offspring will more reliably produce those purple bracts.

Most gardeners know *Dicentra spectabilis* (zone 4–7) through its many years of cultivation as a cottage-garden plant. Usually called bleeding heart, it also has many other common names, including "Dutchman's breeches" and "lady's locket". From late spring into early summer, gently arching, delicate stems, 3 ft. (90 cm) high, present a succession of heart-shaped pink-red buds that, on opening, reveal inner petals of pure white. The foliage is distinctly beautiful: lush, medium green, divided, and almost fernlike, it makes a perfect setting for the flowers.

Most species of dicentra come from moist, wooded habitats in mountainous regions, often growing on stream banks. Cool, moist, but well-drained, slightly alkaline soil brings the best results. The direct sun of midsummer often leads them to become dormant prematurely. Hybrid dicentras are good companions for hostas and ferns and enjoy similar conditions. Their light, fernlike foliage is a useful contrast to heavier subjects and is every bit as important as the flowers. (See also pages 92–93.)

Dicentra spectabilis originates from Siberia, China, and Korea, where the

Dicentra formosa

pure white form *Dicentra spectabilis* 'Alba' is also found. Other species originate from North America, Japan, and the Himalayas. Though less well known, many are excellent perennial plants for the garden.

Dicentra eximia (zone 5–7) is native to eastern United States. The cool blue-green, finely divided leaves grow to 20 in. (50 cm) long; pale to dark pink flowers hang daintily from arching stems, 12 in. (30 cm) high, above the leaves, appearing in late spring and intermittently through to early autumn.

Dicentra formosa (zone 3–8), native to western North America, has deeply divided medium green leaves, blue-green beneath, which form a tight, fern-like clump up to 24 in. (60 cm) high. In

Dicentra 'Bacchanal'

Euphorbia griffithii 'Fireglow'

late spring and early summer, slender stems up to 3 ft. (90 cm) high bear rosy pink buds, which open to pink flowers that fade to white. This species and the white form, *Dicentra formosa alba* (zone 3–8), make excellent ground cover under shrubs and in semi-woodland.

Dicentra macrantha (zone 4–8) is much sought after: In late spring its short stems, 22 in. (55 cm) high, bear creamy yellow flowers, each up to 3 in. (8 cm) long; the foliage is similar to that of *Dicentra spectabilis*. This Chinese beauty is not easy to grow, requiring shelter from the weather and protection from slugs. Moist but well-drained soil with plenty of organic matter is a must.

A SELECTION OF GOOD DICENTRA HYBRIDS

All of the following grow to about 12 in. (30 cm) high.

Dicentra 'Bacchanal' (above) (z. 3–9) Fine green foliage and deep red flowers.

Dicentra 'Langtrees' (see page 106) and *Dicentra* 'Pearl Drops' (z. 4–8) Both have silver-gray leaves and pink-flushed white flowers.

Dicentra 'Luxuriant' (z. 4–8) Fine foliage with showy red flowers.

Dicentra 'Stuart Boothman' (z. 3–9) Blue-gray foliage and dark pink flowers.

Euphorbia griffithii 'Fireglow' (zone 5–7) can be invasive, with vigorous upright shoots growing from spreading underground rhizomes. In late spring its flame-colored stems are topped with bright orange-red flower heads framed by orange-flushed bright green leaves. The color fades as the stems reach 40 in. (1 m) high in midsummer. In fall stems and leaves color orange-red on plants in full sun, before dying down in winter. This is an excellent perennial for moist, fertile soil in sun or shade.

Euphorbia mellifera (zone 9–11) has stout shoots clad in lance-shaped leaves and forms a rounded bush 6 ft. (2 m) high in a sheltered site. A native of Madeira, it is not regarded as being very hardy but it seems to tolerate low temperatures if soil is well drained. In late spring orange-brown flower heads appear; these are honey-scented, hence the Latin name *mellifera*. The flowers are followed by waxy, rounded capsules. (For other euphorbias see page 113.)

Hesperis matronalis (sweet rocket) (zone 6–8) has been in cultivation since early times. It forms a loose rosette or clump of oval, pointed, dark green leaves, from which arise stems 3 ft. (90 cm) tall with loose heads of fragrant, four-petaled, pale lilac to purple flowers.

The scent is of stocks, which are close relatives. The pure white *Hesperis matronalis* var. *albiflora* is a great addition to a blue and white border; it also has a double form, 'Alba Plena'. *Hesperis matronalis* 'Lilacina Flore Pleno' has double lilac flowers.

Sweet rocket prefers full sun or light shade, in rich, moist but free-draining, slightly alkaline soil. Often a short-lived perennial or biennial, it should be cut back hard after flowering. The resulting flush of new growth will help with longevity, provided the plant is not crowded by neighbors or in wet soil. Ideally, leave one plant to set seed: it will produce plentiful seedlings, which can be transplanted. A member of the cabbage family, this plant is prone to attacks by flea beetle, which can be controlled with a suitable insecticide.

Hesperis matronalis

Irises are treasured for their extensive color palette and the exquisite beauty of their complex flowers. Each of these is made up of three outer petals, known as "falls," which may be pendent, reflexed, or spreading, and may have distinctive beards or crests; and three, usually smaller, inner petals known as "standards." These inner petals are often erect, but they may be horizontal or pendent. Many have evolved petal-like flaps to the flowers, and some have ruffled or frilly petal edges. The foliage is often swordlike and upright, but

The architectural forms of *Euphorbia mellifera* and *Acanthus spinosus* combine well with stone and ceramic.

Iris lazica

many irises have distinctive fans of strap-shaped leaves. Most are deciduous, although a few are evergreen.

Irises originate from diverse natural habitats. In the garden they are grouped according to both physical makeup and growing conditions. Some irises like dry, sunny situations. *Iris bucharica* (zone 4–8), for example, thrives in a hot, sunny site with free-draining soil, and in these conditions it is hardy. Unlike other irises, it has short, broadly lance-shaped leaves in sheaths at intervals up rounded stems. In late spring, as the stems reach

8–16 in. (20–40 cm) high, the upper-most leaf axils bear pale to lemon yellow, sometimes white, flowers.

A native of Turkey and the Caucasus, *Iris lazica* (zone 7–8) is similar to the winter-flowering *Iris unguicularis* (see page 179) in its fans of dark evergreen foliage, up to 12 in. (30 cm) high. In late spring, it has stemless, lavender-blue flowers, with partly white falls spotted and veined lavender, each with a yellow stripe. Unlike other Unguicularis irises, it will thrive in light shade and moist soil.

The so-called crested irises prefer moist, humus-rich soil in full sun or part shade; many of these flower in spring. *Iris cristata* (zone 4–8), a native of the eastern United States, forms a fan of fresh, green, lance-shaped leaves. Stemless blooms consist of blue-lilac petals, each with a blotch of white and a yellowish orange crest on each fall. This striking iris grows only 6 in. (15 cm) tall; there is also a white form, *Iris cristata* 'Alba'. Broad, pale green leaves

make up the fan of *Iris milesii* (zone 5–8), and branching stems bear purple-splashed, yellow-crested, lavender-pink flowers. It grows to 3 ft. (90 cm) tall.

Lunaria annua (honesty or silver dollar) (zone 7–9), prized for its silver, papery, moonlike seedpods, is a biennial but can be perennial in the garden, since it seeds so freely. In late spring and early summer, as the stems reach 32 in. (80 cm) high, fine stalks carry clusters of four-petaled purple, sometimes white, flowers; these are followed by the translucent seedpods, which are often dried for winter arrangements. An undemanding plant, it succeeds in many situations, although it is best in rich, moist, free-draining soil, in partial shade or full sun. Thin self-sown seedlings so that each one has space to develop. Purple honesty is an excellent mixer in the spring garden, superb with English bluebells and lovely with the rich silky shades of hardy hybrid rhododendrons.

(continued on page 126)

Bearded irises

The largest selection of irises available comprises the modern cultivars of bearded irises, producing their distinctive flowers in an immense variety of colors from mid-spring into early summer. They are hybrids of often complex origin, although they are frequently incorrectly referred to as hybrids of *Iris germanica*. Growing from large, rounded surface rhizomes, they are classified by the height of the flowering stem. While the larger cultivars produce bold fans of sword-shaped, light green to green-blue foliage, the dwarf varieties often have a more random, dense arrangement of leaves; they also tend to flower earlier in the season than the medium to tall ones.

All need full sun to thrive and ripen the rhizomes. They like good drainage but benefit from moisture in the early part of the year and through the flowering period. They enjoy reasonably fertile soil, with plenty of organic matter added. Bearded irises can be planted as container-grown plants in spring or as bare, semi-dry rhizomes in fall. If planting bare rhizomes, group them in threes, 12 in. (30 cm) apart. They need to be set on or just below the soil surface; if they prove difficult to anchor in position, hold them in place with short canes or wire hoops.

Most varieties need lifting, dividing, and replanting every three to four years, or when the rhizomes become overcrowded (see page 20). Many of the medium to tall bearded irises need support, as a windy, wet day can flatten the stems. Once the flowers fade, the foliage often becomes marked and can be quite unsightly. If leaves start to brown at the tips, they can be trimmed back to two-thirds or half their original height. Although this looks a little unnatural, it is tidier and less obtrusive than the fading foliage.

If bearded irises have one fault, it is their relatively short flowering season. Because the rhizomes need to ripen in the sun, they are not suitable for planting among other perennials that will crowd and shade

In a softly harmonious planting, white *Geranium* clarkei 'Kashmir White' provides light cover at the feet of *Iris* 'Desert Song'.

them. Early tulips can provide interest at the start of the season. *Nerine bowdenii* (zone 9–10) and *Amaryllis belladonna* (zone 8–10) are excellent to bring autumn color to iris beds, particularly at the base of a wall. Low-growing sedums, such as *Sedum acre* (zone 5–8) and *Sedum kamtschaticum* 'Variegatum' (zone 7–10), can be planted to cover the soil between the plants.

GOOD DWARF BEARDED IRISES

'Brannigan' (above) (z. 3–8) Rich royal blue flowers with darker ink blue fall petals.

'Green Spot' (z. 3–8) Greenish white with spotted green fall petals and yellow markings. Very early flowers.

'Mrs. Nate Rudolph' (z. 3–8) Soft lavender-gray flowers flushed with gold.

'Southern Clipper' (z. 3–8) Plentiful fresh light blue flowers with darker spots.

GOOD MEDIUM BEARDED IRISES

'Aunt Martha' (z. 3–8) Frilly, pale yellow petals spotted white.

'Jasper Gem' (z. 3–8) Red-brown flowers flushed gold.

'Rare Edition' (above) (z. 3–8) Eye-catching dark purple flowers with purple-edged white falls.

Dwarf bearded irises (z. 3–8), height 8–16 in. (20–40 cm), start to flower in mid-spring, just before the taller varieties. They will prolong the interest in a bed devoted to bearded irises and combine well with low-growing plants such as helianthemums (z. 5–8), *Helichrysum italicum* (z. 8–10), and *Artemisia schmidtiana* 'Nana' (z. 3–7). Their upright leaves and bold flowers contrast with the fine foliage of most sun-loving plants. **'Laced Lemonade'** (above) is a pretty cultivar with frilly, soft yellow petals and white beards.

Medium bearded irises reach 16–28 in. (40–70 cm) tall. These have all of the dramatic flower quality of the tall varieties but without the problems of support; they are suited to more exposed sites and sit well at the front of a mixed border. They tend to flower earlier than the tall varieties, after the dwarf cultivars. In a border devoted to bearded irises they provide the essential link in the flowering season between tall and dwarf. **'Langport Wren'** (above) (z. 3–8) has magenta-brown flowers, strongly suffused black.

Tall bearded irises, growing to 28–36 in. (70–90 cm), flower from late spring into early summer. These are the classic flag irises of the English garden, producing perhaps the most exotic and flamboyant blooms in the border. They benefit from some additional support when in full flower because of the weight of the blooms. They do not like to be crowded by their neighbors, but associate well with peonies, daylilies (hemerocallis), and geraniums. The flowers of **'Caliente'** (above) (z. 3–8) are deep velvety red-brown, suffused chocolate, with gold beards.

GOOD TALL BEARDED IRISES

'Dancer's Veil' (z. 3–8) Beautiful white ruffled flowers flushed violet.

'Frost and Flame' (z. 3–8) Iced white petals and tangerine-flamed beards.

'Jane Phillips' (z. 3–8) Soft powder blue, ruffled blooms. Vigorous.

'Stepping Out' (z. 3–8) Flowers of palest lavender, edged with purple.

'Top Flight' (z. 3–8) Deep apricot flowers with ruffled petals.

Lunaria annua var. albiflora

Lunaria annua var. *albiflora* 'Alba Variegata' (zone 7–9) has cream-edged leaves and white flowers, while *Lunaria annua* 'Variegata' (zone 7–9) is similar but has pinkish purple flowers. Of those with green foliage, *Lunaria annua* var. *albiflora* (zone 7–9) has white flowers, and *Lunaria annua* 'Munstead Purple' (zone 7–9) is dark red-purple.

Lunaria rediviva (perennial honesty) (zone 4–8) forms a strong clump up to 24–36 in. (60–90 cm) tall, with more refined apple green foliage, the margins gently toothed. The pale lilac flowers, carried loosely, are pleasantly fragrant and followed by the distinctive seed-pods, which are narrower than those of biennial honesty. Left to itself, perennial honesty will self-seed and become semi-naturalized. It is superb for providing tall ground cover in semi-shade and is most attractive in a woodland setting. (See Good Companions, below).

Mimulus (monkey flower or musk) is native to the Americas, South Africa, Asia, and Australia. Some of the species that are native to the United States, including **Mimulus cardinalis** (zone 6–9), with showy, scarlet flowers and **Mimulus aurantiacus** (zone 7–10), with bright orange blooms, will freely naturalize in the right conditions.

Mimulus **Highland hybrids** (zone 7–10) are garden cultivars with lush growth and many bright flowers, their bold, simple colors rivaling those of the annual bedding plants. From late spring into early summer, 8 in. (20 cm) stems carry numerous trumpet-shaped flowers of orange ('**Highland Orange**'), pink ('**Highland Pink**'), rose-pink ('**Highland Pink Rose**'), red ('**Highland Red**') or yellow ('**Highland Yellow**'). Mimuluses thrive in moist, well-drained soil in full sun or light shade. By midsummer supplementary feeding may be required.

Other colorful cultivars are hybrids between the species *Mimulus guttatus* (zone 7–10) and *Mimulus luteus* (zone 5–8). The early-flowering **Magic** and **Mystic** series (zone 7–10) offer a wide range of shades, including pastels.

Ranunculus aconitifolius

Ranunculus is a wonderful genus that includes many varied and garden-worthy plants; however, the notorious perennial weed *Ranunculus repens* (creeping buttercup) (zone 3–9) is the one that most gardeners will know. Native to temperate regions, ranunculus grow in a variety of conditions. Rich, moist soil is a basic requirement, although some dislike over-wet soil, especially in winter. Full to light shade is preferred, but some tolerate full sun.

Ranunculus aconitifolius (zone 5–8), commonly known as bachelor's buttons, produces palmate, glossy, dark green leaves on branched stems of up to 24 in. (60 cm). It is a favorite for its many white flowers, opening from red-tinged buds in late spring to early summer.

GOOD COMPANIONS

Perennial honesty, *Lunaria rediviva* (1) (z. 4–8), is good in combination with snowdrops such as *Galanthus nivalis* (2) (z. 4–8) as the emerging honesty covers the fading foliage of the snowdrop.

The fine silver foliage of *Anthemis punctata* ssp. *cupaniana* (3) (z. 3–9) complements the blue-green leaves of *Cerinthe major* 'Purpurascens' (4) (z. 5–9). Both enjoy poor, well-drained soil.

Solomon's seals (Polygonatum)

Commonly known as Solomon's seal, polygonatums are native to woodlands of North America, Europe, Asia, and Siberia. These are appealing garden plants, most with arching, leafy stems from which hang dainty, usually white, tubular flowers in late spring. Their natural elegance lends them both to structured contemporary plantings and to seminaturalistic settings. Some species are found on chalk as well as acid soils, often in moist but well-drained places, although they may tolerate drier sites if shaded; they are ideal in a light woodland planting. Their potential to thrive in most gardens is evident: They will share a shady corner with pulmonarias, primulas, *Arum italicum*, hellebores, ferns, and evergreen grasses such as *Carex pendula*. Late summer brings an early turn toward winter dormancy for Solomon's seal; by autumn, leaves and stems will become a pleasant shade of creamy yellow.

Polygonatum × hybridum enjoying a shady corner.

Several species are commonly cultivated, including *Polygonatum multiflorum*, *Polygonatum odoratum*, and *Polygonatum × hybridum*—these are so alike that few gardeners are aware of which one they grow.

Polygonatum odoratum (z. 4–7) has arching stems, 34in. (85cm) high, of oval olive green leaves, with a charming cascade of white teardrop buds from the upper leaf axils. The white tubular flowers are lightly tipped with green, and are followed by rounded black fruit. **'Flore Pleno'** has double flowers strongly marked in green. *Polygonatum odoratum* var. *pluriflorum* **'Variegatum'** has attractive cream-edged foliage.

Polygonatum biflorum (z. 4–7) is an impressive architectural plant, commonly growing to about 40 in. (1 m) tall, although many specimens reach double that height. It is similar to other Solomon's seals, but the leaf undersides are finely hairy and veined. The flowers are greenish white and are borne singly or in clusters of two to four.

Polygonatum stewartianum (z. 5–8) is distinctly different from other Solomon's seals: upright, rounded, boxy stems of medium green flecked with reddish purple are clad in tiers of lance-shaped foliage. Above each tier appear clusters of up to four bell-shaped, pale creamy pink flowers with faint red flecks. Height 8–36 in. (20–90 cm).

Polygonatum × hybridum **'Striatum'** Has medium green leaves with creamy white stripes and green-tipped white flowers. Height 3 ft. (90 cm). Grows much more slowly than most.

Ranunculus aconitifolius 'Flore Pleno' (zone 5–8) is the double form, made up of layered, pure white petals.

The meadow buttercup, *Ranunculus acris* (zone 4–7), is considered a weed by some gardeners, but it is certainly worthy of a place in a wildflower meadow. *Ranunculus acris* 'Flore Pleno', 16–32 in. (40–80 cm) high, is the usual form cultivated, producing double, dark yellow flowers between late spring and early summer. Both will do well in full sun, but dislike wet soil.

Ranunculus constantinopolitanus (zone 6–8) forms a tidy clump of foliage. Stems 8 in. (20 cm) high are clad with attractive medium green, deeply divided leaves; bright yellow, cuplike flowers appear from mid-spring to midsummer. The double form *Ranunculus constantinopolitanus* 'Plenus' bears blooms with layers of bright yellow petals; the central ones are lime green.

Ranunculus ficaria (zone 4–7), the lesser celandine, 2 in. (5 cm) tall, with rounded, glossy leaves and bright yellow flowers in mid-spring, is an invasive weed. Don't be fooled by the fact that it quickly goes dormant after flowering; dig it out before it dies back. However, the cultivar 'Brazen Hussy' is a well-behaved plant, with glossy, chocolate brown foliage that sets off the yellow flowers (see Good Companions, below right).

Tiarella 'Spring Symphony'

Smilacina racemosa (zone 3–8) flowers from mid- to late spring and is an impressive sight when in full bloom. The plant forms a mass of unbranched stems, 32 in. (80 cm) tall, carrying oval, pointed leaves, their veins prominent on the fresh medium green of the new growth. At the top of each stem, a conical head of short, branched stalks is crowded with small, star-shaped, white to cream, scented flowers. Often the flowers are succeeded by bright red berries, which stand out against the creamy yellow autumn foliage.

In the wild, smilacinas can be found growing in rich, moist, well-drained soil, enjoying the partial or full shade of light woodland, in parts of Asia and in North and Central America. In cooler climates full sun will be tolerated. They are not suited to alkaline soil, which always

results in poor growth. Many plants enjoying the same conditions work well with smilacinas, especially neighbors of striking form such as rodgersias, ligularias, rheums, or evergreen ferns.

Smyrnium perfoliatum (commonly called perfoliate Alexanders) (zone 6–10) is a slow-growing biennial, but seeds itself readily, especially on light soils, and combines perfectly with perennials. Its lime green spring flowers and foliage offer a lighter alternative to euphorbias and a taller, more definite form than that of alchemilla. It grows to 24 in. (60 cm) tall. (See page 118.)

Tiarellas are commonly known as foam flower, because of the frothy flowers that rise above the low green foliage. Happy in a range of soils, as long as the ground is moist and free draining, they grow best in shade, although they do perform adequately, if slowly, in full sun. They combine well with hostas, bergenias, and pulmonarias and with evergreen grasses and ferns.

Tiarella 'Spring Symphony' (zone 4–9) forms a tight, semi-evergreen clump about 16 in. (40 cm) high. The deeply divided, maple-like leaves are medium green with an attractive red-brown stripe, bronzing in winter. Dark red flower spikes push through the foliage, forming candle-like heads of numerous starry white flowers, which open from pink buds in early spring right through to autumn.

Smilacina racemosa

Tiarella cordifolia

mildew, but this is easily controlled with a commercial fungicide.

Growing as thick ground cover, the stems of *Veronica peduncularis* 'Georgia Blue' (zone 4–8) are clad in rounded, toothed, glossy, medium green leaves, tinged purple with age. From early spring until early summer, a mass of small, saucer-shaped sapphire flowers covers the 4 in. (10 cm) stems.

The variety *Veronica austriaca* ssp. *teucrium* 'Knallblau' (zone 4–7) produces plentiful blue spikes above lush gray-green foliage, from late spring. Growing only 10 in. (25 cm) tall, it is perfect for a patio container or for the edge of a border. The lovely *Veronica austriaca* ssp. *teucrium* 'Crater Lake Blue' (zone 4–7) is taller, reaching 18 in. (45 cm), with equally arresting flowers.

Veronica gentianoides (zone 4–7) is an old garden favorite. Tight winter rosettes develop thick, rounded, dark green leaves, slowly forming a mat. In late spring to early summer, these produce stems 16 in. (40 cm) tall, with a succession of pale to medium blue flowers. *Veronica gentianoides* 'Alba' is white, usually with a hint of blue.

Veronica spicata (zone 5–8) is tidy and compact in habit. Stems up to

Veronica gentianoides

24 in. (60 cm) tall bear lance-shaped, softly hairy leaves and generous spikes of small, bright blue flowers to the end of summer. The cultivars tend to be smaller plants, only about 12 in. (30 cm) high: 'Heidekind' has green-gray foliage and raspberry pink flowers; 'Red Fox' is deep pink. *Veronica spicata* ssp. *incana* is outstanding, with silver-gray foliage and silver-white stems carrying deep blue flowers.

Late spring is a time when the pool side and bog garden are at their best: irises and primulas are joined by a host of perennials with bright flowers and lush foliage (see pages 74–79).

Tiarella cordifolia (zone 3–7) produces more rounded, heart-shaped leaves of a lighter green, each with three to five distinct points and a jagged margin (see Good Companions, below right), while those of *Tiarella trifoliata* (zone 4–7) are palmate and medium green, each with three distinct points. *Tiarella wherryi* (zone 5–9) is a parent of many of the new hybrids. Its rounded leaves have three sharp points and are light green flushed to varying degrees with reddish maroon. The airy heads of white flowers often show a hint of pink. All three species range in height from 8–20 in. (20 to 50 cm).

Tiarella 'Iron Butterfly' (zone 4–9) is one of many new selections; it has large, deeply divided medium green leaves, with a striking dark red-black stripe on each segment, and flowers similar to those of *Tiarella* 'Spring Symphony' (zone 4–9). *Tiarella* 'Jeepers Creepers' (zone 4–9) differs in its spreading habit, forming a dense carpet of green with red-black veining. It is an attractive ground-cover plant, useful in dappled shade. Both grow 12 in. (30 cm) high.

Species of *Veronica* (speedwell) are widespread throughout Europe. Some colonize the margins of rivers and streams; others are found in moist meadows, light woodland, and sunny grassland and on rocky hillsides. In the garden they are easy to grow in sun or in partial shade. Some are prone to

GOOD COMPANIONS

Tiarella cordifolia (1) (z. 3–7) and *Vinca minor* 'Argenteovariegata' (2) (z. 5–8) make a successful partnership for ground cover in shade.

Ranunculus ficaria 'Brazen Hussy' (3) (z. 4–7) and the winter aconite, *Eranthis hyemalis* (4) (z. 3–8); the ranunculus flowers after the aconite, extending the season of interest.

Early summer

As the borders start to billow in early summer, herbaceous perennials come to the fore. This is the season for their variety show; there is no holding back, just sheer floribundance. Stately spikes of delphiniums and lupines rise above mounds of geraniums and lady's mantle. The exotic blooms of poppies, peonies, and daylilies punctuate the planting. Foliage plays second fiddle now, a supporting role to the mass of flowers and riot of color.

Cultivars of *Alcea rosea* (hollyhock) are at their best growing from the dry soil at the base of a sunny wall.

Acanthus (bear's breeches) are truly architectural perennials with striking foliage and statuesque flower spikes, borne from late spring into midsummer. A number of species are found in dry, rocky areas in the Mediterranean region and so enjoy free-draining, fertile soil; winter wet is not appreciated. Although acanthuses will grow in partial shade, full sun results in better flowering. Watering during periods of drought in summer will help maintain the quality of the foliage. *Acanthus spinosus* (zone 5–8) is the most impressive species. The dark green, thistlelike leaves can be up to 40 in. (1 m) long on a mature plant. Its spires of hooded flowers reach skyward, often attaining 5 ft. (1.5 m). The blooms are produced in succession: pure white, tubular, two-lipped flowers, each with a pink-purple hoodlike bract. It is best planted as an individual specimen, against a south-facing wall, alongside a path, or on the edge of a terrace; give it space to be admired.

Acanthus mollis (zone 8–9) equals the height of *Acanthus spinosus*, but has much broader, less thistlelike leaves, and its white flowers with purple-shaded bracts appear much later in summer. *Acanthus* 'Summer Beauty' (zone 6–9), a garden hybrid producing 4 ft. (1.2 m) spires of white

130

Acanthus spinosus

Achillea filipendulina 'Gold Plate'

Achillea 'Summerwine'

flowers with purple bracts, has proved very popular in recent years. Its impressive, dark, glossy leaves, 40 in. (1 m) long, are similar to those of *Acanthus mollis* but more deeply cut. *Acanthus dioscoridis* (zone 6–9) is less common but equally garden worthy. Reaching no more than 16 in. (40 cm) high, its spikes of medium pink flowers and green bracts appear above variable foliage. *Acanthus hungaricus* (zone 5–9) produces dark green, spineless leaves 24–36 in. (60–90 cm) long, and towering spires up to 40 in. (1 m) high, clad in white or pale pink flowers with purple-shaded green bracts.

Achilleas (yarrow) add color and different flower form to any sunny border. Each platelike head is made up of many tiny, daisylike flowers in various shades: creamy white through pinks, spicy oranges and reds, pure white, and golden yellow. Stiff stems carry the flowers above fine fernlike, often aromatic foliage in gray, silver, or green.

Achilleas are hardy plants that thrive in many situations. Some are found wild in rough grassland and meadows, and on roadside verges and wasteland. Shorter species, forming matlike growth, grow in mountainous regions, the harsh conditions resulting in silver-gray foliage. In the garden, achilleas grow on most well-drained soils; full sun is preferred, but partial shade is acceptable. Usually reaching a height of 28–36 in. (70–90 cm), many showier achilleas need support. All have a long flowering period, from early summer right to early fall. When the blooms are past their best, cut the stems back to the base, water thoroughly, and apply a light dressing of fertilizer; the plants should flower again within a few weeks.

OTHER ACHILLEAS WITH GOOD COLOR

Achillea clypeolata (z. 4–8) Exquisite feathery silver foliage, and small heads of golden yellow flowers, less showy than most, on stems 20 in. (50 cm) tall.

Achillea 'Fanal' (z. 3–9) Gray-green foliage and vibrant heads of bright red, yellow-eyed flowers.

Achillea millefolium (z. 2–9) cultivars are all around 24 in. (60 cm) high, with fine, feathery, dark green leaves. 'Cerise Queen' has bright magenta-pink flowers with white centers. 'Lilac Beauty' has divine pale lilac flowers. 'Paprika' has pretty pink and cherry red flowers with yellow centers.

Achillea sibirica var. *camschatica* 'Love Parade' (z. 3–9) Shiny, dark green, finely toothed foliage and tightly packed heads of soft pink flowers.

Achillea 'Walther Funcke' (z. 3–8) Captivating orange-red flowers in broad, flat heads.

PLANTING PARTNERS

Achilleas look wonderful planted randomly among ornamental grasses such as *Stipa calamagrostis* (z. 4–8). The simple upright foliage of the grass contrasts with the solid, platelike achillea flowers, which seem to float among the stipa's moving leaves.

Achillea filipendulina (zone 2–9) is the tallest of the species, reaching over 40 in. (1 m) high. The most popular cultivar is 'Gold Plate', with large golden flower heads 6 in. (15 cm) across. 'Cloth of Gold' is similar, and *Achillea* 'Moonshine' (zone 2–9) offers a soft pale yellow alternative. All are excellent companions for *Salvia nemorosa* (see page 166). *Achillea* 'Coronation Gold' (zone 3–9), often reliably evergreen, has silver-gray foliage and flowers of rich golden yellow. *Achillea* 'Salmon Beauty' (zone 4–8) has fine, feathered, dark green foliage and salmon pink flower heads, while *Achillea* 'Summerwine' (zone 4–8) is a deep cherry red that goes on flowering well into autumn. *Achillea* 'Terracotta' (zone 3–8) is a well-named favorite, producing delightful dusky orange flowers that turn yellow with age.

Achillea ptarmica (sneezewort) (zone 2–9) is very different, with narrow, dark green leaves and branched stems bearing buttonlike, gray-white flowers; 'Boule de Neige' is pure white, flowering at 20 in. (50 cm).

Aconitums (zone 3–7), commonly known as aconite, monkshood, and wolfsbane, are popular garden plants: Their distinctive foliage, bold, upright form and striking flowers over a long period all guarantee them a place in any border. Most do especially well in moist soil in partial shade. (See page 46.)

Like all plants in the mallow family, alceas (hollyhock) (zone 7–9), thrive in full sun. For well over 300 years the patient gardener has propped and tied up these ungainly beauties, overlooking the rust-spotted, insect-nibbled foliage for the sake of the glorious summer flowers. Hollyhocks do best in rather dry, well-drained conditions, thriving near the coast and alongside sunny walls.

The most garden-worthy hollyhocks are selections of *Alcea rosea*. Usually ranging in height from 5–8 ft (1.5 to 2.5 m), their towering stems are clothed in rounded, light green leaves, each with three to seven shallow lobes. Lightly cupped, funnel-shaped flowers in shades of yellow, white, pink, or purple open in succession from halfway up the stem. The double-flowered forms, such as the mixed *Alcea* 'Chater's Double', have layer upon layer of ruffled petals,

Alcea rosea 'Nigra'

Alcea rugosa

resembling the blooms of a peony. *Alcea rosea* 'Majorette' has a bushy habit, with stems about 40 in. (1 m) tall, useful for smaller gardens; the flowers are semidouble in pastel colors. Few flowers are as dark as those of *Alcea rosea* 'Nigra': black at first glance, they have a dark red, velvet sheen. *Alcea rugosa* is a lovely species, with spikes over 6 ft. (2 m) tall. The flowers are clear pale yellow, the leaves lobed and less heavy than those of *Alcea rosea*. Where it is happy, it is a good self-seeder.

Often confused with *Alcea*, the various forms of *Althaea* come close in height, although their stems are usually numerous and much finer. The flowers,

borne throughout summer, are smaller and carried on short stalks on almost the entire length of the stems. Given some support, althaeas will prove their worth in any herbaceous border. *Althaea armeniaca* (zone 3–10) has deep rose-pink flowers, a color also found in *Althaea cannabina* (zone 4–10), along with pleasant shades of lilac-pink.

Baptisias (false indigo) are natives of the eastern and southern United States, where they grow in woodland and grassy scrub on dry, sandy, acid soils. In the garden they are drought-tolerant, hardy plants enjoying free-draining soil and a sunny aspect. Gray-green stems, up to 5 ft. (1.5 m) high, are clad in leaves made up of three oval leaflets, blue-green maturing to soft green. Airy spikes of pealike flowers in early summer are followed by large, often inflated seedpods. Early frosts blacken the stems and foliage, which, along with the dark pods, are useful for floral decoration. *Baptisia australis* (zone 4–8) is the most widely grown. Its upright stems terminate in a 20 in. (50 cm) spike of rich blue flowers (see Good Companions, right). *Baptisia alba* (zone 5–8) is often half the height and has narrower leaflets; its stunning

Baptisia australis

HOLLYHOCK RUST

Hollyhocks are notorious for their susceptibility to rust, a fungal disease that appears as reddish brown spots all over the foliage. A severe infestation can drastically affect performance. To avoid this problem, hollyhocks are often treated as annuals or biennials: plants are destroyed after flowering to prevent the fungus from overwintering. New stock is planted in spring to flower the same summer. Rust is less of a problem in coastal areas.

white flowers sometimes have delicate purple markings on the upper petals. *Baptisia alba* var. *macrophylla* (zone 5–8) has broader foliage and white flower spikes up to 24 in. (60 cm) high. *Baptisia* 'Purple Smoke' (zone 4–9) is a selection from hybrid seedlings found in the North Carolina Botanical Gardens. Dark stems carry dusky purple flowers in spikes up to 24 in. (60 cm) tall.

Campanulas (bellflower) perform throughout the garden, providing tight, low-growing clumps, spreading, trailing mats, and include some of our favorite border perennials. Some species and varieties flower all summer long. Early summer sees some of the best border campanulas at their peak. (See page 40.)

The European annual cornflower, *Centaurea cyanus* (zone 7–9), once commonly grew in cornfields, where it became a persistent weed. Its slender growth topped in dark blue flowers was a real spectacle in early summer. The cornflower is a popular garden flower today, and there are a number of equally lovely perennial species. *Centaurea hypoleuca* (zone 4–7) forms a spreading clump of broad, deeply divided, pale green leaves, gray-white beneath. Borne on 24 in. (60 cm) stems, the early summer flowers are light to deep pink, each pincushion-like center surrounded by a feathery ruff. Needing full sun and moderately fertile, free-draining soil, it mixes well with lavender and rosemary. *Centaurea hypoleuca* 'John Coutts' is a rich, deep rose-pink and flowers intermittently until early fall; it was a favorite of the British garden designer, Graham Stuart Thomas, who likened the seed heads to "silvery daisies."

Long cultivated in cottage gardens, *Centaurea montana* (zone 4–8) is a very easy perennial to grow. It forms a mass of medium green foliage and rather ungainly stems up to 18 in. (45 cm) high. These bear one or more large, inky blue cornflower heads, more

Centaurea hypoleuca 'John Coutts'

Centaurea montana

Cephalaria gigantea

spidery than most, with centers of pinkish purple. (See Good Companions, below.) The flowers reach their peak in early summer; if plants are then cut back hard, new foliage appears, along with occasional later flowers. The white form, *Centaurea montana* 'Alba', looks wonderful with the vibrant deep blue flowers of *Anchusa azurea*. *Centaurea montana* 'Carnea' is a pink-flowered form, while 'Parham' boasts large heads of deep lavender-blue, and those of 'Violetta' are a striking violet-blue.

Cephalaria gigantea (zone 3–7) is a surprising perennial, a truly statuesque plant, which can reach heights of up to 8 ft. (2.5 m). It is often mistaken for a scabious, to which it is closely related.

From early to midsummer, its branched stems hold numerous primrose yellow flower heads, which make marvelous partners for blue delphiniums. It likes rich soil with adequate moisture and will grow either in sun or in partial shade.

GOOD COMPANIONS

Centaurea montana (1) (z. 4–8) and *Papaver orientale* 'Allegro' (2) (z. 3–8) create the classic combination of cornflowers and poppies in the perennial border.

The indigo spires of *Baptisia australis* (3) (z. 4–8) mix well with the graceful, pure white spikes of *Epilobium angustifolium* 'Album' (4) (z. 2–9). Both enjoy well-drained soil in full sun.

Delphiniums

The garden scene has its leading players, but few hold center stage with such splendor as the delphiniums. Their impressive flowers and stunning colors make them the most popular perennials: the very essence of the summer garden.

Few genera claim such worldwide distribution; only the polar regions and Australia lack native species. Many have enchanting, simple flowers resembling a pointed hat or bonnet, occasionally hooded and often spurred. From these, numerous hybrids have evolved to exuberant beauty and proportions.

There are annual and biennial types, but it is the perennials that dominate the summer border. They produce deciduous clumps of divided, pale to dark green leaves, from which emerge tall spikes or spires in early summer and often again in early fall. These carry blooms of numerous shades, both subtle and vibrant, not only much-loved blues but lilacs, purples, pinks, and whites. Most species and hybrids are usually considered short-lived; however, attention to their needs will bring years of loyal service, especially from *Delphinium elatum* hybrids (zone 4–7).

Delphiniums need some space. If they are crowded or shaded by vigorous neighbors, the resulting dampness and poor light can have disastrous effects. They also need shelter from strong winds. Plant them in a fertile, well-drained soil in full sun.

Twiggy or metal grow-through supports should be put into position before new growth exceeds 12 in. (30 cm), with the large-flowered hybrids needing a stout cane to match their ultimate height. For the most impressive blooms, thin out the young shoots in spring, to two or three shoots on young plants and five to seven shoots on mature clumps. The unwanted shoots should be removed at the base with a sharp knife and can be used as cuttings. Routine feeding throughout the growing season with a high-potash liquid fertilizer reaps dividends. Once the blooms have

Statuesque spires of blue delphiniums are set against a yew hedge, with the dramatic silver foliage of the cardoon, *Cynara cardunculus*, in front.

faded, the spikes should be cut back hard to encourage plants to produce a second flush of flowers.

In the twentieth century, plant breeders including Vetterly, Reinelt, Samuelson, and Barber all contributed new forms that are still popular today. In England, the breeding of delphinium hybrids was started in earnest by Somerset nurseries Kelway of Langport, in 1875, and Blackmore and Langdon in 1901.

Most commonly available delphiniums fall into one of three groups: the Elatum group (zone 4–7), with stately upright spikes; the similar but shorter Pacific hybrids (zone 4–7); and the Belladonna hybrids (zone 3–8), with looser, branched spikes. (See also page 41.)

Delphinium hybrids of the Elatum group (z. 4–7) produce some of the showiest flowering spikes, usually 5–6 ft. (1.5–2 m) tall, tightly packed with large blooms. In the best varieties these are semidouble and consist of large outer petals and an inner smaller cluster, often in a contrasting color. *Delphinium* 'Lord Butler' (above) is shorter than most, at 40 in. (1 m), with white-centered sky blue flowers.

OTHER GOOD ELATUM GROUP DELPHINIUMS

Delphinium 'Cassius' (z. 4–8) Rich blue flowers overlaid with pinkish purple, with golden brown centers.

Delphinium 'Faust' (z. 4–8) Statuesque spikes of aquamarine-purple.

Delphinium 'Fenella' (z. 4–8) An old variety, still held in high esteem; the flowers are true deep blue with black centers.

Delphinium 'Gillian Dallas' (z. 4–8) Lavender-blue flowers with gently frilled edges and white eyes.

Delphinium 'Langdon's Royal Flush' (z. 4–8) A shorter hybrid, at 40 in. (1 m) tall. Rich pink flowers with creamy white centers.

Delphinium 'Moonbeam' (z. 4–8) One of the finest pure whites.

Delphinium nudicaule (z. 8–9), a short-lived perennial usually grown as an annual, has flowers in vibrant scarlet-red, orange-red, or yellow. Grows only 24 in. (60 cm) high, with finely divided foliage.

Delphinium 'Völkerfrieden' (z. 4–8), a Belladonna Group hybrid, has graceful flowers of brilliant gentian blue. Mixing well with fellow perennials, Belladonna delphiniums rarely exceed 4 ft. (1.2 m) tall, with finely cut foliage and slender, branched spikes bearing loosely arranged, small, long-spurred, bonnetlike flowers.

OTHER GOOD BELLADONNA GROUP DELPHINIUMS

'Atlantis' Vivid gentian blue with dark eyes; a good cut flower.

'Casa Blanca' Pure white flowers.

'Cliveden Beauty' Flowers in a lovely, refreshing sky blue.

Delphinium grandiflorum 'Blue Butterfly' (z. 4–7) is a short-lived perennial often grown as an annual. It has bright turquoise-sapphire flowers with black eyes, borne on slender, branched stems only 24 in. (60 cm) high, with finely divided foliage. In well-drained soil in full sun, it can survive for a few years.

Delphinium Pacific hybrids (z. 4–7) are often available from garden centers. They have semidouble flowers and are similar to those of the Elatum group but are shorter, at only 4 ft. (1.2 m), and not as long-lived. However, they are easily replaced on a regular basis; they grow quickly and, being raised from seed, are not expensive.

OTHER GOOD SEED-RAISED DELPHINIUMS

Black Knight Group (z. 4–7)

Blue Bird Group (z. 4–7)

Cameliard Group (z. 4–7)

Guinevere Group (z. 4–7)

King Arthur Group (z. 4–7)

Summer Skies Group (z. 4–7)

Cirsium rivulare 'Atropurpureum'

Dianthus 'Gran's Favorite'

Dianthus 'Widecombe Fair'

Cirsiums have become firm favorites in recent years for their tall stems of thistlelike flowers. They like a sunny position on moist, well-drained soil, where they will flower intermittently from early summer to early fall. *Cirsium rivulare* 'Atropurpureum' (zone 5–8) is the most desirable, with rosettes of dark green thistle foliage and 40 in. (1 m) stems carrying very dark red pincushion flowers. It combines well with pinks, purples, and blues, and its light see-through habit makes it valuable for use at the front of the border.

A long history of travel and trade between Europe, Asia, and South Africa has seen the evolution of *Dianthus* as some of the best-loved flowers for the garden and for cutting. From mountain slopes and meadows, numerous species have been collected and hybridized to deliver the dazzling beauties we know as carnations and pinks. From the tight, mounded, needlelike growth of alpine varieties to the looser, longer, lance-shaped leaves of border perennials, they all thrive in well-drained, alkaline soil with plenty of sun.

Carnations are not popular border plants, but they are good in the cutting garden. They are taller than pinks, with stems 24–36 in. (60–90 cm) high, each carrying up to six large double flowers. By midsummer, an established plant produces ample blooms for cutting. The creamy yellow petals of *Dianthus*

'Bookham Fancy' (zone 4–9) are solidly margined in royal red. 'Bookham Perfume' (zone 4–9) is crimson and very fragrant. 'Eva Humphries' (zone 4–9) has white flowers edged purple.

Pinks offer a neater, more compact alternative, flowering at 10–18 in. (25–45 cm) tall. Early summer sees the first blooms, ideal along a path, where their scent can easily be enjoyed. Most modern cultivars repeat flower. Lovely *Dianthus* 'Doris' (zone 3–9) is pale salmon pink. 'Bovey Belle' (zone 4–9) has deep pink flowers and silver-blue foliage. 'Joy' (zone 3–9) is vivid salmon red. 'Gran's Favourite' (zone 3–9) is fragrant, with pale pink flowers laced and centered with red. All these are double; 'Widecombe Fair' (zone 5–9) is semidouble, blush pink, and fragrant. (See also pages 71 and 81.)

Dianthus barbatus (sweet William) (zone 3–8) is a hardy, short-lived

PINKS FOR FOLIAGE

Although grown mainly for their fragrant, long-lasting flowers, garden pinks are extremely valuable for their blue-gray foliage. Evergreen and healthy, the fine, pointed leaves look particularly attractive in winter and make textural mounds or mats at the border's edge. The dwarf alpine varieties, such as *Dianthus* 'Pike's Pink' (z. 5–9), are also useful in winter patio containers.

perennial that is traditionally grown as a biennial for bedding. Stems 28 in. (70 cm) high bear clusters of small single, sweetly aromatic flowers. A true cottage-garden plant, it has richly colored blooms that impart a period character to any planting scheme. They are usually a mix of shades of pink and red to purple, sometimes bicolored, with contrasting banding or paler, suffused eyes; the darker shades are increasingly in demand. *Dianthus barbatus* Nigrescens Group (zone 4–8) and the almost black *Dianthus barbatus* 'Sooty' (zone 4–9) are wonderful plants for rich, dark color schemes.

Dianthus carthusianorum (zone 5–9) is not well known but deserves to be more widely used. Growing to 12 in. (30 cm) high, with well-branched stems and fine gray-green leaves, it produces small double, strong pink flowers all summer (see Good Companions, page 142). The flowers are borne in clusters, like those of sweet William but looser, and the individual blooms are like those of a miniature border pink. It is a good choice in a sunny border with roses.

Digitalis, the foxgloves (zone 4–8), are useful both for naturalizing and in the garden border. Their versatility enables them to fit into both traditional borders and more naturalistic plantings. They provide both subtle color and elegant spikes in the early summer garden. (See pages 47 and 56–57.)

The herbaceous **geraniums** are adept at stitching together the patchwork of the summer border. These accommodating plants perform well over a long period and most types are robust. The leaves vary in size, and some are very aromatic. Most are deciduous; some, like *Geranium cinereum*, are evergreen. (See also pages 47–48 and 67.)

Geranium × *cantabrigiense* (zone 5–7) has inherited the dwarf habit and evergreen foliage of *Geranium dalmaticum* and the strongly aromatic

Geranium cinereum 'Ballerina'

foliage of *Geranium macrorrhizum* (see page 62). From early into midsummer, pale pink or white flowers appear on spreading stems, only 12 in. (30 cm) tall.

Geranium cinereum (zone 5–7) is a star, forming an evergreen rosette of fine gray-green foliage topped with upward-facing, white to pink flowers in early to midsummer. Its slowly spreading growth, 6 in. (15 cm) high, makes it ideal for the edge of a raised border or a container. The cultivar **'Ballerina'** has medium pink flowers finely patterned with threadlike, pinkish red veins, leading to dark eyes. **'Purple Pillow'** has gorgeous vibrant purple blooms.

Geranium subcaulescens (zone 5–7) is of similar height, but more vigorous, and from late spring into early summer boasts dazzling magenta-pink flowers, enhanced by dark eyes.

All these are neat, compact plants, ideal on scree or in rock gardens or for

Geranium cinereum 'Purple Pillow'

the edges of paths. The more vigorous and sprawling geraniums are superb border perennials, mixing readily with other plants. *Geranium clarkei* (zone 5–7) reaches 20 in. (50 cm) high and spreads freely through the border, bearing large blooms in succession from early to late summer. Its native origin is recognized in the named selections **'Kashmir Pink'**, **'Kashmir Purple'**, and **'Kashmir White'**.

The upward-facing, funnel-shaped flowers of *Geranium endressii* (zone 4–7) are pale pink, darkening with age as the petals recurve. They appear from early summer into fall, among evergreen foliage on 18 in. (45 cm) stems.

One of only a few herbaceous perennials that provide autumn leaf color, *Geranium himalayense* (zone 4–7) forms a spreading mat of foliage, 18 in. (45 cm) high, which gives way to loose clusters of lilac-blue to deep blue,

Geranium clarkei 'Kashmir White'

saucer-shaped flowers in early summer. **'Gravetye'** boasts larger blue flowers; it is a parent of *Geranium* 'Johnson's Blue' (zone 4–8), the popular blue geranium (see page 48 and Good Companions, page 149). **'Plenum'** (often available as 'Birch Double') has double purple-pink flowers flushed with blue, which gives a pearly finish. It forms a compact, spreading clump, 20 in. (50 cm) high.

Geums, like the closely related potentillas (see page 82), are not noted for the size of their blooms; however, they compensate with strength and vibrancy of color. In shades of yellow, orange, and red, the usually saucer-shaped flowers appear from late spring into summer. They are borne on slender stems above either a prostrate rosette or a more upright clump of softly hairy medium green leaves, with rounded, toothed leaflets. Geums are easy to grow in full sun in fertile, well-drained soil, although *Geum rivale* (zone 3–7) prefers richer, moister conditions.

Geum **'Mrs. J. Bradshaw'** (zone 4–7), 18 in. (45 cm) tall, is perhaps the most striking, with scarlet-orange flowers of glowing intensity, brilliant with early summer blues and purples such as *Iris sibirica* 'Tropic Night' (zone 4–8). *Geum coccineum* (zone 5–8) grows taller, to 24 in. (60 cm), with flowers of rich orange-red; **'Cooky'** is apricot-orange. *Geum* **'Lady Stratheden'**

Geum coccineum 'Cooky'

SEASONS: EARLY SUMMER

137

Daylilies (Hemerocallis)

One of the major attractions in the perennial or mixed border, hemerocallis are known as daylilies because each flower supposedly lasts one day (around ten hours). Established plants produce a succession of blooms over a few weeks, with many performing repeatedly from late spring to late summer.

Native to China, Korea, and Japan, daylilies are found growing on the forest edge, on hillsides, in rich river valleys, and in meadows. They are very hardy perennials, which may be deciduous, semi-evergreen, or evergreen. The grasslike, medium to dark green foliage is tough and resilient, forming dense clumps that make effective ground cover. In gardens, daylilies prefer moist, free-draining conditions, but many will succeed on wet sites and by water. All will grow in partial shade, but they perform best in sun. In cooler areas, they are best planted where the sun can bake them, perhaps against a sheltered wall. The smaller-flowered varieties, such as *Hemerocallis lilioasphodelus* (zone 4–8), can be naturalized in unmown grass.

From the 13 species in cultivation, breeders and gardeners have produced countless cultivars, certainly in excess of 40,000. Every attribute of the original species—flower size, shape, color, scent, quantity, and period of bloom, along with foliage characteristics and height—has added to the wonderful mixing pot.

Daylily flowers come in a number of different forms, including triangular, circular, double, spidery, and star-shaped. Colors include whites and creams through yellows, oranges, and reds to deep purples, often with contrasting details in the throat. Some are nocturnal, opening in the middle of the afternoon and lasting into the night; in some cultivars, the life of individual flowers has been extended by breeders.

Hemerocallis 'Hyperion' (z. 4–10) produces large, lilylike pale yellow flowers, borne on slender stems above the clump of narrow foliage; the blooms are nocturnal and have a sweet fragrance. Midsummer flowering. Height 28 in. (70 cm).

Hemerocallis fulva **'Flore Pleno'** (z. 2–8), introduced in 1860, is a beautiful double cultivar with elegant orange-brown flowers in mid- to late summer. These are longer lasting than most daylilies and surprisingly graceful for a double variety. A gorgeous combination with blue nepetas. Height 26 in. (65 cm).

Hemerocallis **'Gentle Shepherd'** (z. 4–10) has ivory blooms like those of *Lilium regale* but with a hint of green in the throat. This is a cool and stylish daylily, perfect with white-variegated hostas, and follows on from white peonies and poppies in the summer border. Height 26 in. (65 cm).

Hemerocallis lilioasphodelus (z. 4–8) has pale yellow, elegantly pointed flowers on graceful stems above fine foliage. The nocturnal blooms are lightly and sweetly scented. Flowering in early summer, it combines well with blue *Iris sibirica* cultivars such as 'Flight of Butterflies' (z. 4–8). Height 40 in. (1 m).

Hemerocallis **'Stafford'** (z. 4–10) is an ever-popular variety with strong red-brown flowers that have pointed petals and golden yellow throats. Free-flowering over a long period from mid- to late summer, it is reliable and an excellent choice for hot color schemes, combining well with achilleas and early crocosmias. Height 28 in. (70 cm).

Hemerocallis **'Little Grapette'** (z. 4–10) is a compact variety with lovely small purple flowers with a silver bloom produced over a long period from midsummer onward. Delightful planted with purple heucheras. Height 12 in. (30 cm).

Hemerocallis **'Summer Wine'** (z. 4–10) is one of the loveliest cultivars, bearing warm burgundy-pink flowers in early summer. The blooms have lightly waved and ruffled petals and yellow throats. Rich and sophisticated when planted with purple foliage shrubs such as *Cotinus coggygria* 'Royal Purple' (z. 4–8) and *Physocarpus opulifolius* 'Diabolo' (z. 2–7). Height 28 in. (70 cm).

OTHER GOOD DAYLILIES

Hemerocallis **'Anzac'** (z. 4–10) Velvet red flowers, with yellow throats and a faint yellow stripe on each petal. Midsummer flowering. Height 28 in. (70 cm).

Hemerocallis **'Cherry Cheeks'** (z. 4–10) Evergreen foliage and bright pink flowers with reflexed, white-striped petals and yellow throats. Blooms in midsummer. Height 28 in. (70 cm).

Hemerocallis citrina (z. 3–8) Nocturnal, star-shaped, fragrant flowers in midsummer; green to pale yellow with brown tips. Height 4 ft. (1.2 m).

Hemerocallis **'Edge of Darkness'** (z. 4–10) Midsummer lavender flowers with purple petal edges and eyes. Height 24in. (60cm).

Hemerocallis **'Eenie Weenie'** (z. 4–10) A good dwarf cultivar with neat, compact foliage and yellow flowers from early into midsummer. Height 12 in. (30 cm).

Hemerocallis **'Pandora's Box'** (z. 4–10) Compact, with maroon-eyed cream flowers in midsummer. Height 12 in. (30 cm).

(zone 4–7) is of similar size and has bright yellow, semidouble flowers. *Geum* 'Borisii' (zone 3–7) is compact with medium orange flowers on 12 in. (30 cm) stems. *Geum rivale* (zone 3–7) has pendent, bell-shaped flowers in dusky pink or darker orange-red. With slender, arching stems, 8–24 in. (20–60 cm) tall, this species has a softer habit.

Heucheras (zone 4–8) originate from the Rocky Mountains. Enjoying massive popularity in gardens today, modern varieties offer a wonderful choice of foliage (see pages 88–89 and 93). However, some cultivars also have good flowers, borne over a long period in summer. Heucheras have been hybridized with their near relatives *Tiarella* to produce × *Heucherella* (zone 4–8), also responsible for some valuable flowering cultivars. Growing on moist, well-drained, neutral soils, both form dense clumps of rounded to heart-shaped, semi-evergreen to evergreen leaves. They prefer light shade, tolerating full sun only in moist sites.

Heuchera 'Raspberry Regal'

A FEW GOOD HEUCHERAS AND HEUCHERELLAS FOR FLOWERS

Heuchera 'Cherries Jubilee' (z. 4–8) Stems of showy, cherry red flowers above rich chocolate brown foliage.

Heuchera cylindrica 'Greenfinch' (z. 4–8) Popular with garden designers for its unusual green-cream flowers on 3 ft. (90 cm) stems. Handsome, rounded, dark green leaves, overlaid or mottled with metallic silver.

Heuchera 'Ebony and Ivory' (z. 4–8) Ruffled, dark ebony-purple foliage and large, bell-shaped ivory white flowers.

Heuchera 'Fireworks' (z. 4–8) An explosive display of coral pink-orange flowers above bronzed ruffled foliage.

Heuchera 'Firefly' (z. 4–8) Dark green foliage and dark red stems bearing bright red, fragrant flowers; an established favorite.

Heuchera 'Magic Wand' (z. 4–8) Almost luminous pink-red flowers, double the size of most. Dark green leaves are flushed silver-bronze and finely edged in red.

Heuchera 'Raspberry Regal' (left) (z. 4–8) A profusion of fresh pink flowers on straight stems above copper and burgundy foliage.

× *Heucherella alba* 'Rosalie' (z. 4–8) A profusion of pretty pink, tubular bell-shaped flowers against rounded, maplelike red-flushed leaves.

× *Heucherella* 'Dayglow Pink' (z. 4–8) Distinctive foliage with chocolate brown veining and stems of profuse fluorescent pink, tubular bell-shaped flowers. Looks glorious against the bold blue-gray leaves of *Hosta sieboldiana* var. *elegans* (see page 107) (z. 4–8).

Their fine green or red-brown stems usually reach 16–26 in. (40–65 cm) high, at which point they lightly branch to bear numerous tubular flowers.

Incarvilleas (hardy gloxinia) (zone 6–8) are found in mountainous regions from Afghanistan to northwestern China. The plants form thick taproots and are robust, although they detest

---

over-wet conditions, especially in winter. An ideal situation is a sunny raised bed of rich, gritty soil. Foliage varies from species to species: Most form a rosette of dark, glossy green leaves, each made up of a number of leaflets. The flowers, which are borne in early summer to midsummer, are all trumpet-shaped, opening to five well-defined petals.

Incarvillea delavayi

The most common garden species is *Incarvillea delavayi*, which grows to 18 in. (45 cm). Its height makes it suitable for the perennial or mixed border. Thick stems each carry around ten gloxinia-like flowers, which are rose-pink with clear yellow throats, followed by long, angular seed capsules. 'Bees' Pink' is a more subtle pale pink. 'Snowtop' is pure white. *Incarvillea mairei* is a Himalayan beauty of distinction, its bright pink flowers with white markings and yellow throats sitting proudly above the glossy, dark foliage on stems 6–16 in. (15–40 cm) high.

Iris sibirica (Siberian iris) (zone 4–8) is one of the highlights of early summer. Its upright, grasslike clumps of foliage grow to 32 in. (80 cm) high and produce much taller stems each with about five flowers. Parent of an ever-increasing list of cultivars, *Iris sibirica* prefers slightly acid soil, which must be reliably moist, and a site in full sun or partial shade. The elegant flowers occur in shades of blue through to purple-mauve, as well

Iris ensata thrives in the spring water of the rill at Hestercombe Gardens, Somerset, in England.

as the white of *Iris* **'Sibirica Alba'** (zone 4–8). Intricate markings at the base of each lower petal (fall) often include a golden yellow flush and dark stripes or veins. (See also pages 75–76.)

Iris laevigata (zone 5–8) and its cultivars thrive in acid soil, rich in humus. They grow in the moist to wet conditions at the edges of a pond or stream and are suited to a bog garden. The flamboyant flowers of *Iris ensata* (zone 5–8) will also grow in the border, provided the soil is rich, deep, and moist. Additional watering in summer may be necessary to keep the foliage in good condition and build the plants for the following season. Many beautiful named varieties are available, in colors from white through pinks to the deepest blues and purples. (See also page 76.)

Knautias are close relatives of *Scabiosa* (scabious) and were previously known by this name. Their dainty pincushion flowers are carried on fine stems above felty rosettes of foliage, and appear throughout summer, often repeating in fall. They are easy to grow on any soil, but they do need full sun. *Knautia macedonica* (zone 5–8) has pleasing gray-felted leaves and glorious deep crimson-red flowers. It is useful in the mixed border, particularly when combined with other gray-foliage plants. *Knautia macedonica* **Melton Pastels** lacks the depth of color of the species, but it is still a pretty plant. Three colors are available: pink-lilac, lavender-pink, and crimson-red. All these reach heights of around 30 in. (75 cm); *Knautia macedonica* **'Mars Midget'** is

---

A SELECTION OF IRIS SIBIRICA HYBRIDS

'Butter and Sugar' (z. 4–8) Gorgeous flowers with creamy white standards and butter yellow falls.

'Dance Ballerina Dance' (z. 4–8) Ruffled white-lilac standards above falls of darker lilac edged white.

'Flight of Butterflies' (z. 4–8) Masses of smaller flowers of sapphire blue with darker veining. (See page 75.)

'Papillon' (z. 4–8) Soft medium blue flowers.

'Tropic Night' (z. 4–8) Dark velvety purple, veined blooms. Mixes well with *Carex elata* 'Aurea' (z. 5–9).

'White Swirl' (z. 4–8) Produces outstanding white flowers.

Knautia macedonica Melton Pastels

141

Leucanthemum × superbum

Leucanthemum × superbum 'Aglaia'

dwarf at only 16 in. (40 cm) high, with numerous small ruby red flowers.

Leucanthemum × superbum (zone 4–7), once named *Chrysanthemum maximum*, has long been enjoyed for its show of flowers from early to late summer. It is fondly known as the shasta daisy, and is a tough, robust garden plant. A native of grassland, it thrives in moist, well-drained soils, and its simple to elaborate white flowers stand out in a sunny herbaceous border or brighten

the partial shade of a mixed planting. It forms a clump of toothed, glossy, dark green leaves and carries its flowers on stems 10–36 in. (25–90 cm) high. The taller cultivars often need some support.

Each usually pure white flower head can be up to 5 in. (12 cm) across. Single forms have bold yellow centers, while the double cultivars are often paler and sometimes fringed around the centers.

Lychnis (campion or catchfly) include low-growing alpine perennials, as well as larger, more familiar border plants. Most have upright, usually branched stems with often hairy leaves and loose heads of five-petaled flowers in shades of red and pink in addition to white.

They are undemanding plants, most requiring only moderately fertile, free-draining soil. Ideally grown in full sun, they will tolerate partial shade. Some species self-seed successfully, and this is certainly part of their appeal.

The alpine campion, *Lychnis alpina* (zone 5–7), forms a compact tuft of growth, with dark green leaves. In summer, stems 6 in. (15 cm) high each bear a cluster of saucer-shaped purple-pink flowers with notched petals. *Lychnis flos-jovis* (flower of Jove or Jupiter) (zone 4–8) is another alpine species, with a mat of white-hairy leaves and 12 in. (30 cm) stems topped with loose clusters of white, pink, or scarlet flowers in early summer.

Lychnis coronaria (dusty miller or rose campion) (zone 4–8) is an upright plant, with woolly, gray-silver leaves and silvery-white stems, 32 in. (80 cm) high, of rounded, vivid magenta flowers, often with pale eyes. Borne in loose clusters, these open one at a time over a long period in summer and seed themselves freely. (See Good Companions, below.) A number of color forms are available, such as **Atrosanguinea Group**, deep blood red; **'Alba'**, which is (continued on page 144)

SOME FINE CULTIVARS OF LEUCANTHEMUM X SUPERBUM

'Aglaia' (above right) (z. 4–9) Delicate, fringed, semi-double flowers on 24 in. (60 cm) stems.

'Cobham Gold' (z. 4–9) Double flowers with yellow centers fading through pale lemon to white. Height 24 in. (60 cm).

'Esther Read' (z. 4–7) Pure white double, stunning with the blue flowers of *Agapanthus campanulatus* (z. 7–10). Height 28 in. (70 cm).

'Snowcap' (z. 4–7) A dwarf at 18 in. (45 cm) high, with single flowers, freely borne. Ideal for the front of the border.

'Sunshine' ('Sonnenschein') (z. 4–7) Single, creamy yellow flowers with dark yellow centers. Height 28 in. (70 cm).

'Sunny Side Up' Bold and refreshing, with large double, pure white flowers with deep yellow centers. Height 24 in. (60 cm).

GOOD COMPANIONS

The raspberry pink flowers of *Dianthus carthusianorum* (1) (z. 5–9) make a vivid combination with the wine-colored leaves of *Heuchera* 'Plum Pudding' (2) (z. 4–8).

The bright magenta blooms of *Lychnis coronaria* (3) (z. 4–8) are striking with the lavender-blue flowers and sage green foliage of *Lavandula stoechas* ssp. *pedunculata* (4) (z. 7–8).

Lupines (Lupinus)

Mixed hybrid lupines fill a box parterre at Anne's Grove Gardens, County Cork, Ireland.

Lupines are a welcome addition to any garden. Their stems, up to 3 ft. (90 cm) tall, are an imposing sight as the dense spikes of pealike flowers open from the bottom up. Cultivars come in shades of yellow, pink, red, and blue to mauve, as well as white and some striking bicolors. The clumps of large, softly hairy, palmate leaves are especially attractive when droplets of water are trapped in the center of the leaflets.

Lupines have a long history of cultivation; some were used by the Romans for animal fodder. *Lupinus luteus* (zone 6–10), with fragrant yellow flowers, was the only lupine grown in gardens in Europe until the 17th century, when the first American perennial lupines arrived. The wonderful garden lupine was born of these original species, helped by devotees like George Russell, who started a hybridization program to improve color range and size and shape of flower.

Reliably blooming in early summer, lupines are best planted among other perennials that can take over later in the season. Slightly acid, fertile, well-drained soil is ideal; heavy, wet clay is not appreciated. Full sun brings the best results, although light shade is tolerated. To encourage further blooms, remove spikes right to the base immediately after flowering.

Cultivars are often propagated from cuttings. These are taken from the young shoots in spring, cut right at the base, just above the roots. Today, many modern varieties come true from seed.

Lupinus 'The Governor' (Band of Nobles Series) (z. 6–10) is a popular lupine, with strong spikes of bold, deep blue and white bicolored flowers. They look striking against the silver leaves of *Elaeagnus* 'Quicksilver' (z. 3–6) or rising through a cloud of white valerian, *Centranthus ruber* 'Albus' (see page 43) (z. 4–8).

OTHER GOOD LUPINES

'Chandelier' (z. 4–8) A subtle combination of medium and pale yellow.

'My Castle' (z. 4–8) Lovely flowers of deep lipstick pink.

'Noble Maiden' (Band of Nobles Series) (z. 4–8) White maturing to creamy white.

'The Chatelaine' (Band of Nobles Series) (z. 4–8) Bicolored flowers in boldly contrasting white and rose pink.

'The Page' (Band of Nobles Series) (z. 4–8) Subtle bicolored flowers of red and medium pink (left) .

143

white; and 'Oculata', which is white with a pink flush. *Lychnis × walkeri* 'Abbotswood Rose' (zone 5–8) is similar to *Lychnis coronaria* but is only about 24 in. (60 cm) high, with bright pink flowers. *Lychnis × arkwrightii* 'Vesuvius', 18 in. (45 cm) high, has chocolate stems and foliage, a perfect setting for the clusters of star-shaped, orange-red flowers in early summer.

Although most lychnis thrive in well-drained conditions, some prefer a richer, moister soil. *Lychnis flos-cuculi* (ragged robin) (zone 3–7), good for wildflower meadows, has loose heads of purple-pink flowers with raggedly divided petals, on stems up to 28 in. (70 cm) tall, in late spring and early summer. *Lychnis chalcedonica* (Jerusalem or Maltese cross) (zone 2–8) produces domed heads of star-shaped, bright orange-red flowers in early and midsummer and freely self-seeds. It is a more upright

Lychnis chalcedonica

plant, with bristly stems 40 in. (1 m) high. *Lychnis viscaria*, German catchfly, has slender spikes of bright purple-pink, saucer-shaped flowers, borne on dark red-brown stems, 18 in. (45 cm) tall, in early and midsummer. 'Splendens Plena' has double, bright pink flowers.

Lysimachias (loosestrife) are seldom praised despite their appearance in so many gardens, where they perform year after year. Growing naturally in damp meadows and woodland, they thrive on

Lysimachia punctata

rich, moist, free-draining soil in full sun or partial shade. They are superb border plants, and quickly become established. (See also pages 91 and 101.)

Lysimachia punctata (zone 4–8), the best-known species, has whorls of golden yellow flowers borne from early summer onward on pale green, upright stems 40 in. (1 m) high. It is a useful plant since it requires no support and has enough foliage to dilute the brightness of the flowers. Roughly the same height, and in bloom at the same time, *Lysimachia ephemerum* (zone 6–8) has erect stems of narrow gray-green leaves topped by candlelike spires of numerous starry white flowers.

Lysimachia clethroides (zone 4–8) is glorious in bloom, especially when planted in drifts. Reaching 24 in. (60 cm) tall, it has tightly packed spikes of pure white flowers, which open from the bottom up; the top of each spike dramatically arches or curls with age. Flowers start appearing early in summer and carry on throughout the season. *Lysimachia clethroides* 'Geisha' is a recent Japanese introduction, which has a jagged creamy margin to the leaf.

Lysimachia nummularia (creeping Jenny) (zone 5–7) is a valuable ground-

The bright magenta blooms and silver foliage of *Lychnis coronaria* contrast with the lush green foliage and deep blue flowers of *Iris ensata*.

cover plant for shady banks and under shrubs; its creeping stems carry fresh green leaves and yellow flowers from early summer onward. **'Aurea'** is a lovely yellow-leaved form (see page 95).

Lythrum salicaria (commonly called purple loosestrife) (zone 4–8) thrives in a moist site, producing tightly packed spires of starry, purple-red or purple-pink flowers over long periods from early summer. (See page 77.)

Malvas (mallow) are closely related to lavateras and hollyhocks but are of more modest stature, at around 40 in. (1 m) tall. The funnel-shaped blooms are white, pink, or purple, as well as striking shades of blue, and are borne from early summer to fall. Liking good drainage and lots of sun, malvas suit planting in gravel and are excellent with roses and sun-loving shrubs.

Malva alcea (hollyhock mallow) (zone 5–8) has delightful purple-pink flowers. *Malva moschata* (musk mallow) (zone 3–8) is pale pink and has finely divided leaves with a gentle musk scent. *Malva moschata* f. *alba* is a pure white form.

Malva sylvestris (zone 7–9) has open funnel-shaped flowers, in colors ranging from pink through purple to blue. Those of **'Brave Heart'** are large and purple, but **'Primley Blue'** steals the show: Its pale blue flowers have dark purple-blue veins, and, at 8 in.

A purple form of *Malva sylvestris* associates well with old roses and with other sun-loving perennials.

SHRUBBY MALLOWS

Lavateras are woody-based plants that grow quickly to produce a spectacular show of funnel-shaped blooms throughout summer into fall. They are related to malvas and are often sold alongside them as perennials. They enjoy the same conditions and suit coastal gardens. Although shrubby, they are short-lived, and on wet soils may need replacing every two or three years.

Malva alcea

(20 cm) tall, it sits nicely at the front of a border with shorter campanulas and dwarf agapanthus.

Nepetas are unquestionably good companion plants, presenting their airy flower spikes over a long season from early summer until autumn. Most are in blue and purple shades, but some are white or yellow. A number of hardy species and garden cultivars are universally known as catmint, although not all types stir cats to the same degree. (See pages 42, 67, and 69.)

145

Peonies (Paeonia)

Throughout gardening history peonies have been much treasured plants, a prominent statement of good taste and prosperity. Rich red young growth soon matures into bold, leathery, deeply cut blue-green foliage, with beautiful saucer- or bowl-shaped flowers carried above the leaves at heights of up to 40 in. (1 m). Most flower in early to midsummer. The blooms may be single, semi-double, or fully double; those described as "anemone-formed" have a single or semi-double layer of smaller petals at the center. Colors include white and cream to yellow, and shades of pink and red, often blushed, tinted, or streaked, with the occasional bicolor; most have a central eye of yellow stamens, which is often hidden in fully double forms.

The majority of herbaceous peonies are hardy, easily grown perennials with winter-dormant tuberous roots. They are often sold in fall as bare-root tubers. Careful inspection should reveal at least three firm reddish buds or eyes. Plant immediately in moist, free-draining soil enriched with well-rotted manure. Whether using bare tubers or container-grown plants, never plant too deeply: The top of the tuber should be no more than 1 in. or so (2 cm) below the surface. Plant any deeper and your peonies will not flower.

Long, cold winters bring the best results with peonies. Where temperatures rarely drop below 50°F (10°C), plant in a cool, shady site; otherwise full sun to partial shade is preferred. In full sun individual blooms fade more quickly; those planted in shade will have fewer, longer-lasting flowers.

The greatest threats to new growth are frost and botrytis (a fungus that causes buds and stems to wilt). If shoots develop early, protect with floating row cover. If botrytis develops, apply a fungicide. Still, damp air tends to accentuate this condition, so always allow plenty of space around the plants.

Taller varieties will need some support (see pages 24–25). Peonies appreciate an annual mulch of well-

Paeonia officinalis 'Rubra Plena' is the old-fashioned double red peony of cottage gardens. Round, green, red-veined buds open into balls of silky ruby red petals, which are delightfully scented. The medium green foliage with broad leaflets is the perfect setting for the attractive horned seed heads that follow the flowers. Height 30 in. (75 cm).

rotted manure or compost. This increases the soil's organic content and conserves water, helping to keep the foliage in good condition. Healthy leaves through the summer build the plants up so they are ready to flower freely the following year. Fall is the best time to divide peonies (see page 21).

Although there are two native North American species of peony, most garden peonies are cultivars of the Chinese species *Paeonia lactiflora* (zone 4–8). This species arrived in the United States from China in the 1830s. The peonies of the English-style cottage garden are forms of the European species *Paeonia officinalis* (zone 4–9). All have large, rounded buds, are lightly fragrant, and make wonderful cut flowers.

OTHER GOOD PEONIES

Paeonia anomala (z. 5–8) Wavy red-purple petals surrounding a golden yellow center. Height 20–24 in. (50–60 cm).

Paeonia lactiflora 'Charm' (z. 4–8) Large, ruffled, ruby red flowers, red and yellow at the center. Height 36–40 in. (90–100 cm).

Paeonia lactiflora 'Dinner Plate' (z. 4–8) Large, double, soft lilac-pink blooms, gently fragrant. Height 30–40 in. (75–100 cm).

Paeonia lactiflora 'Karl Rosenfield' (z. 4–8) A lovely deep red double. Height 28–32 in. (70–80 cm).

Paeonia lactiflora 'Raspberry Sundae' (z. 4–8) Large, double, pink-red flowers streaked with white. Height 30–36 in. (75–90 cm).

Paeonia lactiflora 'Sarah Bernhardt' (z. 4–8) Double, scented, pink flowers. Height 36–40 in. (90–100 cm).

Paeonia officinalis 'Alba Plena' (z. 4–9) Large, double flowers with white ruffled petals. Height 24–30 in. (60–75 cm).

Paeonia officinalis 'Rosea Plena' (z. 4–9) Pale pink and very double. Height 26–30 in. (65–75 cm).

Paeonia tenuifolia (z. 3–8) Deep velvety red, single flowers with golden centers. Height 20–28 in. (50–70 cm).

Paeonia mlokosewitschii (Molly the Witch) (z. 5–8) One of the loveliest species peonies. Emerging early with coppery young foliage, it may need frost protection. The pale yellow, kingcup-like flowers are not long lived but are very beautiful, especially against the backdrop of purplish leaves. Height 24–36 in. (60–90 cm).

Paeonia lactiflora 'Bowl of Beauty' (z. 4–8) has glorious bowl-shaped flowers. The shining pink outer petals hold a rich creamy center of numerous smaller petals. Occasionally fully double, plain pink flowers appear early in the season. The plant is upright in habit with reddish stems and shining, dark green leaves, which remain attractive all year. Height 3 ft. (90 cm).

Paeonia lactiflora 'Duchesse de Nemours' (z. 4–8) has very double flowers of creamy white, flushed yellow at the base of the petals, with a light and lovely fragrance. The blooms are sumptuous and extravagant against the handsome dark green foliage. Height 3 ft. (90 cm).

Paeonia lactiflora 'Lord Kitchener' is an old cultivar dating from the Edwardian era. It is upright in habit, with dark foliage, reddish stems and semidouble, bright scarlet blooms with yellow centers. Height 3 ft. (90 cm).

Papaver rupifragum 'Flore Pleno'

bristly medium green leaves starts to die down after flowering; by late summer any remaining foliage is unsightly. The cup-shaped flowers are up to 6 in. (15 cm) across, borne individually on stout, unbranched stems, usually 24–36 in. (60–90 cm) high. Some forms collapse under the weight of the blooms, so some support is needed, either from well-chosen neighboring plants or from artificial supports.

Persicaria (formerly *Polygonum*) (zone 4–7) species are widespread in the northern hemisphere. The hardy perennial types are popular garden plants,

The much-loved annual, biennial, and perennial poppies, *Papaver*, provide a kaleidoscope of color. The large blooms of *Papaver orientale* (oriental poppy) sit well in the perennial or mixed border, while those of *Papaver nudicaule* and annual *Papaver rhoeas* are simply stunning en masse or drifting through cottage or wild gardens. Native to many countries, all need moderately fertile, free-draining soil and full sun.

Papaver nudicaule (zone 4–9), the Icelandic or Arctic poppy, is a short-lived perennial forming tufts of blue-green, divided leaves. Numerous solitary, bowl-shaped, fragrant flowers in white, yellow, orange, or pale red are borne on wiry stems 12 in. (30 cm) tall, appearing from early summer onward. There are a number of good garden selections.

Papaver rupifragum 'Flore Pleno' (zone 6–9) is wonderful along the edge of a gravel path or on scree. Compact tufts of gray-green foliage produce fine stems, 16 in. (40 cm) high, which carry solitary, double tangerine orange flowers from early summer. This is a hardy, short-lived perennial, which self-seeds.

Papaver orientale (oriental poppy) (zone 3–8) contributes a breathtaking display of glorious, oversized blooms, which steal the show for a few weeks in early summer. Its clump of long, divided,

SOME RECOMMENDED PAPAVER ORIENTALE CULTIVARS

'Allegro' (above) (z. 3–8) Scarlet-orange petals with black blotches at the base. A shorter variety, 18 in. (45 cm) high; popular but rather inelegant.

'Beauty of Livermere' (see page 55) (z. 3–8) Glorious dark red blooms on strong, upright stems 3 ft. (90 cm) high.

'Black and White' (below) (z. 3–8) Pure white petals with black basal blotches, which may bleed crimson into the petals.

'Cedric Morris' (z. 3–8) Large flowers made up of frilly, pale pink petals with dark basal blotches.

'Curlilocks' (below) (z. 3–8) Glowing orange-red flowers with cut edges to the petals; pretty and unusual.

'Karine' (z. 3–8) A lovely shade of apricot-pink with crimson-marked petals.

'Manhattan' (z. 3–8) Unusual lavender-rose, ruffled petals.

'Orange Glow' (z. 3–8) Large amber-orange flowers.

'Patty's Plum' (see page 45) (z. 3–8) Large, ruffled flowers of soft gray-purple.

'Picotée' (below) (z. 3–8) Pure white petals with an edge of clear orange.

growing in sun or partial shade on almost any moist soil, including heavy clay. Varied in both habit and form, they range from low-growing, ground-cover subjects to stately border plants (see also page 48). Some are valuable for their attractive stem and foliage color. *Persicaria virginiana* 'Painter's Palette' (zone 4–8) produces intricately patterned leaves in cream, brown, and salmon pink (see page 101); while *Persicaria microcephala* 'Red Dragon' (zone 5–8) has purple-green foliage with striking brown and silver markings (see page 87).

Persicaria affinis 'Superba' (zone 4–7), with rich dark green, evergreen foliage, makes an excellent ground-cover plant, 10 in. (25 cm) high. From early summer onward, it has short spikes, 4 in. (10 cm) high, of tightly packed flowers that open blush pink and turn deep crimson with age. With the onset of autumn, the foliage turns bronze, then red-brown, looking wonderful with the remaining flowers. *Persicaria affinis* 'Darjeeling Red' (zone 4–7) is a slightly taller plant, with flowers that mature to rich red; 'Donald Lowndes' ages to deep pink.

Persicaria bistorta 'Superba' (zone 4–6) is larger, very useful in damp borders. Its large evergreen leaves are conspicuously veined. Stems of up to 30 in. (75 cm) in height are topped with dense cylindrical spikes of pale pink flowers from early summer onward.

Persicaria vacciniifolia (zone 4–7), growing only 8 in. (20 cm) high, has red, spreading stems with small, dark green leaves that turn rich red in autumn. Candlelike heads of numerous large, dark pink, bell-shaped flowers are borne in mid- to late summer.

Polemoniums (Jacob's Ladder) are easily pleased border plants, happy in most conditions. From a winter-dormant clump develop ladderlike leaves of medium to dark green. In early summer,

Persicaria bistorta 'Superba' is an excellent long-flowering perennial that thrives in moist soil.

erect or arching stems bear loose or clustered, tubular to funnel-shaped flowers in white, blue, lilac-mauve, pink, or yellow. Most seed themselves freely.

Polemonium caeruleum (zone 4–7) is the best known, its upright stems, 24–36 in. (60–90 cm) high, carrying funnel-shaped, lavender-blue flowers with pretty golden stamens. *Polemonium caeruleum* ssp. *caeruleum* f. *album* is the white form. *Polemonium caeruleum* 'Brise d'Anjou' has leaves boldly variegated with creamy yellow. *Polemonium* 'Lambrook Mauve' (zone 4–7) is of

Polemonium 'Lambrook Mauve'

similar stature; its pale lilac flowers blend effortlessly with both pale and dark pink geraniums and with roses. *Polemonium carneum* (zone 4–9) has

GOOD COMPANIONS

Scabiosa caucasica 'Clive Greaves' (1) (z. 4–9) looks delightful among clouds of *Gypsophila paniculata* 'Bristol Fairy' (2) (z. 4–8). Both plants enjoy alkaline soil in full sun.

The upright spikes of *Verbascum chaixii* 'Album' (3) (z. 6–8) look perfect above the soft mounds of *Geranium* 'Johnson's Blue' (4) (z. 4–8) .

Rehmannia elata

Sidalcea 'Party Girl'

flowers of pale pink, purple, lavender-blue, or yellow, carried on stems 16 in. (40 cm) in height. **'Apricot Delight'** is a pleasing apricot-pink form.

Polemonium pauciflorum (zone 6–9) is distinct in having large, pendent, narrowly tubular flowers of pale yellow-green, on stems 20 in. (50 cm) high. *Polemonium yezoense* **'Purple Rain'** (zone 6–9), 24 in. (60 cm) tall, has nodding, bell-shaped, pale blue flowers and green-purple leaves, lovely when mixed with fine silver foliage, such as that of *Artemisia* 'Powis Castle' (zone 6–10).

Rehmannia elata (zone 8–9), the Chinese foxglove, is somewhat rare in gardens, perhaps because it is considered tender, although in its native China, where it lives on cliff tops and in rock crevices, it survives low temperatures. The key to success in the garden is to give it well-drained soil; wet conditions, especially in winter, spell disaster. It prefers a sunny situation. The plant has softly hairy, medium green foliage and lightly branched stems reaching 5 ft. (1.5 m); from early summer until the first frosts, these carry large medium pink, foxglovelike flowers with prominent divided lower lips and throats of pale yellow spotted red. If pinched at the tips, the lush growth will branch and maintain a modest height.

Rehmannias are fairly coarse-looking but have beautiful flowers produced

over a long period. Partner them with silver-foliage subjects, such as artemisias or herbaceous geraniums to conceal the lower part of the plants.

Scabiosa (scabious or pincushion flower) are often found in grassland and meadows across Europe, Africa, and Asia. They all like open, sunny situations and good drainage and generally thrive in alkaline soil. Scabious flowers are popular with bees and butterflies, so are widely used in wild gardens. Some are annual or biennial. The perennial species are popular garden plants that produce a long succession of flowers from early summer into autumn. (See page 82.)

Sidalceas (prairie mallow) are natives of North America. The species *Sidalcea candida* and *Sidalcea malviflora* make an arresting sight, creating drifts of creamy white or pink flowers in the moist, free-draining soils of meadows and river plains. Sidalceas are wonderful plants for the perennial border. They form dense clumps of kidney-shaped

leaves, from which arise erect, lightly branched stems, 12–36 in. (30–90 cm) tall, carrying a succession of shallow, funnel-shaped flowers over a long period from early summer onward.

Sidalcea candida (zone 5–8) is an old garden favorite, loved for its spikes of cream or white flowers. *Sidalcea malviflora* (zone 5–8) has pink to pink-lilac blooms, and **'Alba'** is a silky white form. There are numerous garden forms that have larger flowers, 2in. (5cm) across, on spikes reaching 28–36 in. (70–90 cm) in height. *Sidalcea* **'Croftway Red'** is a rich, deep pink. **'Elsie Heugh'** produces showy purple-pink, fringed flowers. **'Party Girl'** lives up to its name with bright pink flowers, and is over 40 in. (1 m) in height. **'Rosanna'** is a lovely satin, rosy pink, and **'Wine Red'** is pinkish red.

Stachys is usually associated with the wonderful silver mat of foliage belonging to *Stachys byzantina* (zone 4–8) and its cultivar **'Silver Carpet'** (see pages 103 and 105), but there are other species and cultivars with exceptional flowers. *Stachys macrantha* (zone 5–7) forms a clump of wrinkled, veined, dark

Stachys macrantha

green leaves and erect stems, 24 in. (60 cm) high, bearing short, dense spikes of tubular, hooded, pinkish purple flowers all summer. 'Nivea' is a white form; 'Robusta' is very floriferous in a lovely shade of purple. Of similar height and habit is *Stachys officinalis* (zone 5–8), with more rounded heads of small pink, white, or reddish purple flowers. 'Alba' is a white form, 'Hummelo' has purple flowers, and 'Saharan Pink' is bright medium pink.

Verbascums (mullein) (zone 6–8) have become more popular as easy-to-grow garden plants in recent years. Tall, upright flower spikes and felty leaves are their main features, useful for adding a different shape and texture to the border. As a rule, the tall species are biennial, the flower stems arriving in the second year, after which the plant often dies. The shorter species are regarded as perennials, albeit short-lived; the same is true of the garden hybrids.

Verbascum chaixii 'Album'

SOME VERBASCUM HYBRIDS

Verbascum 'Buttercup' (z. 6–8) Green, disease-resistant foliage and pretty yellow flowers. Height 40 in. (1 m).

Verbascum 'Cotswold Beauty' (z. 6–8) A lovely shade of apricot-buff with dark eyes. Height 40 in. (1 m).

Verbascum 'Helen Johnson' (z. 6–8) Pinkish orange-brown flowers above gray-green foliage. Height 3 ft. (90 cm).

Verbascum 'Jackie' (z. 6–8) Popular, with lovely pale apricot flowers on well-branched stems. Height 16 in. (40 cm).

Verbascum 'Jackie in Pink' (right) (z. 6–8) Delicious medium pink flowers, which age attractively to pale pink in light shade. Height 16 in. (40 cm).

Verbascum 'Pink Domino' (z. 6–8) Purple-eyed, deep pink flowers. Height 4 ft. (1.2 m).

Verbascum 'Raspberry Ripple' (z. 6–8) Creamy pink flowers with raspberry red centers. Height 24 in. (60 cm).

Verbascum 'Jackie in Pink'

The yellows of the tall species have been crossed with the white, pink, violet, or dark purple of shorter species, such as *Verbascum phoeniceum,* to produce a wonderful palette of bold and pastel shades. Deciduous or semi-evergreen leaf rosettes give rise to a number of stems, each clad in numerous tightly packed, saucer-shaped flowers, often with darker eyes, from early to late summer. (See also page 104.)

Verbascum chaixii is a particularly useful plant that flowers for a long period and needs no additional support. It has gray leaves and yellow flowers with purple stamens, carried on spikes up to 5 ft. (1.5 m) tall in early summer. 'Album' is a white form (see Good Companions, page 149). Both mix easily with most perennials and provide graceful vertical interest in the border.

Verbascums are happiest in full sun on poor, free-draining, alkaline soil. Fertile, wet soil produces tall, floppy growth and may result in mildew. The species are easily raised from seed, and some self-seed freely; garden hybrids can be propagated by root cuttings.

Late summer

Late summer is one of the richest seasons for perennials: warm pinks, blues, and purples sit alongside the hot hues of crocosmias and alstroemerias. Deciduous shrubs, their flowers largely over, present no competition to this colorful display. Without late perennials the garden would be quiet and somber; with their help, the borders are alive and singing.

Agapanthus africanus

Agapanthus africanus 'Albus'

The gray-green and white striped foliage of *Iris pallida* 'Variegata' stays looking good into late summer. It contrasts beautifully with the vibrant purple blooms of *Verbena rigida*.

Agapanthuses (African blue lily) are long-cultivated and widely naturalized plants, popular for their large, rounded heads of tubular, bell- or trumpet-shaped flowers in shades of blue or white, borne throughout summer. All form strong clumps of broad or narrow, fleshy, grasslike leaves, which may be evergreen or deciduous. They are at their most dramatic against a simple uncluttered background of a wall or evergreen shrub; the flowers are ideal for cutting.

Agapanthuses thrive in moist, well-drained, fertile soil with plenty of sun. They dislike winter wet, especially in low temperatures; deciduous species should be given a dry mulch of bark or bracken and evergreen forms should be grown in containers that can be moved to a frost-free position. Well-established, mature plants produce the most flowers; avoid dividing clumps too often.

Agapanthus africanus (zone 9–10) has evergreen foliage and deep blue, trumpet-shaped flowers on stems up to 3 ft. (90 cm) in height; 'Albus' is pure white. *Agapanthus campanulatus* (zone 7–10) has deciduous foliage with pale to dark blue trumpet flowers on stems 32–48 in. (80–120 cm) high; **var. albidus** is white.

SOME FINE AGAPANTHUS HYBRIDS

'Blue Giant' (z. 8–10) Impressive heads of ink blue flowers with dark stripes, carried on 40 in. (1 m) stems.

'Blue Triumphator' (right) (z. 7–10) Shorter than 'Blue Giant' with medium blue, slightly pendulous flowers.

'Bressingham White' (z. 8–10) Similar to 'Blue Triumphator' but white.

'Lilliput' (z. 8–10) Dark blue flowers on stems reaching no more than 16 in. (40 cm) high. Other dwarf cultivars include **'Gayle's Lilac'**, **'Snowball'**, and the sky blue **'Streamline'**.

'Loch Hope' (z. 7–10) Large, bright blue flower heads on slender stems up to 5 ft. (1.5 m) in height.

'Tinkerbell' (z. 7–10) Unique, with its dwarf, variegated foliage of green and creamy white. Not the hardiest agapanthus; shy in producing its pale blue flowers. Height 12 in. (30 cm).

Agapanthus 'Blue Triumphator'

The distinctive species *Agapanthus caulescens* (zone 8–10) forms a short, fleshy stem sheathed in broad, deciduous foliage. Its bell-shaped flowers are violet-blue, on stems to 40 in. (1 m) tall.

Over the years many wonderful garden hybrids have been produced and have recently become more widely available through micropropagation. The hardy *Agapanthus* Headbourne hybrids (zone 7–10) are perhaps most commonly grown (see page 64).

Agastaches are underestimated plants. Their spikes of tightly packed, tubular flowers and bracts are very long lasting and come in shades of white, orange, pink, blue, and purple. The gray-green leaves are aromatic and vary from narrow to broad and nettlelike, carried on upright stems. There are species native to the United States and Asia; all are drought-tolerant, thriving in fertile, well-drained soil in full sun.

Agastache urticifolia (zone 5–8) has upright, 24 in. (60 cm) stems of nettle-like leaves, topped in summer with spikes of pink-blue flowers. 'Alba' is a white form. *Agastache rugosa* (zone 8–10) is similar in habit. **'Golden Jubilee'** is a striking cultivar: An over-wintered crown of crinkled green-purple foliage grows into an upright, bright golden yellow plant, a perfect setting for the lavender flowers (see page 92). A hybrid of *Agastache foeniculum* (see page 50), *Agastache* 'Blue Fortune' (zone 5–9) has showy mauve-blue spikes on stems 30–36 in. (75–90 cm) high. These are all hardy, popular forms.

Of the more tender agastaches, the following are worth growing for their flowers, borne from midsummer until fall. *Agastache aurantiaca* 'Apricot Sprite' (zone 7–10) has 16 in. (40 cm) stems laden with pale orange flowers. *Agastache* 'Painted Lady' (zone 6–9) produces compact, gray-green foliage on 20 in. (50 cm) stems topped with captivating flowers of pink-orange.

AGAPANTHUSES IN POTS

Agapanthuses flower more freely when their roots are restricted, so growing them in pots is ideal. In summer they can be placed in full sun and kept well watered. With the onset of colder weather, they can be moved to a sheltered position near the house, or overwintered in a greenhouse or a sunroom.

Agastache 'Tutti-frutti' (zone 5–8), 60 cm (24 in.) high, is very aromatic with lipstick pink flowers.

Astrantias (zone 5–8) are delightful plants, both subtle and elegant. From a clump of glossy, deeply divided, palmate leaves, lightly branched stems carry a number of unusual pincushion-like flower heads, set against ruffs of sharply divided, colored bracts. The flowers appear from midsummer onward and can be cut for drying.

(continued on page 155)

Agastache 'Blue Fortune'

Agastache 'Painted Lady'

153

Peruvian lilies (Alstroemeria)

Alstroemerias, the Peruvian lilies, provide luxuriant color in the late summer border. Originating from South America, they have tuberous roots and form spreading clumps of erect, fleshy, gray-green stems with lance-shaped leaves. Loose clusters of intricately patterned, lilylike flowers appear at the tips of the stems for several weeks from midsummer onward. They make excellent, long-lasting cut flowers.

Alstroemerias like full sun and are surprisingly hardy. When planted in free-draining soil, they will survive temperatures as low as 14°F (–10°C); extra protection can be given with a dry mulch of bark or bracken. After two to three years, an established clump will have developed tubers deep enough to avoid all but the most penetrating frost.

Bare-root tubers can be planted 8 in. (20 cm) deep in fall or early spring. Plant pot-grown stock in spring, protecting any emerging shoots from frost with floating row cover. The lush stems, up to 40 in. (1m) high, find their way through adjacent plants that lend support. If accommodating neighbors are absent, artificial support may be required.

Alstroemeria aurea (z. 8–10), a well-established favorite, has bright orange-yellow flowers streaked in red on the inner surface. **'Dover Orange'** has the same red markings on deep orange petals, while **'Lutea'** is canary yellow with brown-flecked inner petals.

Alstroemeria psittacina **'Royal Star'** (z. 8–10) is less hardy than other alstroemerias. It has lightly variegated, dark green foliage with white margins and produces subtle but gorgeous green and dark red flowers.

Alstroemeria ligtu hybrids (z. 7–10) are seed-raised from hybrids of the species *Alstroemeria ligtu* and *Alstroemeria haemantha*. They are hardy and reliable. Flowers are usually in shades of pink, with inner petals flushed yellow and streaked white, red, or purple.

Alstroemeria hybrids (z. 7–10) Demand for alstroemerias as cut flowers has inspired breeders to develop a superb range of hybrids, which are produced in volume by micropropagation. The larger-flowered hybrids make wonderful garden plants, albeit more expensive than species and old garden varieties.

'Spitfire' (z. 8–10) Yellow-flushed pinkish red flowers; gold-variegated foliage.

'Apollo' (z. 8–10) White flowers with yellow throats and inner petals marked in brown.

OTHER ALSTROEMERIA HYBRIDS

'Evening Song' (z. 8–10) Pink-red flowers flushed yellow and flecked mauve.

'Glory of the Andes' (z. 8–10) Fragrant, golden flowers with red-brown markings; variegated leaves.

'Orange Glory' (z. 8–10) Flowers are orange-red flushed golden orange and flecked red-brown.

'Red Beauty' (z. 8–10) Glowing pinkish red flowers flushed with yellow and flecked chocolate-red.

Astrantia major

Campanula 'Kent Belle'

Native to alpine woods and meadows of Asia and Europe, *astrantias* grow easily in most gardens, thriving in moist, rich soil in sun or partial shade. Most self-seed, and some species will naturalize readily.

Astrantia major (zone 5–8) has flowers of greenish pink to purple-red surrounded by white to pinkish white bracts traced with green veining. There are many named selections, all growing 12–36 in. (30–90 cm) high; most bloom again in fall. *Astrantia major alba* has white heads, often tipped green, and is attractive with ferns and *Euphorbia amygdaloides* ssp. *robbiae* (see page 57). 'Claret' is wine red, 'Ruby Wedding' is a lighter shade of red, and 'Rubra' dark wine red. *Astrantia major* ssp. *involucrata* produces greenish white flowers and bracts. 'Shaggy' (previously known as 'Margery Fish') features long, sharply cut bracts with green tips. *Astrantia major* 'Sunningdale Variegated' has large, dark green leaves prettily marked with creamy white (see page 100).

The species *Astrantia maxima* (zone 5–7) has less impressive foliage, but compensates for this with its 24 in. (60 cm) stems of pale pink flowers and medium pink bracts. *Astrantia* 'Hadspen Blood' (zone 5–8), a hybrid of *Astrantia major* and *Astrantia maxima* raised at Hadspen, Somerset, England, is a fine dark red cultivar of similar height, which blooms all season.

Astrantia maxima

Campanulas are a feature of gardens in early summer, and their display is continued by later-flowering varieties as the season progresses. They thrive in neutral to alkaline, well-drained soil in sun or part shade. (See also page 40.)

Campanula carpatica (zone 4–8), often found in rock gardens, is a useful plant for the front of the border, the edge of a path or a container. It forms a neat mound, 12 in. (30 cm) high, of bright, crisp green foliage generously studded with buds and flowers. The upturned, bell-shaped, white to blue blooms appear unfeasibly large and, at times, almost completely obscure the plant. A number of forms have a more compact height of 6 in. (15 cm), often with larger flowers in various shades of lavender to blue. The white *Campanula carpatica* f. *alba* 'White Clips' and blue *Campanula carpatica* 'Blue Clips' are seed-raised selections.

Campanula 'Kent Belle' (zone 5–9) produces rosettes of toothed green leaves and 20 in. (50 cm) stems carrying large, shining purple-blue flowers. The color is striking, the habit ungainly.

Campanula latifolia (zone 3–7) is a tall, upright perennial over 40 in. (1m) high. The large tubular, bell-shaped flowers appear between the uppermost leaves. *Campanula latifolia* var. *alba* is white; 'Brantwood' is deep purple-blue and a more modest height at 30 in. (75 cm).

Astrantia major 'Ruby Wedding'

CAMPANULAS FOR SHADE

Many campanulas are useful plants for partial shade, where they will grow and flower as well as they do in sun. Both *Campanula latiloba* and *Campanula latifolia* varieties are a good choice, as is the robust and floriferous *Campanula lactiflora* (see page 40), which will also colonize unkempt grassy areas.

Campanula latifolia var. alba

From a lush rosette of foliage, *Campanula latiloba* (zone 5–7) produces stout stems, 3 ft. (90 cm) high, clothed in cupped, starry, rich lavender flowers. 'Highcliffe Variety' is deep mauve-blue; 'Percy Piper' is lavender-blue. (See also page 83.)

Campanula punctata (zone 4–8) forms a clump of 12 in. (30 cm) stems bearing flowers of creamy white flushed pink, red spotted within. The blooms are pendent, bell-shaped, and impressively large at 2 in. (5 cm) long. *Campanula punctata* 'Hot Lips' is similar in color and very free-flowering. 'Pantaloons' has gently recurved petals that reveal a protruding inner layer. 'Wedding Bells' is similar but white. *Campanula punctata* f. *rubriflora* 'Cherry Bells' produces numerous rich pinkish red bells on 20 in. (50 cm) stems.

The vigorously spreading *Campanula takesimana* (zone 4–8) has glossy leaves and 20 in. (50 cm) stems with pink-flushed, maroon-speckled, white bells.

Campanula trachelium (zone 4–8), known as bats in the belfry, has nettle-like leaves and woody-based stems up to 32 in. (80 cm) high. The purple-blue flowers are outward-facing, tubular, and bell-shaped, with lightly recurved petals. 'Bernice' has fully double, lilac-blue flowers; var. *alba*, the semi-double 'Alba Flore Pleno', and the fully double 'Snowball' are all white.

Catananche caerulea (zone 6–8) is a charming Mediterranean meadow flower that will succeed in most

CATANANCHE IN GRASS

Catananche caerulea is suitable for naturalizing in grass, growing happily in areas managed as wildflower meadows (see page 54). Its charming blue flowers fulfill the role of cornflowers and are particularly pretty with the soft pink mallow *Malva moschata*.

Catananche caerulea 'Major'

gardens. Also known as blue cupidane or Cupid's dart, it bears solitary dark-eyed, lilac-blue cornflower-like heads, 2 in. (5 cm) across, on slender stems of over 20 in. (50 cm), above a low-growing clump of narrow, gray-green leaves. The generally larger flower heads of *Catananche caerulea* 'Major' are of similar coloring on 18 in. (45 cm) stems; 'Alba' is pure white; 'Bicolor' has a distinct flush of bright purple at the center of each white flower. All will be in bloom from midsummer onward.

These are fully hardy, but short-lived perennials often treated as biennials; they produce flowers more prolifically in

their second year. Full sun and well-drained soil increase longevity.

By midsummer the cornflower blooms of *Centaurea montana* (zone 4–8) are nearly over, but exuberant *Centaurea hypoleuca* 'John Coutts' (zone 4–7) is still going strong (see page 133), and other centaureas are about to reach their peak. These late-blooming centaureas are easily accommodated perennials, requiring free-draining, moderately fertile soil in a sunny site.

Centaurea dealbata (zone 3–8) often needs support, with stems reaching 3 ft. (90 cm). Each white-centered flower head is surrounded by a feathery ruff of bright pink. The divided foliage is light green. *Centaurea dealbata* 'Steenbergii' is rather more aggressive in habit, but its thuggish behavior is forgiven on sight of the gorgeous deep pink flowers with pink-white centers, borne on 24 in. (60 cm) stems. *Centaurea pulcherrima* (zone 5–8) has cream-centered pink blooms on stems 16 in. (40 cm) high.

Preferring a moister soil, *Centaurea macrocephala* (zone 3–8) forms a robust clump of broad medium green leaves, which diminish in size as they (continued on page 158)

Centaurea macrocephala produces bold artichoke-like blooms, making a strong statement in the yellow border with the lighter foliage and flowers of achilleas.

Montbretias (Crocosmia)

Natives of South Africa, crocosmias (montbretia) have been in cultivation since the early 17th century. *Crocosmia × crocosmiiflora* thrives in the mild, damp climates, like those of southwest England, where it has become widely naturalized.

Crocosmias overwinter by means of underground corms, which awake in late spring to produce pleated, sword-shaped leaves 20–40 in. (50–100 cm) long. From midsummer onward, slender, lightly branched, upright or arching stems bear a succession of funnel-shaped flowers up to 2 in. (5 cm) long, in fiery shades of yellow, orange, and red. The rounded, segmented seed capsules that follow are also attractive.

These handsome plants enjoy fertile soil, moist but free-draining. In areas of persistent frost, the shelter of a sunny wall is appreciated. They will grow in partial shade but need full sun to flower well.

Crocosmias can be bought as dry corms, usually in early spring; these are planted 2½–3 in. (6–8 cm) deep in clumps of 9–12. Pot-grown plants can be planted

Crocosmia 'Lucifer' (z. 7–9) is the most popular and widely planted of all crocosmias. It is very robust and reaches 4 ft. (1.2 m) in height. It flowers early, with large, rich red blooms, and looks stunning with the blue-gray foliage of *Rosa glauca* (z. 2–7) and the terracotta and ocher flowers of achilleas.

from late spring onward; where conditions are less than ideal, these tend to be more successful. Lift and divide clumps in spring every few years to maintain vigor and flower quality.

Crocosmia × crocosmiiflora (z. 7–10) is the result of crossing the starry, medium orange flowers of *Crocosmia aurea* with the more tubular, red *Crocosmia pottsii*. One of the hardiest, its vigorous, somewhat invasive growth produces stems of orange, occasionally yellow blooms. It has given rise to a rich array of cultivars, growing to around 24 in. (60 cm).

GOOD CROCOSMIA X CROCOSMIIFLORA CULTIVARS

'Gerbe d'Or' (z. 7–10) Golden yellow buds and canary yellow blooms.

'Jackanapes' (z. 7–10) Unusual bicolored flowers of orange-red and yellow.

'Lady Hamilton' (z. 7–10) Golden yellow flowers flushed with pale orange.

'Solfatare' (z. 7–10) Bronzed foliage and pale orange-yellow flowers.

'Star of the East' (z. 7–10) Fully open, starry, bright orange flowers, paler toward the centers.

'Emily McKenzie' (z. 7–10) Vigorous and free-flowering with long-lasting, dark orange flowers splashed with red.

'Carmin Brillant' (z. 7–10) Produces fiery red flowers.

Crocosmia masoniorum (z. 6–9) is hardier than most, and taller, at over 40 in. (1 m), with striking orange-red blooms. These face upward at the stem tips; with most other crocosmias, the flowers point forward under the stems. 'Rowallane Yellow' (above) is rich golden yellow with orange overtones.

Eupatorium purpureum subsp. maculatum 'Atropurpureum'

Gaillardia pulchella

progress up the stout stems, to 5 ft. (1.5 m) high. Quite unlike the other species, it forms large buds covered in brown, scalelike bracts, opening to a mass of fine golden yellow petals, similar in appearance to a thistle.

Coreopsis verticillata (zone 3–7) is a compact perennial, 12 in. (30 cm) high, with wiry stems and fine narrow leaves. Small, starry yellow flowers are freely borne from midsummer (see page 27). 'Moonbeam' is pale yellow, an easier color to mix with others.

Growing in moist to wet soil in sun or part shade, *Eupatorium purpureum* (zone 5–8) is a landmark of the late summer border. The stems, rising 6 ft. (2 m) or so high, are furnished with tiers of coarse, pointed, medium green leaves, making an effective backdrop to other plants. Domed heads of pink, pinkish purple, or white flowers form at the stem tips from midsummer until early fall. *Eupatorium purpureum* ssp. *maculatum* 'Atropurpureum' is widely grown. The stems are reliably red, the color often spreading to the foliage; the flower heads are richer red.

Eupatorium rugosum (zone 5–8) is less often seen. Its nettlelike foliage reaches 5 ft (1.5 m) or more in height, and clusters of bright white flowers appear at the tips of the stems.

Eupatorium rugosum 'Chocolate' is valuable for the rich deep coloring of its foliage (see Good Companions, below, and see page 90).

Gaillardias (blanket flower) (zone 3–8) provide some of the brightest and most cheerful blooms in the border, the dual coloring of the daisy flower heads shamelessly grabbing attention from midsummer into fall. Two species, both American natives, are the parents of our garden hybrids. The perennial species *Gaillardia aristata* has flower heads with sunny, medium yellow, fringed ray-like petals surrounding blood red,

buttonlike centers, while the ray florets of the annual *Gaillardia pulchella* are mostly red with a variable yellow rim. Both thrive in full sun on grasslands and rocky slopes, the latter species in desert conditions, which makes them undemanding even in the hottest summers.

Gaillardias are short-lived perennials, and are often treated as bedding plants. Give them a free-draining winter location sheltered from wet to increase their longevity. They are easily propagated from seed, most producing flowers within a year; alternatively, try taking root cuttings in fall or winter.

GOOD COMPANIONS

The pale yellow sunflower blooms of *Helianthus* 'Lemon Queen' (1) (z. 4–9) are carried on tall plants and look stunning against the wine and flame autumn foliage of *Cotinus* 'Grace' (2) (z. 5–8).

The dark purple-brown foliage of *Eupatorium rugosum* 'Chocolate'(3) (z. 5–8) mixes well with the red, purple, and pink foliage of *Berberis thunbergii* f. *atropurpurea* 'Rose Glow' (4) (z. 4–8).

Many selections are available; most are 24–30 in. (60–75 cm) tall. *Gaillardia* **'Burgunder'** (zone 3–8) is deep wine red, while **'Dazzler'** has orange-red ray florets tipped with yellow, around deep red centers. **'Kobold'**, one of the most popular, is a compact, bushy plant only 12 in. (30 cm) tall. It produces blood red flower heads tipped with medium yellow for long periods of summer into fall. **'Fanfare'** is a more recent variety. Each flower head has a dark red center surrounded by red tubular ray florets, tipped in bright yellow. It grows to 16 in. (40 cm) and is good for cutting.

Geraniums, prolific in spring and early summer, have yet more to offer in late summer. With neat or sprawling habits and leaves of varying size, shape, and texture, the hardy geraniums are also blessed with variety of flower. (See also pages 48, 67, and 137.)

Geranium **'Ann Folkard'** (zone 5–7) flowers from midsummer into fall, its magenta, black-eyed blooms seeming to float above the foliage. Scrambling stems bear attractive, maplelike leaves of bright yellow-green, maturing to medium green. Growing 24 in. (60 cm) tall, it makes good ground cover and will spread over a large area in sun or semi-shade. (See also page 93.)

Geranium × *oxonianum* (zone 4–8), too, blooms from midsummer to fall, bearing masses of medium pink, starry flowers. Forming a vigorous clump of toothed, segmented foliage, 32 in. (80 cm) high, it makes effective ground cover. **'A.T. Johnson'**, a favorite cultivar, has numerous pale pink flowers. The larger, more widely spaced petals of **'Sherwood'** are white flushed medium pink at the tips, with deep pink veins. *Geranium* × *oxonianum* f. *thurstonianum* has narrow, deep pink petals, often notched at the tips, with white centers to the flowers. The double form **'Southcombe Double'** has multilayered medium pink petals.

Geranium × oxonianum f. thurstonianum

Geranium wallichianum 'Buxton's Variety'

Geranium sanguineum

Geranium sanguineum (zone 4–7) forms a neat mat, 8 in. (20 cm) high, of fine, soft, narrow-fingered green leaves. Upward-facing, cup-shaped flowers hug the foliage; they are deep pink in the species, white in the case of **'Album'**, purple-pink for **'New Hampshire Purple'**, and deep pink-red on the very compact **'Shepherd's Warning'**. The popular *Geranium sanguineum* var. *striatum* grows 4 in. (10 cm) tall and has pale pink flowers with darker veins. *Geranium wallichianum* **'Buxton's Variety'** (zone 5–7) is always sought after. It has superb saucer-shaped flowers, each with a large white center, generously edged sky blue and veined in

bluish purple. Trailing, branched stems, 12 in. (30 cm) high, carry the flowers from midsummer to fall, when they age to shades of pinkish blue and purple.

Few other perennials make such an impact in late summer plantings as the glorious **heleniums** (zone 3–8). Clumps of sturdy stems clothed in lance-shaped medium green leaves are topped with a wealth of daisylike flower heads in shades of yellow through orange-red, with bold yellow to golden brown centers. At up to 5 ft. (1.5 m) tall, they have a dramatic effect mid-border.

In the wild heleniums grow in the moist meadows and prairies of North and Central America. There are annual and biennial heleniums, but those that are commonly grown in gardens are the herbaceous perennial species and their hybrids. All reliably hardy, they are perfect for a sunny border, thriving in fertile, moist, well-drained soil. The shorter ones are self-supporting, but the taller varieties may need support. Most begin to flower in midsummer and go on right through fall. *Helenium* **'Baudirektor Linne'** has satin red-brown petals with brown centers. **'Butterpat'** (zone 3–8) is bright yellow with golden yellow centers. **'Rubinzwerg'** (zone 3–8) has orange-red petals surrounding golden brown

Helenium 'Sahin's Early Flowerer'

Helianthus 'Loddon Gold'

centers. **'Sahin's Early Flowerer'** (zone 3–8) has yellow flowers with orange streaks arriving in early to midsummer on more compact plants, 30 in. (70 cm) high. (See also pages 42 and 52.)

The perennial forms of *Helianthus* (sunflower) are not as well known as the annual varieties, but they are valuable for sunny color in late summer; most reach a relatively modest 5 ft. (1.5 m). They like moist, neutral to alkaline soil in full sun. *Helianthus* 'Gullick's Variety'

(zone 5–8) is extremely free flowering, producing masses of yellow blooms with purple-brown centers. **'Loddon Gold'** (zone 4–8) has fully double golden blooms on very upright, stocky stems. **'Lemon Queen'** (zone 4–9) has vibrant, pale yellow flower heads (see Good Companions, page 158).

Many **inulas** are monumental plants, familiar but often not readily identified by gardeners. Dormant in winter and spring, they grow steadily through the

summer, forming a robust clump of coarse, dark green leaves up to 10 in. (25 cm) long, with stems of bright daisylike flower heads in shades of yellow to orange, from midsummer into fall. Thriving in rich, moist soil and full sun, inulas are good for the edge of a bog garden and for an exotic border.

Inula magnifica (zone 4–8) has hairy stems, almost 6 ft. (2 m) tall, streaked dark brown-purple. In late summer these carry a stunning show of bright, golden yellow flower heads, each up to 6 in. (15 cm) across. *Inula helenium* (zone 4–8), known as elecampane, has smaller, bright yellow flowers, borne on 3–6 ft. (1–2 m) stems in mid- to late summer; it is prized for the medicinal property of its roots.

At about 18 in. (45 cm) high, *Inula ensifolia* (zone 4–8) is altogether smaller, perfect for a patio container or border's edge. In mid- to late summer, bushy growth of gray-green leaves is topped by plentiful heads of golden yellow flowers.

Inula hookeri (zone 4–8) has sunshine yellow flowers with brownish yellow centers, borne on 28 in. (70 cm) stems from late summer into autumn. It prefers partial shade, where its spreading roots and upright stems will quickly colonize uncultivated areas.

ANNUAL SUNFLOWERS

The annual sunflowers need little introduction, being familiar for their giant growth of up to 15ft. (5m), with flower heads as big as dinner plates. While *Helianthus annuus* itself is no more than a towering novelty, many of the new shorter varieties are useful late-flowering plants to fill gaps in the border. Easily raised from seed, they quickly reach heights of around 5ft. (1.5m). They have larger flowers than the perennial sunflowers, in a richer color range; their shades of yellow, russet, orange, and brown associate particularly well with dahlias.

160

Inula hookeri

Kirengeshoma palmata

Monarda 'Croftway Pink'

Flowering in roughly the same period in similar conditions are the closely related *Telekia* and *Buphthalmum*. ***Telekia speciosa*** (zone 6–8) is another bold beauty growing almost 6 ft. (2 m) tall, with large, broad, dark green leaves and branched stems bearing yellow, daisylike flower heads. Tolerating much drier conditions, *Buphthalmum salicifolium* (zone 4–8) is superb for a Mediterranean border; its 24 in. (60 cm) stems of fine foliage bear a succession of bright yellow daisies.

Kirengeshoma palmata (zone 6–8) is a Japanese treasure forming a clump of dark red, slender, gently arching stems, 40 in. (1m) high, clothed in maplelike leaves. In late summer, each stem ends in a lightly branched arrangement of nodding, tubular, canary yellow flowers with slightly recurved, waxy petals. This robust perennial is by nature a woodland plant, requiring lime-free, rich, moist soil in dappled shade. An annual mulch of leaf mold is beneficial.

Monardas (bee balm or bergamot) (zone 5–9) are superb plants native to North America. They form dense clumps of upright stems clad in aromatic, mint-like, medium to dark green leaves, which are sometimes bronzed purple.

The flowers are similar to those of sage and mint, but are much larger. At the top of stems 40 in. (1 m) high, neat, leaflike pink, purple, or red-flushed bracts open to reveal stunning heads of tubular, two-lipped flowers, in white or shades of pink, red, and violet. Often the stem grows beyond the first flowers to develop another tier. Typically the flowers are borne from midsummer into fall. A site in full sun or partial shade is required, in reasonably fertile, moist soil.

Of the many monardas available, most are derived from *Monarda didyma*, a species with bright red or pink flowers above red-tinged bracts. *Monarda*

PREVENTING MILDEW ON MONARDAS

Although monardas are very garden-worthy plants, they are rather prone to powdery mildew. In late summer, it is common to see plants with entirely gray foliage as a result of infestation by the fungus. To try to prevent the problem, do not let the roots dry out from early summer on; plants under stress are far more susceptible. At first signs of attack, spray with a fungicide, and water plants thoroughly.

'Beauty of Cobham' (zone 5–9) has purple-bronzed foliage with pale lilac-pink flowers above pinkish purple bracts. **'Croftway Pink'** has bold heads of medium pink flowers. **'Mahogany'** has rich red-brown bracts and flowers of bright pinkish red. **'Snow White'** is a pure white variety with green bracts. **'Violet Queen'** is rich violet purple, good with orange and red kniphofias.

Oenotheras (evening primrose) are well known for their fragrant flowers, opening at dusk, although some species open at dawn. They are native mainly to the Americas, but some popularly planted biennial varieties have become naturalized in Europe, where they are a fairly common sight on roadside verges. They thrive in fertile, free-draining soil in full sun, but dislike wet conditions.

Oenothera fruticosa (zone 4–8) is a short-lived perennial responsible for many familiar garden hybrids. Upright, branched red stems, up to 32 in. (80 cm) tall and with small dark leaves, bear clusters of deep yellow, funnel-shaped flowers, which open during the day *(continued on page 164)*

Penstemons

There are more than 250 species of penstemon, all natives of the Americas, and the innumerable hybrids derived from them are among our most popular herbaceous perennials. Selected for their bushy, upright habit and large, tubular or bell-shaped flowers, they bloom from midsummer into early winter in mild areas and mostly retain their foliage throughout the year. As a rule, those with broader, larger leaves are less hardy than those with fine, narrow leaves.

When introduced into Europe in the late 1700s, penstemons were regarded as short-lived perennials. The plant hunter Reginald Farrer later described them as having "a crowded hour of glory rather than a longer existence of mere usefulness." Over the years we have learned more about how to grow them; as a result, and through hybridization and selection, penstemons today are hardier than many people realize.

Penstemons thrive in poor, free-draining, slightly alkaline soil, ideally in full sun. In wet conditions

Penstemon 'Raven' is an upright cultivar, reaching 3 ft. (90 cm) in height. The leaves are broad and dark. The spikes of large tubular flowers are carried at the top of the stems from early summer until late fall (z. 7–9). The darkest rich purple, they are a perfect contrast to silver-foliage plants.

some plants struggle to survive the winter. On heavy soils, add grit when planting and spread gravel on the soil surface. Do not plant too deeply. Removing spent flower stems maintains vigor and encourages further flowering. Some species can be grown from seed, and the garden cultivars propagated by cuttings.

Penstemon hybrids always produce healthy shoots at the base of the plant, so it is tempting to cut stems back to ground level and allow the new shoots to take over. However, cutting back hard in spring results in plants that are late to come into flower. It is better just to tidy the plants, removing any remaining seed heads and any dead or damaged growth; the overwintered stems will then start to flower in early summer.

Penstemon pinifolius (z. 8–9), a spreading species, is good for scree. It has needlelike leaves on 16 in. (40 cm) stems with bright red flowers. Cultivars include **'Wisley Flame'** with orange-red flowers, and **'Mersea Yellow'**.

Penstemon campanulatus (z. 7–10) Upright and semi-evergreen, with stems 12–28 in. (30–70 cm) high. Flowers are small and numerous, in shades of pink to purple to violet. Early flowering.

Penstemon **'Andenken an Friedrich Hahn'** (also known as *Penstemon* 'Garnet') (zone 7–10) is an old favorite, one of the hardier penstemon hybrids, with fine foliage and large tubular, bell-shaped wine red flowers. Its light habit and prolific flowers make it perfect for a mixed border, where it provides interest after early shrub roses stop flowering. Height 30 in. (75 cm).

Penstemon heterophyllus (z. 8–9) is a low, spreading plant with lax stems, up to 12 in. (30 cm) high, and narrow, shining green leaves. Small, pink-flushed blue flowers are produced early in the season, usually with intermittent blooms later. **'Catherine de la Mare'** (above) is excellent, with dark green foliage and brilliant blue flowers with lavender-blue markings.

OTHER GOOD PENSTEMON HYBRIDS

All grow 24–36 in. (60–90 cm) high.

'Evelyn' (z. 7–10) Numerous small, bright pink flowers.

'George Home' (z. 6–9) Small wine red flowers.

'Hidcote Pink' (z. 6–9) Pale pink flowers, delicately streaked crimson.

'Stapleford Gem' (z. 6–9) Distinctive lilac-blue flowers flushed pink-purple, with white throats striped purple.

'White Bedder' (also known as 'Snow Storm') (z. 6–9) Conical white flowers that age with just a hint of pink.

'Windsor Red' (z. 6–9) Narrow, white-throated, vibrant red flowers.

Penstemon barbatus (z. 5–8), a hardy species, reaching over 40 in. (1 m) in height. With its blue-green foliage and rosy red flowers with bearded lips, it attracted much attention at the Royal Botanic Gardens, Kew, in England, when it was introduced in 1793.

Penstemon digitalis **'Husker Red'** (z. 3–8) Rosettes of dark green foliage, deep red when young, from which 24 in. (60 cm) stems of small pinkish white flowers emerge as summer progresses.

Penstemon hartwegii (z. 9–11) Stems up to 40 in. (1 m) high carry a glorious show of nodding purple-red tubular bells with white throats.

Penstemon **'Alice Hindley'** (z. 7–10) Large flowers of iridescent lilac-blue are carried on light spikes 3 ft. (90 cm) high. It has a vigorous habit and good foliage. Grown as an alternative to the well-known but somewhat unreliable 'Sour Grapes'.

Penstemon smallii (z. 6–8) Glossy, bronze-green basal leaves and many stems of bearded, lavender-purple flowers, white striped within. Prefers moist soil. Height 24 in. (60 cm).

Oenothera 'Lemon Sunset'

Oenothera speciosa 'Siskiyou'

from late spring to late summer. *Oenothera fruticosa* 'Fireworks' (zone 4–8) is unusual in its dark green, glossy leaves, flushed brown-purple. *Oenothera fruticosa* ssp. *glauca* (zone 4–8) has broader blue-green foliage, tinged red when young. *Oenothera* 'Lemon Sunset' (zone 5–9) is a hybrid with clear yellow flowers.

Oenothera macrocarpa (formerly known as *Oenothera missouriensis*) (zone 4–8) is a superb low-growing species reaching only 12 in. (30 cm). Over a long period from late spring through to early fall, the lax stems carry solitary, large, funnel-shaped, shining yellow blooms, 4 in. (10 cm) across,

which are quite out of scale with the plant; they make an impact wherever they are, but especially in a gravel planting or on the edge of a path.

Oenothera speciosa (zone 5–7) is another low-growing plant with spreading stems, 12 in. (30 cm) high, bearing solitary, saucer-shaped, strongly scented white flowers with yellow eyes, from early summer until early fall. *Oenothera speciosa* 'Siskiyou' is a popular cultivar, with its white

tissue-paper petals edged and flushed in pink; it looks truly wonderful with the rich, brightly colored flower heads of *Verbena* 'Homestead Purple'.

Origanums (zone 5–8) are perhaps best known as the source of the familiar culinary herb oregano, or marjoram, prized for its aroma and flavor and an essential in Mediterranean dishes. Many species make excellent garden plants for their prolific flowers and aromatic, sometimes striking, foliage.

Some species and their hybrids are specifically grown as alpine plants. With their unusual flower bracts, these are distinctly different from most origanum species; they also tend to need more careful cultivation. *Origanum scabrum*

THE HERB OREGANO

Oregano is the dried flowers of wild marjoram, *Origanum vulgare*. In the Mediterranean it is commonly sold bunched, on the stem. The open flowers can be cut from the garden in late summer and hung upside down in a warm, airy place to dry for use throughout the winter. Origanum grown on the driest, poorest soil always has the highest concentration of oils and the best flavor.

(zone 5–8) has prostrate, woody stems bearing scalelike, pinkish red bracts resembling shrimps' tails.

Most species are native to Asia and the Mediterranean, growing in full sun on free-draining, alkaline soil of low fertility. They are at home in a sunny perennial border or the herb garden, their flowers enjoyed by a variety of bees and butterflies.

Origanum laevigatum (zone 5–8) forms a spreading clump of erect, woody-based stems, 24 in. (60 cm) high, with small oval, dark green leaves. Clusters of small, tubular, purple-pink flowers set among dark red bracts give a long season of interest from early

GOOD COMPANIONS

With its yellow leaves and purple-brown flowers, *Origanum vulgare* 'Aureum' (1) (z. 5–8) looks delightful with the violet-blue double *Geranium pratense* 'Plenum Violaceum' (2) (z. 4–7).

The deep blue spikes of *Salvia nemorosa* 'East Friesland' (3) (z. 5–8) make a lovely combination with the pale blue blooms of annual *Nigella damascena* 'Miss Jekyll' (4).

Origanum laevigatum 'Herrenhausen'

Phygelius aequalis 'Yellow Trumpet'

Phygelius × rectus 'Winchester Fanfare'

summer into the autumn. *Origanum laevigatum* 'Herrenhausen' (zone 5–8) overwinters as a mat of purple-green foliage. In spring and summer, young growth is bronzed purple—a perfect backdrop to the purple flowers.

Origanum vulgare (zone 5–8) has woody-based, upright stems of about 20 in. (50 cm), clad in oval, dark green, strongly scented leaves. Tubular flowers of white or pale to dark pink appear in loose clusters from midsummer right through fall. *Origanum vulgare* 'Aureum' is an excellent perennial, its foliage golden yellow in full sun and a lovely lime green in shade (see Good Companions, left, and see page 95).

Patrinia gibbosa

Patrinia triloba (zone 6–9) is a rare jewel, with golden yellow flowers on red-tinted, branched stems. It forms thick ground cover, 16 in. (40 cm) high, of medium green, maplelike leaves, which turn yellow in autumn. Growing naturally on mountain plains in Siberia and Japan, patrinias are hardy plants, thriving in fertile, moist soil in partial or full shade. *Patrinia gibbosa* (zone 6–8) is another garden-worthy species, giving the effect of *Alchemilla mollis* (lady's mantle) late in the season.

Phlox paniculata (zone 4–8) is acknowledged as one of the loveliest of perennials, long grown in the cottage garden and the perennial border. The rounded heads of soft, fragrant flowers in rich and pastel shades are the essence of the summer garden and make wonderful cut flowers. (See page 43.)

Phygeliuses (river bell or wild fuchsia) are sub-shrubs with suckering, upright stems carrying loose spikes of narrow tubular flowers in summer. They are natives of South Africa and in colder climates are often treated as herbaceous perennials, combining easily with other border perennials. Phygeliuses like lots of sun and moist, free-draining soil. Dry

conditions lead to poor growth and few flowers. If they are treated as perennials, phygeliuses can be cut back to around 4 in. (10 cm) in late fall and protected with a dry mulch. New growth emerges the following spring. Most grow to 40 in. (1m) high. In a sheltered spot against a wall, they can reach 10 ft. (3 m) or more if unpruned.

Phygelius capensis (zone 7–9) bears flowers of orange or scarlet-red with yellow throats. *Phygelius aequalis* (zone 8–9) has pale pink-orange, yellow-throated flowers. The cultivar 'Yellow Trumpet' has creamy yellow flowers on light green stems; 'Sensation' is striking, with dark purple-red flowers over dark, glossy foliage.

Phygelius × rectus (zone 8–10) is a garden hybrid derived from the above two species. There are a number of excellent cultivars. 'African Queen' has pale red flowers on dark red stems. The blooms of 'Devil's Tears' are blood red, and those of 'Salmon Leap' are orange and deeply lobed. 'Winchester Fanfare' has lovely dark stems, which bear attractive red-pink flowers.

Physostegia virginiana (zone 4–9), popularly called the obedient plant, has

165

Physostegia virginiana 'Vivid'

Potentilla atrosanguinea and Potentilla nepalensis are the parents of many hybrids; both grow wild in arid grassland, scrub, and alpine meadows in the Himalayas. In the garden, they will thrive in any free-draining soil, preferably in full sun. They grow well on alkaline soil (see page 82).

Salvias are a diverse group of plants including aromatic herbs, woody shrubs, and herbaceous perennials and annuals. Their colorful flowers, long flowering period, and undemanding nature have made them popular for summer bedding. Even perennial species are often given this role, the ease with which they are propagated making them a disposable purchase, especially if they are winter tender. An example is *Salvia farinacea* 'Victoria' (zone 8–10), which has spikes of dark purple-blue flowers from late summer into fall.

Most salvias prefer moderately fertile, free-draining soil in full sun, although they will tolerate a site in partial shade. Hardiness is variable, but good drainage in winter is essential for survival.

Salvia nemorosa (zone 5–8) is perhaps the toughest of the perennial salvias. From a clump of deciduous, wrinkled, oval, dark green leaves arise branched stems, 32 in. (80 cm) tall; these carry tightly packed spires of small tubular, white, pink, and violet to purple

tubular two-lipped flowers, which stay in position when gently nudged to one side, hence its common name. It forms a strongly spreading clump, with stems 24–40 in. (60–100 cm) high carrying lightly branched flower spikes. Each spike is covered in a succession of buds, which open from bottom to top, in white or shades of pink to purple.

There are many garden-worthy forms, all growing well in full sun or in partial shade, wherever the soil is reliably moist and rich. Among the best of these are *Physostegia virginiana* 'Olympic Gold' (zone 4–9), a golden-leaved variety with violet-pink flowers; var. *speciosa* 'Bouquet Rose', with lilac-pink flowers; and var. *speciosa* 'Variegata', with white-margined, dark green leaves and bright pink flowers. 'Summer Snow' is the finest of the whites, only 24 in. (60 cm) tall. 'Vivid' produces dazzling purple-pink flowers on stems around 20 in. (50 cm) tall.

Potentillas (zone 5–8) are best known for their shrubby species, but the herbaceous kinds share their ease of cultivation and versatility in the garden. With spreading clumps of green to silver, strawberry-like foliage, they are an asset to any border or rock garden.

Salvia farinacea 'Victoria'

SALVIA OFFICINALIS

Although really woody sub-shrubs, the varieties of *Salvia officinalis* (common sage) are often offered alongside herbaceous perennials. Preferring a dry, sunny position in the garden, they produce spikes of blue flowers similar to those of many herbaceous salvias. Their aromatic leaves are used for flavoring food. The purple and variegated forms are particularly ornamental and go well with silver-leaved perennials and shrubs, helianthemums, and cistus. (See also page 97.)

GOOD COMPANIONS

Achillea filipendulina 'Gold Plate' (1) (z. 2–9) goes on flowering into late summer and looks good with the late red-brown blooms of *Sanguisorba officinalis* (2) (z. 4–8).

The green-purple foliage and red-purple blooms of *Tradescantia* 'Concord Grape' (3) (z. 5–8) mixes well with the fine golden foliage of *Sambucus racemosa* 'Sutherland Gold' (4) (z. 3–7).

flowers, with violet purple bracts that last from midsummer well into fall. **'Amethyst'** has lilac-pink flowers and soft gray-green foliage. Rather shorter is **'East Friesland'**, which has violet-blue flowers and purple bracts on stems reaching only 18 in. (45 cm) high (see Good Companions, page 164).

Salvia nemorosa was involved in the parentage of the garden hybrids *Salvia × superba* and *Salvia × sylvestris*; they have inherited both its hardiness and its habit. *Salvia × superba* (zone 5–8) boasts vibrant violet blue to purple flowers on stems 24–36 in. (60–90 cm) tall. *Salvia × sylvestris* **'May Night'** ('Mainacht') (zone 4–8) is one of the

Salvia nemorosa 'Ostfriesland' (EAST FRIESLAND)

most useful: Reaching 24 in. (60 cm) high, it is dwarfer than many and self-supporting. The long-lasting flowers are rich violet-blue with violet bracts (see page 43). **'Blauhügel'** has striking blue flowers and grows only 20 in. (50 cm) high; **'Rose Queen'** has pink flowers, and **'Schneehügel'** is white.

Salvia sclarea (clary sage) (zone 5–9) is a short-lived perennial or biennial forming a rosette of large, wrinkled, medium green leaves. In summer of the second year, numerous lilac or pink to

Salvia lavandulifolia

blue flowers and lilac bracts appear on candelabra-like stems up to 40 in. (1 m) tall. *Salvia argentea* (zone 5–8) is another biennial, with silver leaves (see page 103). *Salvia lavandulifolia* (Spanish sage) (zone 5–9) is a short-lived perennial with silver-gray foliage, enhanced by short spikes of lavender flowers on 20 in. (50 cm) stems from early summer onward.

Many species of salvia belong to hot, often arid regions of the United States, Mexico, and Central America. These are less hardy but are useful garden plants, either replaced annually or grown in patio containers that can be moved to a frost-free winter location.

The sub-shrubs *Salvia greggii* (zone 8–11) and *Salvia microphylla* (zone 7–9) grow to about 32 in. (80 cm) tall, with wiry stems and small aromatic leaves, characteristics they have passed on to their hybrid *Salvia × jamensis* (zone 7–10). This has given rise to a number of cultivars that reliably produce a display of flowers all summer and fall, in many shades of pink, red, violet, and purple, as well as creamy yellow to orange. These are hardier than they look and, although often cut back by frost, break into leaf again in late spring. They combine well with other sun-loving perennials, lavenders, herbs, and silver-leaved shrubs. There are many cultivars to choose from: *Salvia × jamensis* **'Raspberry Royale'** is excellent, with vivid raspberry pink flowers in profusion.

Salvia leucantha (zone 8–10) is another bushy sub-shrub, with 32 in. (80 cm) stems and narrow, lance-shaped medium green leaves. From late summer until the frosts, white flowers appear, in lavender-blue to purple bracts. The young shoots and leaf undersides are covered in a distinctive soft white down.

Salvia uliginosa (zone 6–9) has small but numerous, glorious medium blue flowers, borne in short spikes on elegant, slender stems 6 ft. (2 m) tall. In a sheltered site, with a dry mulch of bark or bracken, this Latin American treasure often proves winter hardy.

Salvia leucantha

Tradescantias

Tradescantias (spiderwort, Moses in the bulrushes) (zone 5–8) are natives of the United States. With their spiky, angular stems and leaves, they offer a useful contrast to the soft, broad leaves of many other border perennials. The unusual three-petaled blooms, in white or shades of pink to red and pale blue to purple, have distinctive feathery centers and are borne at the shoot tips in early summer, repeating until fall.

Relatives of the well-known houseplants, these are hardy perennials; those most popular for the garden are the hardy forms of *Tradescantia virginiana* and the cultivars of *Tradescantia* Andersoniana Group.

Reliable summer moisture is essential, and ideally rich, fertile soil in full sun or partial shade. Unless supported by their neighbors, tradescantias benefit from low grow-through supports to prevent plants from collapsing later in the season.

Tradescantia Andersoniana Group 'Sweet Kate' has golden yellow foliage studded with sapphire flowers. It mixes well with gold-variegated plants and is perfect for containers.

OTHER GOOD TRADESCANTIAS

The following all belong to the Andersoniana Group and grow 16–24 in. (40–60 cm) high.

'Bilberry Ice' Short and compact, with soft purple flowers edged in white.

'Charlotte' Pink flowers.

'Concord Grape' Purple-green foliage and rich red-purple blooms (see Good Companions, page 166).

'Danielle' White flowers.

'Isis' Rich royal purple.

'Osprey' Pure white flowers and feathery pink-blue centers.

'Perinne's Pink' Pale pink flowers; blue-green foliage.

'Rubra' Bright pinkish red flowers over a long period.

Sanguisorbas are natives of wet meadows and swamps, popular for their fine stems and bottlebrush flower heads, which appear from midsummer to mid-autumn. Spreading, hardy, deciduous perennials, they have distinctive foliage, each leaf made up of rounded-oblong, toothed leaflets of green or greenish blue. All need moist soil and a site in full sun or partial shade.

The bold blue-green leaves of *Sanguisorba alpina* (zone 4–7) are striking. *Sanguisorba canadensis* (zone 3–7) is upright, growing to 6 ft. (2 m), with apple green foliage and plenty of white flower spikes; good in a naturalistic setting. *Sanguisorba hakusanensis* (zone 4–7) has gray-green foliage and fluffy pink flower heads on numerous stems 32 in. (80 cm) high. It likes a cool position. The lovely *Sanguisorba obtusa* (zone 4–7), from Japan, has lipstick pink flower heads and handsome grayish foliage. It grows to 24 in. (60 cm) high. *Sanguisorba officinalis* (zone 4–8) forms clumps of spindly stems, 40 in. (1 m) tall, with small red-brown flower heads; it is an attractive see-through plant in a mixed border. (See Good Companions, page 166.)

Sanguisorba officinalis

Stokesia laevis

Stokesia is a wonderful plant for the garden and for cut flowers. There is only one species, *Stokesia laevis* (zone 5–10), from the southeastern states. It enjoys fertile, moist, free-draining soil, preferably slightly acid. In a sunny site the evergreen rosette of lance-shaped leaves will produce upright stems of up to 24 in. (60 cm), each with a number of blooms from midsummer to early fall. Each 4 in. (10 cm) flower consists of a central disk surrounded by a ray of raggedly fringed petals.

There are a number of cultivars: *Stokesia laevis* **'Alba'** and **'Silver Moon'** both have pure white blooms; **'Träumerei'** is blush pink; **'Purple Parasols'** has violet-purple petals around a white to blue center; **'Omega Skyrocket'** has lilac blooms on 3 ft (90 cm) stems; **'Blue Star'** is bright blue.

Verbena bonariensis (zone 8–9) is a South American plant that has become naturalized in the southeastern states and California. Stunning when drifting through wild gardens and borders, it has elegant branching stems bearing narrow medium green leaves and small domed heads of numerous lilac-purple flowers, from midsummer until late fall. Its airy stems are popular companions to asters, echinaceas, and achilleas. *Verbena bonariensis* self-seeds on all but the

The violet flowers of *Verbena bonariensis* are carried on tall stems to meet the ripening fruits of *Malus* × *zumi* 'Golden Hornet' as summer mellows into autumn.

TRAILING VERBENAS

Many hybrid verbenas form low, spreading mats, 6–18 in. (15–45 cm) high, which, from midsummer onward, deliver a fine show of flowers, which are perfect for patio containers and hanging baskets, as well as for the edge of a border. The bold flower heads come in white and shades of pink, pale orange, red, and blue to purple, sometimes with distinctive eyes. *Verbena* 'Lawrence Johnston' (z. 5–7) has dark velvet red flowers, while *Verbena* 'Homestead Purple' (z. 5–7) is rich bright purple.

---

heaviest, wettest soils. On light, sandy soils its self-propagation is prolific! It enjoys full sun and reasonable moisture and fertility and in ideal conditions will easily reach 6 ft. (2 m) in height. Shorter plants result on drier soils.

Verbena corymbosa (zone 6–7) blooms all summer, producing loose heads of lovely lilac-pink flowers on 5 ft. (1.5 m) stems, clothed in broader, toothed, medium green leaves. *Verbena rigida* (zone 7–10) dazzles with its pinkish purple flowers, borne in succession until autumn on 20 in. (50 cm) stems (see pages 69 and 152).

Veronicastrums (zone 4–8) are close relatives of veronica, similar in their spikes of flowers but far more statuesque. In full sun or partial shade, they are easy to grow, as long as they have adequate moisture in summer.

Veronicastrum virginicum, a North American native, has whorls of narrow leaves on 6 ft. (2 m) stems. The flowers are white, light blue or pink, and borne in narrow spikes at the tips of the stems from mid- to late summer. It provides useful tall, late spikes in the border and will take over, albeit subtly, where the early-flowering delphiniums leave off.

Veronicastrum sibiricum is a native of China and Japan and has whorls of broader leaves on similarly tall stems. From mid- to late summer the hebelike lilac-blue flower spikes are carried on the stems in upright clusters of five or six. They make a useful contrast to orange crocosmias and yellow achilleas.

Veronicastrum sibiricum

Fall

As dewy mornings develop into mellow days, and colder nights warn of impending frosts, the softer, warm-blooded blooms of summer make way for the brave and beautiful flowers of autumn. Delicate colors and graceful habits belie their hardiness, some continuing their display into early winter. Against the fiery tints of autumn foliage, the rich blues and purples of asters sing out all the louder. Evergreens provide a dark backdrop to the delicate pastel blooms of anemones.

The pale mauve-pink of *Anemone* × *hybrida* 'September Charm' is delightful in dappled shade in the soft light of autumn.

Anemones that flower in fall are delightful perennials that have been grown in gardens for many generations, finding a welcome both in the cottage garden and in the grand perennial border. Popularly known as Japanese anemones, they have maplelike leaves and branched stems of up to 1 m (40 in.) tall, which, from late summer, produce airy clusters of silver buds and simple, saucer-shaped flowers with gold stamens. These anemones enjoy moist, fertile soil and are useful for their shade tolerance. Once established, they spread freely through the border, which may not suit carefully composed plantings.

Varieties belonging to *Anemone hupehensis* (zone 6–9) tend to flower from mid- to late summer, while those coming from *Anemone vitifolia* (zone 4–8) bloom later, continuing into fall. *Anemone* × *hybrida* cultivars are the results of hybridizing the two species.

Anemone hupehensis (zone 6–9) bears either white or pink flowers on stems 32 in. (80 cm) tall. **'Hadspen Abundance'** has pale and darker pink in the same flower, and blooms over a long period. *Anemone hupehensis* **var. *japonica*** (zone 7–10) has flowers

The single pink flowers of *Anemone hupehensis* 'Hadspen Abundance' clash happily with the vibrant autumn shades of heleniums.

with more numerous narrow petals, borne on stems often over 40 in. (1 m). **'Pamina'** is a more compact alternative, at 20 in. (50 cm), and its neatly double flowers are of a beautiful deep pink. **'Prince Henry'** produces lovely semi-double, rose pink blooms.

Anemone × *hybrida* **'Honorine Jobert'** (zone 5–7), with 4 ft. (1.2 m) stems of large, single, pure white flowers, is the finest of the fall anemones (see Good Companions, page 177). It looks stunning when planted against a dark evergreen hedge. **'Queen Charlotte'** produces large semidouble, silky pink blooms on stems 40 in. (1m) tall. **'September Charm'**

Anemone hupehensis var. japonica 'Prinz Heinrich' (PRINCE HENRY)

has an abundance of pale pink blooms. **'Whirlwind'** is white and double, but lacks the sophistication of the single varieties. (See also page 46.)

Asters, which are best known for the Michaelmas daisies of the cottage garden, deliver an unrivaled show of color late in the season. Their daisy flowers have a delightful simplicity and are good mixers both in the border and as cut flowers. Most of the popular hardy perennial species form clumps of upright stems clothed in lance-shaped medium green leaves. Native to much of the northern hemisphere, most enjoy full sun or part shade in moderately fertile, moist but well-drained soil. Although some will tolerate dry conditions, any prolonged extremes of dry or wet will cause stress, increasing susceptibility to powdery mildew in some varieties.

Aster amellus (zone 5–8) provides a good range of shades: flower heads up to 2 in. (5 cm) across are borne on stems of 12–24 in. (30–60 cm). **'Brilliant'** has bright pink blooms; **'Violet Queen'** is rich violet; **'King George'** is lilac-blue. These asters flower for a long period, and their medium green foliage is far less prone to mildew.

Aster ericoides (zone 3–7) delivers a mass of smaller white flowers, on stems 40 in. (1 m) tall, throughout autumn. **'Brimstone'** has unusual creamy white sprays; **'Blue Star'** is sky blue; and **'Golden Spray'** produces waves of golden-centered white flowers with just a hint of pink. **'Pink Cloud'** is a hazy pale pink and is seldom troubled by mildew. Other asters with small flowers in light sprays include *Aster lateriflorus* **'Prince'** (zone 5–7), 24 in. (60 cm) high, with starry white flowers with rosy red centers and purple-red young growth aging to dusky green. Flower arrangers will be familiar with *Aster pilosus* var. *pringlei* **'Monte Cassino'** (zone 4–9), with its graceful sprays of dainty white, yellow-centered daisies and dark green foliage; it grows 40 in. (1 m) tall. (See also page 51.)

Aster × *frikartii* (zone 5–7) is a real autumn treasure, flowering for long periods. Considered by many to be the best, *Aster* × *frikartii* **'Mönch'** has flowers of a wonderful lavender-blue with prominent yellow centers. Growing 24–36 in. (60–90 cm) high, it is resistant to mildew so can be given a place at the front of the border, where its light form will not obscure other plants behind it.

The Michaelmas daisy, *Aster novi-belgii* (zone 2–8), is somewhat blighted by its readiness to succumb to mildew, but with due care can still play a role *(continued on page 174)*

Aster × *frikartii* 'Mönch'

Dahlias

Dahlias have been a gardeners' passion for generations. Species from Central America and Mexico found their way into European gardens from the mid-17th century, and they soon became fashionable blooms of high society. Today their colorful flowers brighten so many gardens and are popular subjects for competition.

Dahlias excel for their variety of flower form, which ranges from small and daisylike to large and spherical, and includes blooms resembling peonies, water lilies, and anemones. The color range, too, is astonishing, from whites and creams to deep reds and purples, including a wide choice of pastel shades. Plants are bushy and grow from tuberous roots, producing stems bearing leaves with toothed, oval leaflets, which in some cases are beautifully bronzed or deep red.

The dahlias with smaller, relatively simple flowers are excellent garden plants, in bloom from midsummer until fall. Their colors suit bold planting schemes, and their flower form looks at home in the traditional border. They are also excellent for cutting.

Dahlias are easy to grow, given fertile, free-draining soil and a sunny position. Dry tubers can be planted where they are to flower in mid-spring, or started into growth under glass in early spring. Pinch the tips of new growth to encourage stout stems. Protect from frost; dahlia shoots are tender and susceptible to cold.

In regions where winters are severe (generally, areas cooler than zone 9), tubers are best lifted when the foliage is knocked back by the first frost. Remove all soil, and lay out the tubers to dry; then place in a dry medium, such as sand, and store in a frost-free, airy location. Check for fungal infections and treat as necessary with a fungicidal dust such as sulfur.

In a sheltered position on free-draining soil, some gardeners succeed in overwintering dahlias outside as far north as zone 7. Dry tubers are inexpensive and readily available and pot-grown plants are sold in early summer, so failures are easily replaced.

Dahlia 'Bishop of Llandaff' (z. 9–11) is very effective for general planting. Dark chocolate foliage, reaching 3 ft. (90 cm) or more high, throws tall stems of semidouble, dark-eyed, bright scarlet flowers. As the blooms mature, golden stamens ring the centers. This is a stunning plant, combining well with *Verbena bonariensis* (z. 8–9). *Dahlia* 'Tally Ho' (z. 9–11) offers a shorter version, at a height of 24 in. (60 cm) or more.

For propagation, softwood cuttings can be taken when tubers start into growth in spring. The cuttings will produce fully developed plants in their first season and tubers by the following fall. Tuber size varies according to variety, but it is improved by feeding with a high-phosphate fertilizer during the growing season.

Dahlia 'Moonfire' (z. 9–11), at 28 in. (70 cm) high, is a favorite for patio containers. Its dark, red-brown foliage is the perfect setting for the numerous single golden orange, red-centered flowers produced in long succession from midsummer until late fall.

Dahlia 'Roxy' (z. 9–11) Single, bright magenta flowers on dark, dusky red stems above chocolate foliage. Height 24 in. (60 cm).

OTHER GOOD DAHLIAS FOR BORDERS

Dahlia 'Arabian Night' (z. 9–11) Small, double, upward-facing flowers of the darkest red. Height 40 in. (1 m) or more. Good for cutting.

Dahlia 'Chimborazo' (z. 9–11) Dark red outer petals with an inner circle of shorter, yellow-tipped petals. Height 5 ft. (1.5 m). Suits informal planting.

Dahlia 'Grenadier' (z. 9–11) Similar to 'Bishop of Llandaff' and equally good. Deep scarlet flowers; excellent dark foliage. Height 3 ft. (90 cm) or more.

Dahlia coccinea (z. 9–11), one of the original species, has small, single, rich orange flowers and dusky green foliage. Height is 24 in. (60 cm).

Dahlia 'David Howard' (z. 9–11) produces delightful small, double, apricot orange blooms above dark bronzed foliage. Height 3 ft. (90 cm). A seedling of 'Bishop of Llandaff', it was discovered in the late 1950s.

Dahlia merckii (z. 9–11) Many small, single flowers in shades of lavender-pink with yellow centers; lush growth and looser habit, 5 ft. (1.5 m) high.

173

among other late flowers (see page 40). The New England aster, *Aster novae-angliae* (zone 2–8), a native of North America, seems resistant to mildew, and its robust stems of bloom, in excess of 40 in. (1 m), produce a reliable, loud display. 'Barr's Pink' has semidouble flowers of lipstick pink with gold centers; 'Mrs. S.T. Wright' is lilac-pink; 'Rubinschatz' is pinkish red, and 'Violetta' violet-pink.

Chrysanthemums are often thought of as beauties planted in neat rows at the back of the vegetable plot, carefully nurtured, supported, and disbudded in order to produce the finest of blooms. Some chrysanthemums are less demanding and grow happily among other perennials in the border, prolonging the flowering season with their mellow shades, including pink, red, and purple, as well as yellow and white. The flowers are borne on woody-based, upright stems, clad with dark green, oval, and deeply or shallowly cut leaves, which are distinctly aromatic. A sunny site in reasonably fertile, free-draining soil is required, enriched with plenty of well-rotted manure for best results.

The **Rubellum Group** (zone 5–9) consists of named selections or hybrids between *Chrysanthemum rubellum* (now *Chrysanthemum zawadskii*) and other notable species. These are hardy

Chrysanthemum 'Clara Curtis'

Chrysanthemum Rubellum Group

border perennials, also good for cutting. All have yellow-centered, daisy flowers on stems usually up to 30 in. (75 cm) high, in late summer and early fall.

Chrysanthemum 'Clara Curtis' is a favorite, with deeply divided foliage and stems carrying long-lasting sprays of single medium pink flower heads. 'Emperor of China' is taller, at over 40 in. (1 m), and has double, pale pink-white flowers with red-bronzed foliage. 'Mrs. Jessie Cooper' has large, semidouble, vibrant red flowers, 4 in. (10 cm) across. 'Nancy Perry' has deep pink, semidouble flower heads.

Rubellum Group chrysanthemums are divided in spring; healthy divisions can be replanted or potted in a frost-free situation to replace any winter losses.

Members of this group tend to be less susceptible to most of the pests and diseases that affect chrysanthemums; they should remain largely trouble free.

The florists' spray chrysanthemums, developed mainly for cutting and for exhibition, are not such hardy creatures. They grow 32–56 in. (80–140 cm) high and flower from late summer into fall. There is a fine range of flower forms: alongside the singles, doubles and semidoubles are the spherical or pompon heads made up of layer upon layer of raylike petals; those resembling a large daisy with a broad central disk are referred to as "anemone centered." The florists' chrysanthemums are usually propagated from basal cuttings, best taken in late spring.

CHRYSANTHEMUM LEAF MINER

This insect pest burrows through the leaf blade between the upper and lower surfaces, manifesting itself as a progressive filigree pattern of light green to buff appearing throughout the leaf. It obviously causes extensive damage to the foliage, so early identification and eradication is desirable. Pick off and destroy affected leaves as they appear. Treat the plant with a systemic insecticide if the problem persists.

GOOD COMPANIONS

The yellow-centered lavender-blue flower heads of *Aster* × *frikartii* 'Mönch' (1) (z. 5–7) sit well above the bright pink blooms of *Nerine bowdenii* (2) (z. 9–10).

As fall progresses, the wispy leaves of *Carex buchananii* (3) (z. 7–9) reflect the warm tones of the fading blooms of *Sedum* 'Autumn Joy' ('Herbstfreude') (4) (z. 4–8).

Chrysanthemum 'Buff Margaret' (zone 5–9) has double, rounded heads 3 in. (9 cm) across in a creamy honey-orange. 'Enbee Wedding' has single pinkish white flowers, effective against a dark shrub or hedge. 'Pennine Oriel' has large, anemone-centered flowers of buff-white with pale yellow centers.

Echinaceas (coneflower) produce their daisylike flower heads on upright, leafy stems from late summer into autumn. After the petals have fallen, the conelike seed heads remain attractive into winter. Most varieties are derived from the rich reddish purple *Echinacea purpurea* (zone 4–8), some especially familiar through their use in prairie plantings (see page 51).

Excellent varieties to grace the autumn garden include *Echinacea purpurea* 'Indiaca', which is similar to the species, but in some flowers there are more petals appearing from the top of the cone. This "double-decker" effect is a random occurrence, not to be found on every bloom. *Echinacea purpurea* 'Razzmatazz' also resembles the species, except that the central cone of each flower head is replaced with a mass of shorter, notched petals, not unlike a fully double dahlia. *Echinacea purpurea* 'Jade' has single flowers with white, green-tipped petals and dark green cones. All grow 40 in. (1m) high.

Two other prairie echinaceas are somewhat lighter in habit, and their flowers consist of much narrower raylike petals around the central cone. *Echinacea angustifolia* (zone 3–8) is dainty and pale pink, and a favorite of butterflies. *Echinacea paradoxa* (zone 4–7) is similar but medium yellow. A new hybrid, *Echinacea* 'Art's Pride' (zone 4–9), shares this flower form, with narrow petals of rich medium orange around each cone; it makes a delightful garden plant and a lovely cut flower.

Like many prairie plants, echinaceas like full sun and rich, well-drained soil

Echinacea 'Art's Pride'

with an adequate supply of moisture. Where conditions are too dry, plants are slow to become established.

Kniphofias (red hot poker or torch lily) (zone 6–9) have long been popular garden plants. Some start to flower from early summer, others peak in late fall. Their bright, torchlike flowers suit hot color schemes and excel with the warm shades of autumn. (See also pages 42 and 68.)

Kniphofia caulescens, also called the Lesotho red hot poker (zone 6–9), grows to 4 ft. (1.2 m) high and provides glorious heads of pinkish orange flowers, which mature to lime yellow as they open from bottom to top. The glaucous, evergreen foliage is also attractive. The flowers of the slightly shorter *Kniphofia* 'Percy's Pride' start off lime yellow, but turn to creamy yellow as they mature. *Kniphofia* 'Erecta', 3 ft. (90 cm) tall, carries its flowers upside down when in tight bud, but on opening, each flower points skyward in a show of fiery orange-red.

Physalis alkekengi (Chinese lantern) (zone 4–7) reaches its full glory in early

fall, when its large, deep orange, papery lanterns glow against its yellowing foliage. In early summer its spreading stems of diamond-shaped leaves and small, starry cream flowers command little attention. By late season, plants carry a succession of blooms alongside developing green lanterns and those already turning orange.

Close inspection of the lanterns reveals a shiny orange berry at the center of each. The berries become more visible as winter progresses and the lanterns lose their color, exposing their intricate skeletal frames.

Physalis likes well-drained soil in sun or partial shade, and is best sited where its vigor will not cause problems. Growing up to 30 in. (75 cm) tall, the stems become rather lax and may need support. The dwarf forms, which grow to 20 in. (50 cm), are more controllable.

Physalis alkekengi

DRYING CHINESE LANTERNS

Chinese lanterns (*Physalis alkekengi*) (z. 4–7) are wonderful for winter decoration in the home. Cut the lanterns as they mature, remove any remaining yellow leaves, and support the stems in a tall vase without water until dry. Wooden skewers or thin canes may be needed to keep the stems straight. Just three stems in a slender ceramic vase make a superb contemporary arrangement.

Sedums

Sedums are well known for attracting butterflies and bees, which search for nectar in the tiny, star-shaped flowers that crowd the flat flower heads. Many are grown in planters and rock gardens, their diminutive foliage borne on trailing stems forming dense mounds or mats, but they also have a role to play elsewhere in the garden. *Sedum kamtschaticum* (zone 7–10), for example, is excellent in scree or to edge the border. Its dark, spoon-shaped leaves and yellow flowers are also useful to fill gaps between bearded iris rhizomes.

The taller herbaceous species form clumps of upright, unbranched stems bearing oval to rounded-oblong, gray-green to blue-green, succulent leaves. They die down in winter, leaving behind a cluster of blue-green succulent buds. The flowers peak in late summer and fall: flat heads of white or pink. When faded, the browned stems and mahogany heads can be left until spring to provide winter interest.

Sedums typically thrive in free-draining, shallow, preferably alkaline soils. Mature clumps tend to

Sedum 'Autumn Joy' ('Herbstfreude') has large, flat heads of rich pink flowers on 24 in. (60 cm) stems. The blooms turn coppery pink then mahogany and last well into early winter.

collapse in fall if grown in moist, fertile sites, so grow-through supports may be necessary; annual division and replanting will also help to avoid the problem. Sedums are easy to propagate by stem cuttings, taken at any time in the growing season.

Sedum telephium (z. 3–8), 24 in. (60 cm) high, has heads of purple-pink flowers above pale gray-green foliage. The cultivar **'Matrona'** has larger, rounded leaves; **'Munstead Red'**, a Gertrude Jekyll plant, has darker foliage with a distinct purple flush and pleasant, rich brown-red flowers. *Sedum telephium* ssp. *maximum* **'Atropurpureum'** has striking purple foliage (see pages 73 and 91).

Sedum erythrostictum (z. 3–10) is little more than 12 in. (30 cm) high, with greenish white flowers. These are particularly attractive in the variegated cultivar **'Frosty Morn'** (above), which has clear white leaf markings. (See also page 97.)

Sedum spectabile (ice plant) (z. 4–8) has light blue-green foliage and stems 18 in. (45 cm) high bearing pink flowers. **'Iceberg'** (above) has pure white flowers above pale foliage. **'Brilliant'** has bright pink blooms; **'September Glow'** is darker. **'Indian Chief'** has rich pink flowers and gray-green leaves with boldly serrated edges, supposedly resembling the feathers of a headdress.

OTHER GOOD SEDUMS

Sedum 'Ruby Glow' (z. 4–8) Forms a sprawling clump to 10 in. (25 cm) high. Leaves are gray and flowers deep wine red.

Sedum aizoon **'Euphorbioides'** (z. 4–9) Forms a spreading clump of 14 in. (35 cm) stems, with green succulent leaves and yellow flower heads.

Rudbeckias are North American natives found growing in moist, often heavy soils of plains and foothills, where they thrive in full sun or partial shade. The hardy herbaceous perennial species *Rudbeckia fulgida* (commonly known as black-eyed Susan) and *Rudbeckia laciniata* are excellent garden plants, easy to grow and reliable, provided they have an adequate supply of moisture as the flowers develop.

Rudbeckia fulgida var. *sullivantii* 'Goldsturm' (zone 4–8) is a striking plant that produces a mass of golden, black-eyed daisy flower heads from late summer well into fall on stems up to 3 ft. (90 cm) high. It is superb planted with grasses or against the dark backdrop of purple foliage. (See page 53.)

Rudbeckia laciniata (zone 4–9) has rather stringy, tall stems up to 13 ft. (4 m) high, with pale, deeply cut leaves. The flowers consist of pale green-yellow cones dressed in recurved, narrow petals of bright yellow. The fuller, more prolific flowers of 'Herbstsonne' make a dramatic impression at the back of the border. 'Goldquelle' is more modest in height, with sumptuous double, bright yellow flowers, which, when fully open, reveal shorter, green-yellow petals obscuring the central cone.

Rudbeckia occidentalis (zone 3–10), 3 ft. (90 cm) tall, is a favorite of garden designers. A collar of sharply pointed green bracts cradles a dark, almost black, egg-shaped cone with a narrow band of bright yellow pinhead anthers. The cultivar 'Green Wizard' has striking flowers with conspicuous green bracts.

Schizostylis coccinea (zone 6–8) is a South African native with showy scarlet blooms. It forms a clump of semi-evergreen, narrow, swordlike medium green foliage, from which 24 in. (60 cm) flower spikes emerge in late fall, each carrying up to eight open, starry blooms in shades of pink, red, or white. There

Rudbeckia occidentalis 'Green Wizard'

Schizostylis coccinea

are a number of named forms and cultivars: **f.** *alba* is white; **'Viscountess Byng'** is dainty pale pink; **'Jennifer'** produces large flowers of medium pink; **'Sunrise'** is a rich shade of salmon pink and **'Major'** a lovely satin red. All look good with silver-foliage plants.

Schizostylises (zone 6–8) are often still in bloom at Christmas, and they make excellent cut flowers. They thrive in a site in full sun with moist, but free-draining soil. In cooler areas, they must be protected from cold, drying winds, with a dry mulch in winter. Even so, the flower spikes may be damaged by frost.

Solidagos (goldenrod) have long been a strong feature of the autumn garden. Excellent plants to encourage wildlife, they are much loved by late-pollinating insects. Their green-gold flowers are good mixers in the border, and they supply light relief from some of the bolder blooms. (See page 53.)

Tricyrtis, the toad lilies, may not be the showiest of autumn flowers, but their muted colors and exquisite beauty suit the season well. Useful plants in shady situations, they bring contrasting form and detail to plantings of ferns and hostas. (See page 59.)

GOOD COMPANIONS

The pure white petals and golden stamens of *Anemone* × *hybrida* 'Honorine Jobert' (1) (z. 5–7) contrast well with the rich burgundy of *Cotinus coggygria* 'Royal Purple' (2) (z. 4–8).

With its delicately patterned flowers, *Tricyrtis formosana* (3) (z. 4–9) makes a good companion for *Heuchera micrantha* var. *diversifolia* 'Palace Purple' (4) (z. 4–7) in semishade.

177

Winter

Most herbaceous perennials retreat safely underground in winter, hiding beneath the surface until the warmer days of spring. Yet in many zones, evergreen perennials still provide foliage interest—heucheras, ajugas, ophiopogons, epimediums, and bergenias are among those that defy the cold—and a few brave souls join the winter-flowering shrubs and produce delicate but hardy blooms. These are all the more welcome as reminders of the pleasures to come, and all the more wonderful in the way that, paying no heed to the elements, they challenge the frost and snow.

When you are considering winter flowers, *Helleborus niger* (zone 4–8), commonly called the Christmas rose, is one of the first that come to mind. A pure white beauty, it will defy the winter gloom, although often waiting until late in the season to produce its finest flowers. From a clump of dark, semi-evergreen, leathery leaves emerge numerous short, reddish brown flower stems, about 12 in. (30 cm) high, each carrying up to three nodding buds of folded white petals. These open to outward-facing, saucer-shaped white flowers, sometimes with a hint of pink, but always aging to a lovely shade of creamy pink before setting seed.

Native to regions of Germany, Austria, Switzerland, Italy, and Slovenia, *Helleborus niger* is a robust, tough perennial. Cultivation in the garden is not always easy; often the plant is given too much shade and moisture, which results in spotting of the leaves and badly marked flowers. In the wild, this hellebore is found growing on limestone in fairly dry coniferous woods or in open meadows. In the garden, an open, well-drained position suits it best, on fertile, neutral to alkaline soil. Some protection from slugs and snails is desirable; a grit mulch over the soil surface is ideal.

A number of named selections are available, often with subtle variations to the excellent flowers of the species.

The brave winter flowers of soft purplish pink *Cyclamen coum* and purest white *Galanthus nivalis* appear among the inky foliage of *Ophiopogon planiscapus* 'Nigrescens'.

Helleborus niger

Iris unguicularis

Iris foetidissima

Iris foetidissima 'Variegata'

Helleborus niger ssp. *macranthus* (zone 4–8) has more glaucous foliage, with larger white flowers. *Helleborus niger* 'Potter's Wheel' has white bowl-shaped flowers with pale green centers. *Helleborus niger* Harvington hybrids are reliable, free-flowering plants with pure white blooms. There are also forms of *Helleborus niger* with marbled or silver leaves. (For other hellebores, see pages 180–81.)

GROWING CHRISTMAS ROSES IN POTS

Helleborus niger can be grown in a pot of loam-based soil mix. Stand the pot in a sunny spot in the garden for the summer, and keep it well watered. In winter, when flower buds appear, move it close to the house. The blooms can be enjoyed without venturing too far into the garden, and the plant will gain some protection from winter wet.

Iris unguicularis (formerly known as *Iris stylosa*) (zone 7–9) produces beautiful fragile blossoms from a dense clump of narrow, evergreen, grasslike foliage 12 in. (30 cm) tall. The deliciously scented flowers are a vibrant blue-mauve; the lower petals (falls) display a flash of yellow, framed in white stripes.

This is a native of countries such as Greece and Turkey; in the garden, the ideal situation for it is the dry soil at the base of a sunny wall. Left undisturbed, a mature plant will produce a succession of blooms, which continue for a whole season. The flowers sit low down in the foliage, so removing damaged or brown leaves will help to reveal the full beauty of the blooms.

Iris foetidissima (zone 6–9) excels, not with showy flowers but with brightly colored seed heads. The plant forms a clump of sword-shaped, dark, evergreen foliage: a useful spiky form against neighboring flowers and foliage throughout the seasons. The rather dull purple flowers, on 16–32 in. (40–80 cm) stems, go almost unnoticed in early summer, but without them the winter treat of scarlet berries nestled in large splitting capsules could never be enjoyed. Stems bearing the distinctive seed heads can be cut for indoor display.

Found naturally in much of Europe, *Iris foetidissima* was often prescribed by medieval herbalists as a purgative. The plant has a pungent smell, like that of raw beef, when the foliage is crushed or damaged, hence its common names "stinking iris" and "stinking gladwyn"; but such an unfortunate odor is quickly forgiven when considering its garden merits. This is a versatile plant, happily performing in almost any free-draining soil and tolerating full sun, but thriving in full to partial shade and alkaline soil.

A small number of varieties to the species are available: *Iris foetidissima* var. *citrina* produces yellow flowers, while *Iris foetidissima* 'Fructu Albo' has unusual white winter berries. *Iris foetidissima* 'Variegata' has deep green foliage striped creamy white. An excellent hardy foliage plant, it tolerates hostile conditions and looks good all *(continued on page 182)*

179

Lenten roses (Helleborus × hybridus)

No garden suitable for the Lenten rose should be without its classic beauty. Its colorful yet subtle shades brighten the darkest days of winter, giving a glimpse of eagerly awaited spring. *Helleborus × hybridus* (zone 5–8) is in fact a large group of garden hybrids, the offspring of *Helleborus orientalis* (zone 6–9) and other hellebore species. Many of the parent species are native to regions of Greece, Turkey, and the Caucasus and have featured in gardens for the past two centuries. *Helleborus × hybridus* began to reach gardeners in the mid-1900s, assisted by many keen enthusiasts and plant breeders.

These hellebores form a clump of semi-evergreen, leathery, medium to dark green leaves, from the base of which appear thick stems, up to 18 in. (45 cm) high, each carrying up to four pendent buds, sheathed in soft new leaves. The buds open to outward-facing, saucer-shaped flowers. The promiscuous nature of the plant has led to great variety in flower color: shades of green, white, cream, yellow, pink, red, and burgundy to slate gray. Pink to dark red speckles are a common feature, as if paint has been flicked from a brush and landed on the flowers in distinct spots or a fusion of tiny flecks.

Some forms of pink to burgundy have darker veining on the petals. A rare delight are those with semi- to fully double flowers; scarcer still are anemone-flowered forms, with short, ruffled petals packed into the center of the more typical outer ones.

Micropropagation of these hellebores has given poor results, so the few named clones command high prices. There are some seedling strains, such as the Ashwood Garden hybrids, Ballard's Group, Blackthorn Group, and the Hillier hybrids. These include the flower forms and colors described above, but because they are seedlings, they show variation.

Helleborus × hybridus (z. 5–8) has beautiful flowers, enchanting both in the garden and for indoor decoration. Unfortunately they wilt and die if stems are cut and put in water. Instead, just the flowers should be picked, and floated on a bowl of water. They look wonderful used in this way, and the exquisite detail of each bloom can clearly be seen.

Helleborus × hybridus planted among hemerocallis (daylilies), which will provide both color and shade in summer as next year's hellebore flowers develop.

CULTIVATING LENTEN ROSES

The many forms of *Helleborus* × *hybridus* are undemanding plants, thriving in most moist, well-drained sites, but preferring neutral to alkaline soil. Vigor is seriously inhibited in very wet or dry conditions. They enjoy the dappled shade of trees or shrubs and look delightful planted with evergreen ferns or spring bulbs, such as snowdrops (*Galanthus nivalis*) (z. 4–8) or *Cyclamen coum* (z. 6–8). Buy pot-grown plants of flowering size; these can be planted at any time. Buying plants in flower is ideal, since the exact color can be seen.

In fall or early winter, before the flowers appear, remove any brown or damaged foliage. Some gardeners prefer to remove all mature foliage, in order to enjoy the emerging flower stems; new leaves will soon be produced once the flowers are over.

As the flowers fade, remove any weeds around the plants and carefully loosen the soil surface. Hellebores seed themselves readily, and seedlings will appear later in the year all around the mother plants. These should be left where they are until the following spring, then transplanted to make room for the next crop. The seedlings will vary in flower color—and hopefully result in some pleasant surprises. Alternatively, the seed can be collected when ripe and sown immediately in a cold frame, protected from birds and mice.

Established plants can be divided, but this may seriously affect the health and vigor of both the mother plant and its offshoots. The best time for dividing or moving plants is late summer or early fall, just as cooler conditions encourage a flush of new root growth.

Ophiopogon jaburan 'Vittatus'

year (see Good Companions, below). Dark purple, semi-evergreen heucheras are glorious against its strong, creamy white variegation. Though prone to rust, its foliage is less susceptible than that of the green form.

Evergreen foliage comes to the fore in the winter garden. With competition from deciduous plants much reduced, those that retain their leaves now take center stage, particularly if the shape or color of the foliage is either unusual or dramatic. ***Ophiopogon planiscapus* 'Nigrescens'** (zone 6–9) is a natural

choice. Few plants come even close to matching its glossy, almost black, broad, grasslike leaves, which grow in tight evergreen tufts (see Good Companions, below). Ophiopogons are members of the lily family, and have charming bell-shaped, purple-white flowers during summer, followed by shiny black berries.

Native to China and Japan, they grow on fertile, moist, but well-drained soil in dappled woodland shade. In the garden, a site in full sun is preferable because it intensifies the blackness of the leaf. The slowly spreading foliage reaches 12 in. (30 cm) in height and forms a thick, weed-suppressing carpet, the darkness of which looks sensational underneath golden-leaved evergreen shrubs such as *Euonymus japonicus* (zone 7–9) and *Choisya ternata* 'Sundance' (zone 8–10).

The foliage of ***Ophiopogon jaburan* 'Vittatus'** (zone 7–8) is less dramatic but perfectly lovely, reaching 24 in. (60 cm) high. Each pale green leaf is striped creamy white, and the small white flowers are followed by violet-blue berries. Not as hardy as *Ophiopogon planiscapus*, it needs good drainage and the shelter of a sunny wall. Protect with floating row cover if temperatures persistently fall below 27°F (–3°C).

***Primula* Cowichan** series (zone 6–8) are rather a surprise in the winter garden. They are members of the Polyanthus Group of primulas and share many of their relatives' attributes, but they should definitely be considered as more than winter bedding plants.

Cowichan primulas produce robust, winter-hardy rosettes of rounded-oblong, bronzed, dark green leaves. From late winter to early spring, they bear elegant, reddened stems, showing off clusters of simple, saucer-shaped, velvet flowers in shades of cream, yellow, and apricot as well as white,

Primula Cowichan series

blue, purple, and deep satin red; each has just a hint of yellow in the center. Compared to many of the more brazen forms in the Polyanthus Group, Cowichan primulas bring a more subtle, sophisticated touch to the garden.

In some zones, plants may start to bloom in early winter and continue through spring. Although a severe frost may spoil the early flowers, a succession of blooms will follow. Grow them in any reasonably fertile, humus-rich, moist but well-drained soil, in full sun or partial shade. Plant them in containers or beneath the bare winter stems of shrubs such as the red-barked dogwood, *Cornus alba* (zone 2–8). After flowering, the foliage rosettes will thicken, forming useful, weed-suppressing ground cover.

GOOD COMPANIONS

The shiny purple-black foliage of *Ophiopogon planiscapus* 'Nigrescens' (1) (z. 6–9) is stunning when planted beneath the bare, powdery white stems of *Rubus cockburnianus* (2) (z. 6–7).

The flame-colored wands of *Cornus sanguinea* 'Winter Beauty' (3) (z. 5–8) contrast with the creamy-white striped foliage of *Iris foetidissima* 'Variegata' (4) (z. 6–9).

Left undisturbed, the mahogany flower heads of sedum stand throughout winter.

BEAUTIFUL REMAINS

As the last summer and autumn flowers fade, many gardeners rush to strip away the remnants of flowers and foliage. But left alone, many border plants will keep their structure, their drying stems a reflection of former glory, yet still captivating in their own right.

Some essential maintenance must be done at this time of year—for example, mulching dormant perennials vulnerable to frost and collecting seed, whether for use next season or simply to avoid self-sown seedlings. But the big cleanup is best left until early spring; the dead growth helps to insulate against hard frosts as well as providing winter interest and often seeds for birds and animals.

Toward the back of the border, the light filigree form of *Foeniculum* (fennel) (zone 5–8) contrasts with the heavier upright rods of faded **verbascums** (zone 6–8). **Echinopses** (zone 6–7) hold their rounded thistle heads, and the flat heads of *Achillea filipendulina* 'Gold Plate' (zone 2–9) turn golden brown. The cones of **echinaceas** (zone 4–8) and **rudbeckias** (zone 4–8) remain deep black-brown, persisting long after the colorful petals have fallen.

Above the tight gray-green rosettes of its dormant winter shoots, *Sedum spectabile* (zone 4–8) still holds stout stems of large, flat chestnut heads, the remnants of its ruby autumn brilliance.

The reddened stems and rounded heads of *Angelica gigas* (zone 4–8), blackened by frost, persist alongside the oblong cones of the teasel, *Dipsacus fullonum* (zone 4–8), and surrounded by **gypsophila** (zone 4–8). *Eryngium × oliverianum* (zone 5–8) retains brown, rounded cones, still encircled by dramatic spiny bracts. The plant known as Chinese lantern, *Physalis alkekengi* (zone 4–7) has intriguing winter remains. The papery lanterns lose their rich orange color, leaving skeletal frames, each imprisoning a shriveled fruit waiting to release its seeds.

Ornamental grasses excel. Plumes of **cortaderias** (pampas grass) (zone 6–9) above arching foliage, feathery spikes of silvery **miscanthus** (zone 5–9), swirling mists of **stipas** (zone 4–8), and fluffy tails of **pennisetums** (zone 5–9) all contribute to the winter scene.

Frost etches the silhouettes of winter, snowfall emphasizes shapes and hides imperfections. Low sun changes color and outline. The winter garden is a magical place above and below ground. While we enjoy the delights of the more minimal landscape, those deciduous herbaceous perennials are waiting expectantly for warmer days to come.

Faded remains of summer glory are transformed by hoarfrost in midwinter.

Authors' choice:
favorite perennial planting groups

There are vast numbers of perennials in cultivation, and this book contains a selection of those that we consider to be the best. From these we have chosen some proven favorites that are easy to grow and rewarding. We have put them together into suggested planting groups that will give a long season of interest as well as providing variety in form or texture. Among these planting combinations you should find one to suit just about any situation in your garden.

1. DARK FOLIAGE AND HOT COLORS FOR FULL SUN
Maximum height 6 ft. (2 m)

 Crocosmia 'Lucifer' (z. 7–9) (page 157) Sword-shaped leaves and rich red flowers.

 Foeniculum vulgare 'Purpureum' (z. 5–8) (page 90) Feathery foliage of soft bronze; yellow flowers.

 Dahlia 'Moonfire' (z. 9–11) (page 173) Dark chocolate foliage and golden orange flowers.

 Lysimachia ciliata 'Firecracker' (z. 5–8) (page 91) Dark foliage and starry yellow flowers.

 Shrub planting partner: *Physocarpus opulifolius* 'Diabolo' (to 10 ft. [3 m]) (z. 2–7) Upright, deep burgundy foliage; a perfect background shrub.

2. LIME AND YELLOW FOR A SUNNY SITUATION
Maximum height 4 ft. (1.2 m)

 Alchemilla mollis (z. 4–7) (page 46) Soft green leaves and frothy lime flowers in summer.

 Hemerocallis 'Hyperion' (z. 4–10) (page 138) Grasslike foliage; pale yellow summer flowers.

 Euphorbia characias (z. 8–9) (page 113) Evergreen, gray-green foliage; early, bold, yellow-green flowers.

 Leucanthemum × *superbum* 'Aglaia' (z. 4–9) (page 142) Yellow-eyed white flowers; dark leaves.

 Shrub planting partner: *Philadelphus coronarius* 'Aureus' (to 6 ft. [2 m]) (z. 4–8) Lime foliage aging to yellow in summer. Fragrant white flowers.

3. BLUE, PURPLE AND MAGENTA FOR A SUNNY SITUATION
Maximum height 40 in. (1 m)

 Geranium psilostemon (z. 5–7) (page 48) Tall habit; vivid magenta, black-centered flowers in summer.

 Penstemon 'Raven' (z. 7–9) (page 162) Purple flowers summer and fall. Upright, evergreen.

 Salvia × *sylvestris* 'May Night' (z. 7–9) (page 43) Violet-blue, late flowers. Compact, upright.

 Heuchera 'Amethyst Myst' (z. 4–8) (page 89) Dark purple, glossy, waved leaves. Evergreen.

 Shrub planting partner: *Buddleia* 'Lochinch' (to 6 ft. [2 m]) (z. 5–9) Silver-gray leaves and large sprays of scented, lilac-blue flowers in late summer.

4. SILVER AND WHITE FOR A DRY, SUNNY SITUATION
Maximum height 40 in. (1 m)

 Eryngium bourgatii 'Oxford Blue' (z. 3–8) (page 67) Silver-gray foliage; silver-blue flowers in summer.

 Artemisia 'Powis Castle' (z. 6–10) (page 103) Finely cut silver foliage on sprawling, shrubby stems.

 Centranthus ruber 'Albus' (z. 4–8) (page 65) Fresh green leaves and frothy white flower heads.

 Stachys byzantina 'Silver Carpet' (z. 4–8) (page 105) Soft, felted silver-gray leaves in a low mat.

Shrub planting partner: *Cistus* × *obtusifolius* 'Thrive' (3 ft. [90 cm]) (z. 8–10) Small, dark, evergreen leaves. White, yellow-eyed flowers.

5. GREEN AND WHITE GROUND COVER IN SHADE
Maximum height 32 in. (80 cm)

  Euphorbia amygdaloides var. *robbiae* (z. 7–9) (page 57) Dark green leaves in whorls on short, upright stems. Lime green flowers in spring.

 Helleborus foetidus (z. 6–8) (page 114) Dark green leaves divided into narrow leaflets. Pale green flowers in early spring. Evergreen.

 Brunnera macrophylla 'Jack Frost' (z. 4–8) (page 106) Attractive silver-green foliage and bright blue forget-me-not flowers in early spring.

 Lamium maculatum 'Beacon Silver' (z. 4–7) (page 62) A mat of green-silver leaves, narrowly edged dark green. Pink-purple flowers in summer.

 Hosta 'Patriot' (z. 4–8) (page 98) Bold, deep green, heart-shaped leaves broadly edged with white. Lilac flowers in midsummer.

 Shrub planting partner: *Skimmia* × *confusa* 'Kew Green' (to 40 in. [1 m]) (z. 7–8) Evergreen, glossy leaves; cream-green scented flowers in early spring.

6. EASY-TO-GROW MIX FOR SUN OR SEMI-SHADE
Maximum height 40 in. (1 m)

 Astrantia major (z. 5–8) (page 155) Starry, greenish pink flowers on straight stems above a mound of foliage through summer and into fall.

 Geranium 'Johnson's Blue' (z. 4–8) (page 48) Dark-veined, lavender-blue flowers in early to midsummer, often again in fall. Attractive cut foliage.

 Penstemon 'Andenken an Friedrich Hahn' (z. 7–10) (page 163) Rounded bush of evergreen foliage. Wine red flowers through summer and fall.

 Paeonia officinalis 'Rubra Plena' (z. 4–9) (page 146) Attractive medium green foliage and large, very double, ruby red flowers in early summer.

 Nepeta 'Six Hills Giant' (z. 4–7) (page 42) Gray-green, aromatic foliage and fine spikes of lavender-blue flowers throughout summer.

Shrub planting partner: *Sambucus nigra* 'Black Lace' (to 6 ft. [2 m]) (z. 5–7) Vigorous, with finely cut, dark leaves. Pinkish flowers in early summer.

7. BOLD FOLIAGE FOR SEMI-SHADE AND MOIST SOIL
Maximum height 6 ft. (2 m)

 Euphorbia griffithii 'Fireglow' (z. 5–7) (page 122) Upright stems crowned with vivid orange-red flowers in late spring. Good autumn foliage color.

 Hosta sieboldiana var. *elegans* (z. 4–8) (page 107) Large, bold, silver-blue architectural leaves. Spikes of pale lilac flowers in midsummer.

 Lobelia 'Queen Victoria' (z. 8–9) (page 76) Shining, rich red-purple foliage. Spikes of vivid scarlet flowers on dark stems in late summer.

 Ligularia 'The Rocket' (z. 3–8) (page 76) Green, toothed leaves on black stems. Spikes of tiny, deep yellow flowers in midsummer.

 Bergenia purpurascens (z. 4–8) (page 111) Bold, leathery foliage that turns deep mahogany red in autumn. Purple-red flowers in spring.

 Shrub planting partner: *Cornus alba* 'Gouchaultii' (to 6 ft. [2 m]) (z. 2–8). Soft green, yellow-variegated leaves, flushed pink. Red winter stems.

8. BLUE AND WHITE FOR SEMI-SHADE
Maximum height 40 in (1 m)

 Hosta 'Halcyon' (z. 4–8) (page 107) Wonderful, elegant blue-green leaves. Spikes of grayish lavender flowers in midsummer.

 Aquilegia alpina (z. 5–7) (page 120) Pretty divided, fernlike leaves of bluish green. Slender stems of inky blue flowers in late spring. Self-seeds freely.

Dicentra 'Langtrees' (z. 4–8) (page 106) Fernlike foliage of silver-gray. Delicate stems of pinkish white flowers in spring.

 Pulmonaria 'Roy Davidson' (z. 4–8) (page 115) Pale ice blue flowers above strongly spotted foliage, which remains fresh all season.

 Iris sibirica 'Flight of Butterflies' (z. 4–8) (page 75) Narrow, upright, swordlike leaves and dainty sapphire blue flowers in early summer.

 Shrub planting partner: *Cornus alba* 'Sibirica Variegata' (to 5ft. [1.5m]) (z. 2–8) Dark green and cream foliage, flushed pink. Red winter stems.

Suffix *i* refers to illustrations. Page numbers in bold type indicate major references; numbers in italics indicate illustrations and captions only. The letter *z.* refers to USDA zones.

INDEX

191

INDEX

INDEX

PICTURE CREDITS
The publishers would like to acknowledge with thanks all those whose gardens are pictured in this book.

All photographs were taken by Andrew McIndoe or Kevin Hobbs with the exception of:

Blackmore & Langdon: 135a
Crûg Farm Plants: 127c
Patricia Elkington: 28c, 123a, 126 Good Companions (3) , 174b
John Hillier: 112 Good Companions (3)
Kelways: 125b, 125d, 146
Notcutts Nurseries Ltd: 87a
Jane Sterndale-Bennett: 89b, 94b, 99a, 120b, 128a, 129a, 177 Good Companions (4)
Terry Underhill: 40b, 61b, 71a, 87c, 95b, 112a, 123b, 124, 126a, 126b, Good Companions 129 (3), 148c, 174a
Whetman Pinks Ltd: 81b, 136a, 136b
Garden Picture Library/Rich Pomerantz: front cover, main image: